THE
100 BEST
STOCKS

TO OWN IN AMERICA

FOURTH EDITION

Gene Walden

Dearborn
Financial Publishing, Inc.

TO LAURIE, WHITNEY AND RYAN

Managing Editor: Jack Kiburz
Senior Associate Editor: Karen A. Christensen
Interior Design: Elizandro Carrington
Cover Design: S. Laird Jenkins Corporation

Printed in the United States of America.

96 97 98 10 9 8 7 6 5 4 3 2 1

Library of Congress Cataloging-in-Publication Data

Walden, Gene.
    The 100 Best stocks to own in America / Gene Walden. — 4th ed.
        p.   cm.
    Includes index.
    ISBN 0-7931-1478-0
    1. Stocks—United States.   I. Title
HG4963.W35   1995   95-24034
332.63'22'0973—dc20   CIP

Contents

Alphabetical Listing of the 100 Best Stocks

Acknowledgments

Without some important contributions from a few key people, this book would not have been possible. Special thanks goes to Larry Nelson, who once again served as the research assistant for this book as he did for the third edition and for *The 100 Best Mutual Funds To Own in America.* He crunched numbers, compiled tables and graphs, sent letters, made calls, checked facts and helped keep the project organized and on schedule.

Edmund O. Lawler, my coauthor on the book *Marketing Masters,* once again did a tremendous job writing some of the profiles for the book as he did for the third edition of *The 100 Best Stocks To Own in America.*

Finally, special thanks goes to my editors, Caroline Carney, Karen Christensen and Jack Kiburz, of Dearborn Financial Publishing, who did a remarkable job of pushing this timely book through the cumbersome editing and publishing process.

Introduction

If you want to make money in business today, the best bet may be to put your money where your mouth is.

In edition after edition of this book, the top-rated stocks have all been companies whose business revolves around products designed for the mouth.

In the first edition, Anheuser-Busch, which sends 87 million barrels of beer across consumers' lips each year, ranked number one. In the second edition, cigarette maker Philip Morris held down the top spot, followed by chewing tobacco producer UST. In the third edition, the top pick was gum maker William Wrigley Jr., followed by UST.

In this fourth edition, once more, it is the mouth that roars. Making another strong showing, this time at number two, is William Wrigley. And the number one pick—drum roll, please—is The Gillette Company. Gillette is not only the world leader in blades and razors, it is also the nation's leading manufacturer of toothbrushes through its Oral-B subsidiary.

Gillette has sales in 200 countries and territories. Nearly 70 percent of its $6 billion in annual revenue comes from foreign operations. Gillette stock has enjoyed an exceptional run the past decade, providing a total return for shareholders of 29.5 percent per year. A $10,000 investment in Gillette stock 10 years ago would have grown to about $133,000 today.

As always, the rest of this edition's 100 best stocks represent a broad blend of industries. As usual, many of the stocks on the list are household names with products or services that are popular worldwide.

Rounding out the top ten, from third through tenth respectively, are **Franklin Resources,** an investment management firm best known for its Templeton family of mutual funds; **Coca-Cola,** the world's leading soft drink maker; **Albertson's,** the nation's fastest-growing supermarket chain; **UST,** the smokeless tobacco leader; **Medtronic,** the world's leading heart pacemaker manufacturer; **Merck,** the nation's top pharmaceutical concern; **Schering-Plough,** another leading pharmaceutical manufacturer and the parent company of Dr. Scholl's (footcare products); and **H&R Block,** the country's largest tax preparation service.

This edition features 21 new companies that were not included in the last edition of the book and 80 companies that continued to perform well enough to make a repeat appearance. Only 35 companies have made the list in all four editions:

Abbott Labs
Albertson's
American Home Products
Anheuser-Busch
Automatic Data Processing
Banc One
Bemis
Bristol-Myers Squibb
ConAgra
R.R. Donnelley & Sons
Fifth Third Bancorp
Genuine Parts
H.J. Heinz
Hershey Foods
Kellogg
McDonald's
Merck
Pall Corp.

PepsiCo.
Philip Morris
Pitney Bowes
RPM
Rubbermaid
Sara Lee
A. Schulman
Shaw Industries
Sherwin-Williams
Torchmark
Tyson Foods
UST
Valspar
Wal-Mart
Walgreen
Walt Disney
William Wrigley

Food and medical companies continue to dominate the Best 100 list. There are 17 food and beverage-related companies and 16 medical companies featured in the book.

Of the 21 new stocks on the list, however, very few are household names. Franklin Resources, at number three, is the highest-ranking of the new additions. Other new names of note include Norwest, a Minnesota-based bank that ranks 13th; Cintas Corp., a business uniform manufacturer that ranks 25th; and motorcycle maker Harley-Davidson, which ranks 65th.

In addition to the 21 new companies, you'll find a couple of new features in this edition:

- **"At a Glance" summary tables.** Each company profile is accompanied by a comprehensive financial summary table with five-year growth records for revenue, net income, earnings per share, dividend, dividend yield, and price-earnings (PE) ratio. For stock price growth, you'll find six-year "high-low-close" charts that graphically depict annual price movements of the stock.
- **Honorable mention stocks.** The honorable mention list includes another 40 stocks that have shown solid growth over the past decade.

FUTURE PROSPECTS

This book makes no pretense of projecting the future performance of any security. The rankings are based strictly on the past performance of the companies. I looked at several factors: Has the company had consistent earnings growth and consistent stock growth for the past ten years (or longer)? Is the company well-diversified? Is it a leader in its market sector? Out of the approximately 2,000 stocks that I evaluated for positions in this book, the companies listed here have all passed with flying colors. They are the 100 major U.S. corporations that have fared the best over the past decade and given their shareholders the most.

While there is no assurance that any of these companies will outperform the market in the years to come, they do have a couple of strong points in their favor. For one, each company featured here has proved its ability to compete as a market leader in one or more areas. Their concepts are working. Their lines of products or services have made an impact in the marketplace, and have been highly profitable over the past 10 to 15 years. Each of these companies has a management team that has also proved capable of turning a buck on a consistent basis. They've ridden the ups and downs of the economy over the past decade, survived the rash of mergers and acquisitions (and probably made a few of their own), weathered the recession and have still come away with an outstanding record of earnings and stock price growth. Presumably most of these companies will continue their success throughout this decade.

While it is certainly possible that companies like McDonald's (29 consecutive years of record earnings), Automatic Data Processing (45 consecutive years of double-digit growth in both earnings and revenues), Torchmark (43 consecutive years of record earnings), and RPM (47 consecutive years of record sales and earnings) could slip into a sudden free fall, after decades of uninterrupted growth, the odds would seem to bode otherwise.

Traditionally, the type of top-quality stocks selected for this book tend to do very well compared with the overall market. For instance, a portfolio of the top 40 ranked stocks of the first edition of this book (published in 1989) would have grown 102 percent over the following five years—a record good enough to outperform 89 percent of all mutual funds for that period!

THE CASE FOR STOCKS

While an individual's first investment priority should be money in the bank—everyone needs a cash cushion to fall back on—stocks should be a key component of any well-balanced portfolio.

Why buy stocks rather than collecting that safe, consistent flow of interest earnings a bank account would offer? Here are some numbers to reflect on:

On average, over the 68 years for which records are available—which includes both the stock market crash of 1929 and the crash of 1987—stocks have paid an average annual return of about 10.5 percent, roughly double the return of bonds, and three times the return of money market funds. The difference is even more dramatic when put in inflation-adjusted terms. A dollar invested in a money market account in 1925 would have grown (inflation-adjusted) to about $2.60 by 1990. That same dollar invested in the broad stock market would have grown to about $77 (inflation-adjusted) during the same period. While stocks may have their ups and downs, if you can live with the volatility, you would be a far richer investor by keeping your money in the stock market.

Sometimes stock market investing requires great patience. Stock performance can vary dramatically from one ten-year period to another. An investor entering the market in 1965, for instance, would have experienced an agonizing 1.2 percent average annual return over the next ten years. But an investor in the market from 1949 to 1958 would have reaped a 20 percent average annual return.

STOCKS OR STOCK MUTUAL FUNDS?

The other issue for many investors is whether to invest in individual stocks or stock mutual funds. The fact is, mutual funds probably should be the investment of choice for many investors—particularly those individuals who haven't the time, the expertise or the resources to invest in a well-diversified selection of stocks.

But if you have an interest in the market, the time to spend researching it and the money to diversify your portfolio, individual stocks can offer several advantages over mutual funds.

First, buying stocks can be challenging, stimulating and, at times, fulfilling. You pit your wits against the market and against the millions of other unseen investors who are also scouring the market for a bargain. It is a test of your insight, your shrewdness. At times it can also be a test of your endurance, or—during downturns in the market—a test of your courage as you hold fast to your position in anticipation of that next market rally.

When you pick a winner, the results can be exhilarating. You watch the price move up. You see the stock split two-for-one. Suddenly your 500 shares becomes 1,000. Your investment grows to a multiple of your initial outlay. You've won at the age-old game of picking stocks. And the victory is a boon not only to your pocketbook, but to your ego as well. It's that psychological reward of picking a winner that motivates so many investors to set aside mutual funds and test their hand in the stock market.

There's also another important—though less publicized—reason to choose stocks over mutual funds. As they say, money is power. But it's only power if you use it as power. That means controlling it yourself and deciding exactly where each dollar is put to work. Socially conscious individuals who wouldn't dream of investing in companies that pollute the environment, produce tobacco products or build weapons of mass destruction unwittingly invest in all those types of companies when they invest in stock mutual funds. Most mutual funds pay little heed to social concerns.

There are, of course, mutual funds that take an ethical approach and avoid investing in companies with questionable ethical connections. The problem is, when you invest in those funds you're still letting someone else decide the fate of your money. After all, you may not necessarily agree with *all* the fund's ideals. You might, for instance, enjoy a beer on a hot afternoon and see no reason to avoid investing in alcoholic beverage producers. You may prefer not to invest in a weapons manufacturing company, but you may think nuclear power is the best thing since windmills. So a mutual fund that invests according to all the popular ethical issues of our time may not be exactly the investment for you. Stocks give you the freedom to make those choices for yourself.

RATING THE COMPANIES

In selecting the 100 companies for this book, I looked at a wide range of financial factors, the most important of which was earnings performance. I wanted companies with a long history of annual increases in earnings per share—because if a company is able to raise its earnings year after year, the stock price will ultimately follow.

Other factors such as revenue growth, stock price performance and dividend yield also played into the screening process, but none carried the same weight as earnings growth.

I made my selections after reviewing the financial histories of about 2,000 major U.S. companies. After narrowing the list to the final 100, the next step was to rank them 1 to 100 based on a six-part rating system. Each category is worth up to four points (except shareholder perks, which is worth a maximum of three points) for a maximum of 23 points. The categories are earnings per share growth, stock growth, dividend yield, dividend growth, consistency and shareholder perks.

I've also tried to bridge the long-term performance with the short-term performance. Stock growth was judged on ten-year performance, while earnings growth and dividend growth were rated based on the most recent five-year period. The dividend yield was rated based on the average yield over the past three years. And finally, the consistency category rated stocks based on year-to-year earnings gains over a ten-year period. That gives the rating system a blend of the long term and the short term. Accompanying each company profile, you will see a ratings chart similar to this:

ABCDE Corp. Ratings Box

Earnings Growth	★ ★ ★ ★	Dividend Growth	★ ★
Stock Growth	★ ★ ★	Consistency	★ ★ ★
Dividend Yield	★	Shareholder Perks	★ ★
NYSE—ABC		**Total**	**16 points**

Each star represents one ratings point. This company scored the maximum 4 points for stock growth and somewhat less for the other categories. The lower left indicates both where the stock is traded (e.g., NYSE—New York Stock Exchange) and the stock's ticker symbol (ABC). The lower right gives the total score.

The following charts offer an exact breakdown of the point system for each category:

Earnings per Share Growth

5-Year Growth Rate	Average Annual Rate	Points Awarded
50–79%	9–12%	★ (1 point)
80–109%	13–16%	★ ★
110–139%	17–19%	★ ★ ★
140% and above	20% and above	★ ★ ★ ★

Stock Growth

10-Year Growth Rate	Average Annual Rate	Points Awarded
155–249%	10–13%	★ (1 point)
250–399%	14–17%	★ ★
400–599%	18–21%	★ ★ ★
600% and above	22% and above	★ ★ ★ ★

Dividend Yield

(Based on dividend yield average over past three years)

Dividend Yield	Points Awarded
0.5 to 1.4%	★
1.5 to 2.4%	★ ★
2.5 to 3.4%	★ ★ ★
3.5% and above	★ ★ ★ ★

Dividend Growth

In one sense, dividend growth may be even more important than the dividend yield. As the dividend grows, the current return on your original investment grows with it. Here's an example:

A stock yielding 2 percent when you bought it ten years ago at $10 a share may still be yielding a current return of only 2 percent, but if the stock has appreciated in value to $100 a share, then that 2 percent yield has now grown from its original 20 cents a share on a $10 stock to $2 per share on the $100 stock—the equivalent of a very generous 20 percent yield on your original $10 investment.

The rating scale is based on dividend growth over the most recent five-year period. However, a few factors can alter the score: If a company has raised its dividend fewer than five straight years, one point is subtracted from the total; if it has raised its dividend at least 10 consecutive years, add a point (unless it is already at the 4 point maximum). If the company pays a dividend of under 0.5 percent, the maximum score it can get in the dividend growth category is 2 points.

Dividend Growth	Points Awarded
39 to 59%	★
60 to 99%	★ ★
100 to 149%	★ ★ ★
150% and above	★ ★ ★ ★

Consistency

A company that has had a flawless run of increases in earnings per share over the past ten years would score four points. The consistency of the stock price growth is not taken into account here because the volatility in a stock price can often be dictated by market factors beyond the control of the company. But if the company is strong and growing steadily, the stock price, over time, should reflect that.

- **Score: 3 points.** A company that has had a nearly flawless run of earnings increases—with gains nine of the past ten years.
- **Score: 2 points.** A company that has had a fairly consistent growth record, with earnings increases eight of the past ten years.
- **Score: 1 point.** A company that has been somewhat inconsistent, with earnings increases seven of the past ten years.
- **Score: 0 points.** Theoretically, a company with a very volatile growth record would score no points here, although no company can make the top 100 list if it has had fewer than seven years of increased earnings out of the past ten.

Shareholder Perks

This category carries a maximum of three points. The grading in the perks category is very stringent. Most companies score two points or less. Only a handful scored a full three points.

Without question, this has been both the most admired and the most questioned category of the rating system. Investment purists question its validity, while other investors looking for a little extra for their investment dollars have really taken the perks concept to heart.

But even investment purists should appreciate the investment value of the most common perk, a dividend reinvestment and stock purchase plan, offered by about 75 of the 100 companies in the book. These programs enable shareholders not only to reinvest their dividends in additional shares automatically, but also to buy more stock in the company either commission-free or for a nominal fee (usually under $5).

For example, Coca-Cola shareholders may buy up to $60,000 a year in additional shares through the company plan, and McDonald's shareholders may make up to $75,000 a year in commission-free stock purchases. May Department Stores puts no upper limit on its program.

The only drawback to such plans is that the shareholder has no control over when the stocks are purchased. Most companies have a date set each month or each quarter (depending on how the plan is set up) to make all shareholder stock purchases. You should also note that shareholders must pay income taxes on their dividends, even though the dividends are automatically reinvested in additional stock. These programs are perfect for investors who want to build a position in three or four companies at a time with relatively small monthly contributions (minimum contribution limits range from $10 to $50 per payment). The savings can be immense.

For instance, normally commission costs even through a discount broker would run, on average, at least $40 per stock purchase per month—a total of $160 per month for four stocks. That adds up to $1,920 per year. With the free reinvestment plans, you can either put that $1,920 into your pocket or invest it in additional stock. Either way, the commission-free programs are a great perk, and well worth the two points my system awards to each company that offers such a program.

Many companies offer other interesting perks as well. Some firms send welcome kits with free samples of their products to new shareholders of record. Others serve a free lunch at the annual meeting and give away a nice package of sample products. Anheuser-Busch shareholders who attend the annual meeting are welcome to sample the brewer's full line of beers and snacks. Shareholders are also offered a discount on admission to the company's amusement parks, including Busch Gardens, Sea World, Sesame Place and Adventure Island. Each Christmas, the William Wrigley Jr. Company sends shareholders about 20 packs of Wrigley's gum.

Hershey is one of several companies that puts together Christmas gift boxes that their shareholders may buy (at discount prices) to send to friends or business clients. Shareholders simply send in their money along with the names and addresses of their friends, and the company does the rest.

While shareholder perks may not contribute to a company's investment performance, it can generate goodwill among shareholders. One investor called me to report that he had had great success with several stocks from a previous edition of the book, but saw his Marriott stock fall prey to hard times in the lodging industry. "But," he added, "I've used Marriott's 50 percent shareholder discount on lodging rates on several business trips, and it has already saved me a couple hundred dollars."

Breaking Ties

The 100 companies are ranked in order by points. The company with the most points is ranked first, and the company with the fewest points is ranked 100. To break ties between companies with identical point scores, the company with the higher total return on shareholder investment gets the higher ranking. If two companies tie on both total points and return on shareholder investment, the company with the higher total revenue gets the higher ranking.

Performance Graphs

At the end of each profile, you will see a five-year financial "At a Glance" summary of the company's performance, including revenue, net income, earnings per share, dividend, dividend yield and price-earnings (PE) ratio.
    I have also included a "high-low-close" stock growth chart.

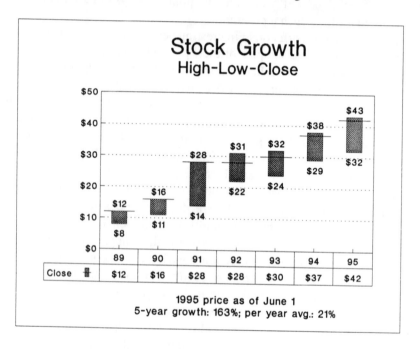

This stock growth graph shows:

- The yearly stock price range (all figures are adjusted for stock splits), with the low price for the year at the bottom of each graph block, and the high price for the year at the top of the block. A horizontal line through each yearly graph block marks the closing price for the year. The closing price for each year is also listed at the bottom of the graph.
- The graph shows the price range for 1989 through June 1, 1995. The price range indicated is for the 52-week period from June 1, 1994, to June 1, 1995.
- The stock's five-year growth percentage through 1994 and the per year average growth percentage (both shown below the graph).

    Now you're ready to begin making this book work profitably for you.

How To Use This Book Profitably

Think of this book as a sales catalog for investment shoppers. You can page through it, look over the merchandise and make your selections.

Let's assume that you have $20,000 to invest in stocks. Here is the process I recommend that you use to select the best stocks for *you* based on the entries in this book:

Begin by reading through the 100 profiles and narrowing your choices to 10 to 12 stocks by asking these questions:

- *Are they companies you like?* Are they involved in business activities that you think have a strong future?
- *Are they located in your part of the country?* This is not essential, but it *is* easier to follow companies based close to home because the local press tends to give those companies better coverage so you can stay better informed on your investment.
- *Do they represent a diverse cross-section of industries?* Spread your choices around. You might select a food company, a medical products firm, a heavy manufacturer, perhaps a publisher, a retailer, or a computer or data processing company. Choose no more than two or three companies from the same industrial segment. By making a broad selection, you can minimize your losses if one sector goes sour.

The next step is to narrow that list of 10 to 12 favorites to the four to six companies that you will ultimately invest in.

If you wish to use a stockbroker or financial advisor, call your advisor, read your list of choices and ask if he or she has any current research on those stocks. If so, find out which ones the broker recommends, and buy the stocks through your broker. If you are interested in enrolling in the dividend reinvestment plan or in receiving the special perks your chosen companies might offer, instruct your broker to put your stocks in your name rather than holding them at the brokerage office in "street name." Most dividend reinvestment plans and perks programs are available only to shareholders of record.

GOING IT ALONE

If you have no broker, or wish to go it alone through a discount broker, here are some steps you can use to narrow your list to the four to six companies you will ultimately invest in:

1. *Write or call those 10 to 12 companies to request their annual report and their 10-K report (which is a suppliment to the annual report), then skim through the reports.* (The phone numbers and addresses of each of the 100 companies are listed in this book along with their corporate profiles.)
2. *Go to the library and look up the most recent articles on those stocks and request any other information the library may have on your selections.* If it's a local company, there's a good chance your library will have an entire file on the firm. Make sure the company hasn't become involved in any major scandals or business problems.
    The library may also have two or three investment research books you can use to check up on your stock selections. *Value Line Investment Survey* and the Standard & Poor's report both offer up-to-date information and recommendations on hundreds of companies.
3. Keep an eye on the stock prices of the companies you are interested in. Find out what range each stock has been trading in over the past few months. Then select the four or five stocks that appear at present to be the best values. Timing can be very important in your overall success. All stocks fluctuate greatly in price, tugged along by the current of the overall market. But some stocks vacillate more than others. For instance, you could have bought Walt Disney stock in 1973 for $27 a share, and sold it for a mere $4 a share a year later. You could have reinvested in the stock in 1976 at $15 a share and sold out in disgust in 1984 at $11.50 a share. Or, on the other hand, you might have bought the stock for that same $11.50 a share in 1984 and sold out with a grin for more than ten times that price ($136 a share) in 1990. So even with stocks like Disney that qualify as a 100 Best entry, timing can make a significant difference.

WHEN TO BUY

Volumes have been written on this topic. But the best advice may have come from Baron von Rothschild in the mid-1800s. He said, "Buy when the enemy is at the gate and sell when you hear your cavalry's bugle sounding charge."

Wall Street has a popular adage that reinforces that concept: "Pessimism is always most rampant just before the market hits bottom."

Two extraordinary buying opportunities have arisen in the past several years. The first came in 1987 following the October "Black Monday" crash. The crash frightened many investors out of the market, but those who bought when everyone else was selling got in on the bottom of a market that grew more than 50 percent over the next 18 months.

The second great opportunity came during Iraq's occupation of Kuwait, when oil prices were rising, and the world was transfixed on the Middle East crisis. The market dropped about 15 percent in the months after Iraq invaded Kuwait, then roared back more than 20 percent in a three-month span that began the day the Allies began the bombing.

But barring war or disaster, the best strategy for most investors is a steady, persistent, long-term investment program.

In evaluating the Best 100 stocks for my newsletter, *The Best 100 Update* (a twice-yearly report available for $12.95; 800-736-2970), I found that the stocks that tend to do the best are those that are trading at a lower price today than they were two years earlier. Often, their depressed price indicates that the stock and its segment have been out of favor on Wall Street, and may be poised for a turnaround. In the in-depth evaluations I made of stocks the first and third editions of this book, I found that the portfolio of Best 100 stocks that were trailing their price of two years earlier grew during the succeeding year or two at a rate of more than double the Dow Jones Industrial Average.

While investors may strive to buy stocks while they are well below their peak prices, market experts advise against buying a stock on its way down. Or as they say in the brokerage business, "Don't fight the tape." Wait until a falling stock has bottomed out and shown some upward momentum before buying.

Benefits of Dollar Cost Averaging

One of the easiest and most effective investment strategies is called *dollar cost averaging,* and it's as simple as this: Pick a number, any number—$100 for instance—and invest that amount every month (or every quarter or every year) in the same stock. Period. It's that simple.

Elementary as it sounds, however, the dollar cost averaging method is also a very effective technique for beating the market. The reason? By sticking to a set sum each time you invest, you automatically buy fewer shares when the stock price is high and more shares when the price is low.

The following table illustrates the advantages of dollar cost averaging. The table assumes that the stock price fluctuates somewhat each month (and lists the monthly price of the stock). The table compares the number of shares purchased through a dollar cost averaging strategy with the number of shares purchased through a method in which the investor buys a set number of shares each month.

EXAMPLE OF DOLLAR COST AVERAGING

(Investing a set dollar amount each month versus buying a set number of shares each month).

	Jan	Feb	Mar	Apr	May	June	July	Aug	Sept	Oct	Nov	Dec	Totals
Stock Price[1]	$ 10	9	12	13	9	10	8	7	9	12	10	11	
Investor A Dollar Cost Averaging[2] Investment:	$100	100	100	100	100	100	100	100	100	100	100	100	$1,200
Shares	10	11.1	8.3	7.7	11	10	12.5	14.3	11	8.3	10	9.1	123.5 shrs
Investor B Set Quantity[3] Investment	$100	90	120	130	90	100	80	70	90	120	100	110	$1,200
Shares	10	10	10	10	10	10	10	10	10	10	10	10	120 shars

1. Indicates average stock price each month.
2. Assumes investor invests $100 a month in the stock.
3. Assumes investor buys 10 shares of the stock per month.

As the table indicates, using the dollar cost averaging method investor A would have purchased 3½ more shares than investor B who bought a set amount of shares each month, even though both spent a total of $1,200 during the year.

Tip: The dollar cost averaging method is most effective when you can make your purchases at no commission (or minimal commissions) through a company's dividend reinvestment and voluntary stock purchase plan.

Such plans are ideal for dollar cost averaging because they enable you to buy fractional shares and to make regular contributions (some companies offer stock purchase options once per month, others once per quarter). However, if the company you're interested in has no stock purchase plan, the brokerage commissions you would have to pay to make regular investments in the company's stock would greatly diminish the advantages of a dollar cost averaging plan. Most of the 100 top performers in this book offer a dividend reinvestment and voluntary stock purchase plan.

PICKING WINNERS

There is no infallible system for predicting tomorrow's market winners—only ratios and theories and computer-generated formulas that seem foolproof, but aren't. For investors who trade actively in stocks, the key to beating the market is not so much which stocks to buy, but when to buy them and when to sell them. And that's about as easy to predict as next month's weather.

Even Wall Street's finest can't consistently outfox the market. Stock mutual funds offer an interesting example. Despite being actively managed by some of the sharpest, most well-supported analysts in the investment industry, the average rate of return of stock mutual funds traditionally trails the overall market averages. Generally speaking, history has shown that you can do better just buying and holding a representative sample of stocks—without ever making a single trade—than most mutual fund managers do with their wealth of investment research, their finely honed trading strategies, and all their carefully calculated market maneuvers.

Nor do investment newsletters, on average, fare any better than the mutual fund managers at timing their trade recommendations, according to Mark Hulbert, publisher of the *Hulbert Financial Digest* newsletter. "Most newsletters have not kept up with the Standard & Poor's 500," says Hulbert. In fact, in tracking the seven-year performance of a sampling of investment newsletters, Hulbert found that the ones that recommended the greatest number of buys and sells (switches) were the ones that did the worst.

"We've also conducted some studies that show that in the case of most newsletters, if you had bought and held the stocks they recommended at the first of the year, you would have done better than if you had followed all of their trading recommendations throughout the year," Hulbert adds.

The moral? For sustained, long-term growth, it's hard to beat a buy and hold strategy. Buy good companies with the intention of holding onto them for many years.

The Strategy of Benign Neglect

Most of us know someone who bought a few shares of a stock many years ago, stashed the certificates in a drawer and then discovered years later that the stock had grown to a multiple of the original cost. Benign neglect is often the smartest policy for stock market investors.

Besides avoiding the difficulties of making timely buying and selling decisions, the buy and hold approach offers some other excellent advantages:

No commission costs.   Let's assume that you turn over your stock portfolio just once a year. You sell out all the stocks you own and buy new stocks that you think have greater short-term potential. Typically, you would incur about a 2 percent commission to sell the old stocks and a 2 percent commission to buy new ones—a total of 4 percent in round trip commissions. That means, for instance, that a respectable 12 percent gain on your investments would suddenly shrink to 8 percent after you've paid off your broker. That commission may not seem like much at the time, but over the long term, it can add up to a significant amount. See the chart on the next page, which illustrates the hidden costs of a buy-and-sell approach.

Tax-sheltered earnings.   A buy-and-hold strategy is one of the best tax-advantaged investments available today. You pay no taxes on the price appreciation of your stocks until you sell them—no matter how long your keep them. (You are taxed, however, on any stock dividend income.)

However, every time you sell a stock, the federal government taxes you up to 33 percent on your gains (for most working professionals). And state taxes would very likely nibble away another 3 to 5 percent. That means each year Uncle Sam bites off more than a third of your investment profits. So you're looking at losing 36 percent of your gains, plus the brokerage house commission, every time you sell a stock at a profit. How does that translate into real dollars?

Let's assume that (1) you start with an investment of $10,000, (2) your stock portfolio appreciates at a rate of 12 percent per year and (3) you sell your stocks, take the profit and buy new stocks once a year. The following chart compares your performance with that of a buy-and-hold investor with an identical 12 percent compounded average annual appreciation rate:

The Hidden Costs of a Buy-and-Sell Approach

$10,000 investment @ 12% annual growth	Buy-and-hold (No commission and no taxes)	Buy-and-sell results[1]	
		With commission[2]	And with taxes[3]
After 1 year	$11,200	$10,800	$10,512
After 5 years	17,600	14,700	12,850
After 10 years	31,000	21,600	16,400
After 20 years	96,500	46,600	27,200
Total 20-year profit: (minus initial $10,000)	$86,500	$36,600	$17,200

1. Assumes investor sells all stocks in portfolio one time per year (and reinvests in new stocks).
2. Assumes commission of 2% to buy and 2% to sell (an annual total of 4% of total portfolio price).
3. Assumes 32% federal and 4% state tax (an annual total of 36% of profits).

As you can see, over a 20-year period, the buy-and-hold portfolio could earn five times the profit of a buy-and-sell approach—even though both portfolios earn an average annual return of 12 percent.

Less emotional wear and tear.   By adhering to a buy-and-hold strategy you also avoid the high anxiety of trying to buy and sell stocks actively— of watching the financial pages each day to see how your stocks have fared, and of the inevitable disappointment of watching them rise and fall, then rise and fall again. Every stock goes through many ups and downs each year. There are *no exceptions*. The market moves like the tide of the ocean—it ebbs and flows—and every time it moves, it carries with it the broad market of individual stocks. Typically, about 70 percent of a stock's movement is attributable to the stock market itself. If the broad market is moving up, almost any stock you pick will also rise, but if the market is in a tailspin, almost any stock you pick—even those with record earnings— will fall with it. The remaining 30 percent of the movement of a stock is attributable to its industry group and to the performance of the company that issued the stock.

You skirt much of the emotional pressure the market inflicts if you invest with a buy-and-hold approach. You don't have to concern yourself with the inevitable daily ups and downs—or even the yearly ups and downs—of the market. Because over the long term, if you've bought stocks of good, solid, growing companies, the value of your portfolio will eventually reflect the strong performance of those companies. That's why it's crucial to select your stocks carefully. Because these are "one-decision stocks," that one decision takes on much greater importance.

When not to buy

Assuming that you've selected 10 to 12 prospective stocks, that you've researched the companies and you're ready to buy, what financial factors should you look at to decide which four to six of those 10 to 12 stocks represent the best value at the time?

The easiest way to select your finalists might be through the process of elimination: weed out the stocks that appear to be overvalued and invest in the others.

To assist you with your elimination process, here are two of the most common "don'ts."

Don't buy when a stock is at an all-time high.   Stocks constantly rise and fall. A noteworthy adage in the securities industry that goes like this: "The market always gives you a second chance." In almost every case, when a stock reaches an all-time high, it will eventually drop back in price, bounce back up, then drop back again. Nothing goes in a straight line. If you see that a stock is at its all-time high, it's probably not a very good value at that time. Prior to the October 1987 crash, many stocks were at or near their all-time highs, which is one reason why many investment experts claimed—correctly—that there were few good values in the market.

Don't buy when the price-earnings ratio is unusually high. It sounds complicated, but the *price-earnings (PE) ratio* is actually a very simple formula that offers yet another barometer of a stock's relative value. And best of all, the PE ratio is listed along with the company's stock price in the financial section of most newspapers, so you don't have to calculate it yourself.

Specifically, the ratio is the current price of the stock divided by the company's earnings-per-share.

Example:

ABC Corporation's stock price is $30.
Its earnings-per-share is $3.

$$\frac{\text{Stock price}}{\$30.00} \div \frac{\text{Earnings-per-share}}{\$3.00} = \frac{\text{PE ratio}}{10.0}$$

PE ratios are like golf scores—the lower the better. Generally the, PEs of most established companies are in the 10 to 20 range (although a handful of the stocks listed in this book have PEs over 20 and a few have PEs under 10). The real key, however, is not how the PE of one company compares to the PE of another, but how a company's current PE compares to its own previous PE ratios.

In this book, at the end of each company profile, you will see a financial summary "At a Glance" section that shows the PE ratio for the past six years. (The PE ratios in this book were calculated based on the earnings of the company's most recent four quarters, just as they are in the daily newspaper.) You might use that PE ratio as a guidepost to provide a relative point of comparison.

If you find in comparing the company's current PE (as listed in your morning newspaper) with its past PE range (as listed in this book) that the PE is near or above the high end of its past range, that could be an indication that the stock is relatively overvalued.

One more way to save

Once you've decided which stocks to buy, you may be able get more for your money by taking one more step.

Call around to several discount brokerage firms to find out which firm has the lowest minimum. Then buy your stocks through the discounter with the lowest minimum and have the broker put the stocks in your name (rather than "street name") and mail you the certificates. Buy a few shares—whatever you feel comfortable with—enroll in the company's dividend reinvestment and stock purchase plan, and make your subsequent stock purchases through the company. You may never have to pay commissions again!

WHEN TO SELL

Probably the most common mistake investors make in selling their stocks is that they tend to sell their winners to take a (fully taxable) profit and hold onto their losers in hopes that those stocks will someday rebound. That's an excellent way to assemble a portfolio full of losers. Prevailing wisdom in the investment business—for what it's worth—calls for just the opposite approach: "Cut your losses and let your profits run."

With that in mind, you might consider following a couple of basic strategies for selling stocks:

When news is grim.   If a company you own stock in comes under legal siege or becomes involved in some type of disaster or health controversy, take your lumps and get out as fast as you can dial up your broker.

Sell when the stock price drops relative to the market.   Barring disaster, you might also want to set up some other type of safety valve for your stocks. For instance, if the stock drops 10 to 20 percent while the market in general is moving up, it might be time to move on to something more promising. Some investors use a 10 percent/10 percent rule in which they sell a stock when it 1) drops 10 percent from its recent high and 2) drops 10 percent relative to the market. For example, if your stock drops 10 percent from $100 to $90, it meets the first criterion. But if the market has also gone down with it, then the stock still hasn't met the second criterion. If, on the other hand, the broad market has stayed the same or moved up while your stock dropped 10 percent, then it's time to sell—based on the 10 percent/10 percent rule.

More patient investors might lean toward a modified version of this: call it the 20 percent/20 percent rule. If your stock drops 20 percent and drops 20 percent relative to the market, sell it and move onto something more promising.

Sell when earnings drop.   Investment professionals sometimes call it the "cockroach theory." When you see one disappointing earnings report, that may mean more bad periods loom around the corner—just as the sight of a single cockroach usually means that other bugs in are hiding under the sink or behind the cupboard. Money managers who follow the cockroach theory get out of a stock at the first sign of trouble—even if it means taking a small loss—to avoid taking a bigger loss later should the bad news continue.

But timing is a tricky business. As Mark Hulbert puts it, "You need to approach those decisions realizing that more than half the time you're inclined to sell you would be better off holding than selling. So you'd better make sure there's a preponderance of evidence in your favor before you sell."

That's why your buying decision is so important. This guide can help steer you to 100 of the best stocks of the past ten years. Here's hoping you can cull from this collection some of the all-star stocks of the next ten years.

The Gillette Comp..

Prudential Tower Building
Boston, MA 02199
617-421-7000

Chairman and CEO: Alfred M. Zeien
President and COO: Michael C. Hawley

Earnings Growth	★ ★ ★	Dividend Growth	★ ★ ★ ★
Stock Growth	★ ★ ★ ★	Consistency	★ ★ ★
Dividend Yield	★ ★	Shareholder Perks	★ ★ ★
NYSE—G		**Total**	**19 points**

In every five o'clock shadow looms another prospect. Across six continents and 200 countries, where there's stubble, there's Gillette.

The Boston operation is the dominant producer in the razor blade market both in the United States and around the world. But Gillette means more than just a close shave. With its Oral-B and Paper Mate brands, Gillette is also the world leader in toothbrushes and writing instruments.

Few U.S. companies rely more on foreign sales than Gillette. Some 68 percent of the company's $6.07 billion in annual revenue comes from its foreign operations. The company has 57 manufacturing plants in 28 countries.

Razors and blades make up Gillette's largest segment, accounting for 39 percent of total revenue and 69 of total operating profit. The company controls about 65 percent of the U.S. razor blade market. Gillette's leading razor brands include Sensor, Good News, CustomPlus, Atra and Trac II razors.

Gillette's other key segments include:

- **Toiletries and cosmetics** (19 percent of revenue). Gillette manufactures Right Guard, Gillette and Soft & Dri deodorants, White Rain shampoo,

Epic Wave home permanents, Jafra skin care products and Gillette shaving creams and gels.
- **Stationery products** (13 percent of revenue). Gillette is the world's leading manufacturer of writing instruments and correction fluid. It makes Paper Mate, Parker, Flair, Flexigrip and Waterman pens, and Liquid Paper correction fluid.
- **Braun products** (22 percent of revenue). Gillette's German subsidiary is one of the leading manufacturers of electric shavers in both Europe and North America. The company also makes toasters, clocks, coffee-makers, food processors and other household appliances.
- **Oral-B products** (7 percent of revenue). Oral-B is the leading marketer of toothbrushes in the United States and several international markets. It also manufactures dental floss and other dental care products.

Gillette was founded in 1903 by King C. Gillette, who introduced a safety razor with a compact brass shaving head and a sleek wooden handle. It came with 20 steel blades, and sold for $5. The company has 32,800 employees and 27,000 shareholders.

EARNINGS-PER-SHARE GROWTH ★ ★ ★

Past 5 years: 131 percent (18 percent per year)
Past 10 years: 391 percent (17 percent per year)

STOCK GROWTH ★ ★ ★ ★

Past 10 years: 997 percent (27 percent per year)
Dollar growth: $10,000 over 10 years (including reinvested dividends) would have grown to $133,000
Average annual compounded rate of return (including reinvested dividends): 29.5 percent

DIVIDEND YIELD ★ ★

Average dividend yield in the past 3 years: 1.5 percent

DIVIDEND GROWTH ★ ★ ★ ★

Increased dividend: 17 consecutive years
Past five-year increase: 108 percent (16 percent per year)

CONSISTENCY ★ ★ ★

Increased earnings per share: 9 consecutive years
Increased sales: 12 straight years

SHAREHOLDER PERKS ★ ★ ★

Good dividend reinvestment and stock purchase plan: voluntary stock purchase plan allows contributions of $10 to $5,000 per month.

Shareholders who attend the annual meeting receive an excellent selection of products. At a recent meeting, shareholders were given a tote bag with Gillette's logo on the front, containing a Sensor razor for women, a can of Gillette Series shaving gel, a container of ClearGel antiperspirant, a tube of Jafra hand treatment, a bottle of White Rain Essentials shampoo, a Flexigrip ball-point pen and Oral-B dental floss. The company also occasionally sends out new products or coupons to all its shareholders of record. It recently mailed its shareholders a Sensor razor, plus a coupon for $1 off a package of blades.

GILLETTE AT A GLANCE

Fiscal year ended: Dec. 31
Revenue and net income in $ millions

	1989	1990	1991	1992	1993	1994	5-year Growth Avg. Annual (%)	Total (%)
Revenue ($)	3,819	4,345	4,684	5,163	5,411	6,070	10	59
Net income ($)	285	368	427	513	591	698	20	145
Earnings/share ($)	.68	.80	.97	1.16	1.33	1.57	18	131
Div. per share ($)	.24	.27	.31	.36	.42	.50	16	108
Dividend yield (%)	2.3	2.0	1.6	1.4	1.5	1.5	—	—
Avg. PE ratio	15.3	17.3	20.1	22.7	21.0	21.6	—	—

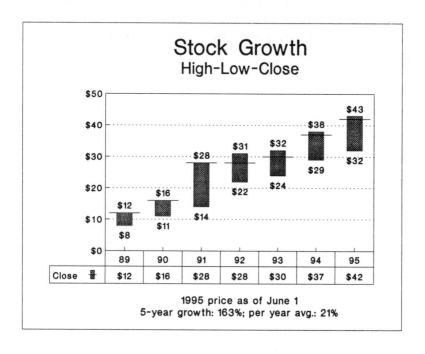

Stock Growth
High-Low-Close

	89	90	91	92	93	94	95
Close	$12	$16	$28	$28	$30	$37	$42

1995 price as of June 1
5-year growth: 163%; per year avg.: 21%

William Wrigley Jr. Company

410 North Michigan Ave.
Chicago, IL 60611
312-644-2121

President and CEO: William Wrigley

Earnings Growth	★ ★	Dividend Growth	★ ★ ★ ★
Stock Growth	★ ★ ★ ★	Consistency	★ ★ ★ ★
Dividend Yield	★ ★	Shareholder Perks	★ ★ ★
NYSE—WWY		**Total**	**19 points**

Double your pleasure. Double your fun. And double your money about every three years with an investment in the William Wrigley Jr. Company. The company's stock price has grown more than tenfold over the past decade, establishing new highs every year from 1983 through 1994. The company has also racked up 14 straight years of increased dividends and 12 years of record sales and earnings.

William Wrigley is the world's leading gum manufacturer. The 102-year-old, Chicago-based operation has managed to keep sales and profits growing through global expansion and brand extension.

Wrigley is sold in more than 100 countries and territories and operates subsidiaries in 26 foreign countries. The company has been pushing aggressively into the former Soviet bloc countries of Russia, Hungary, Poland, Yugoslavia and Czechoslovakia. The company also has a factory in the Guangdong Province of the People's Republic of China that opened in 1993. Foreign sales account for about 45 percent of the company's $1.6 billion in annual sales.

The company's largest markets outside the United States are Australia, Canada, Germany, the Philippines, Taiwan and the United Kingdom.

Brand extension has paid big dividends for Wrigley. The company has added about 15 new brands in recent years. Wrigley's top grossing brands continue to be Spearmint, Doublemint, Juicy Fruit and Big Red. Its Extra sugar-free gum (available in several flavors and as bubble gum) is the nation's top selling sugar-free brand. The sugar-free line is also beginning to sell well in European markets, thanks to the company's marketing emphasis on the "dental benefits" of sugar-free gum.

Other Wrigley brands include its new WinterFresh brand, along with Freedent, Orbit, Hubba Bubba and Sugarfree Hubba Bubba (original and grape).

Wrigley also owns Amurol Products, which manufactures children's novelty bubble gum and other confectionery products, including Big League Chew, Bubble Tape gum and Reed's hard roll candies.

Wrigley was founded in 1891 by William Wrigley Jr., the late grandfather of current president William Wrigley, 61. Wrigley was a baking soda salesman who first offered gum as a premium to customers who bought his baking soda. The gum quickly became more in demand than the baking soda, so Wrigley did what any smart marketer would do—he switched products. In 1893, he introduced his first flavors of Wrigley's gum, Spearmint and Juicy Fruit, and an American institution was born. The Wrigley Company has 7,000 employees, 24,000 shareholders.

EARNINGS-PER-SHARE GROWTH ★ ★

Past 5 years: 92 percent (14 percent per year)
Past 10 years: 409 percent (18 percent per year)

STOCK GROWTH ★ ★ ★ ★

Past 10 years: 937 percent (26 percent per year)
Dollar growth: $10,000 over 10 years (including reinvested dividends) would have grown to $128,000
Average annual compounded rate of return (including reinvested dividends): 29 percent

DIVIDEND YIELD

Average dividend yield in the past 3 years: 2.0 percent

DIVIDEND GROWTH

Increased dividend: 14 consecutive years
Past 5-year increase: 100 percent (15 percent per year)

CONSISTENCY ★ ★ ★ ★

Increased earnings per share: 13 consecutive years
Increased sales: 13 consecutive years

SHAREHOLDER PERKS ★ ★ ★

Good dividend reinvestment and stock purchase plan: voluntary stock purchase plan allows contributions of $50 to $5,000 per quarter.

Wrigley also sends out a gift package to all its shareholders each Christmas that includes several packs of Wrigley's gum, personally selected by the company chairman and president, William Wrigley.

WRIGLEY AT A GLANCE

Fiscal year ended: Dec. 31
Revenue and net income in $ millions

	1989	1990	1991	1992	1993	1994	5-year Growth Avg. Annual (%)	5-year Growth Total (%)
Revenue ()	992.9	1,111	1,148.9	1,287	1,429	1,597	10	61
Net income ()	106	117	129	141	175	201	14	90
Earnings/share ($)	.90	1.00	1.09	1.27	1.50	1.73	14	92
Div. per share ($)	.45	.49	.55	.62	.75	.90	15	100
Dividend yield (%)	3.1	2.9	2.7	2.2	2.0	1.9	—	—
Avg. PE ratio	16	17	19	23	25	27	—	—

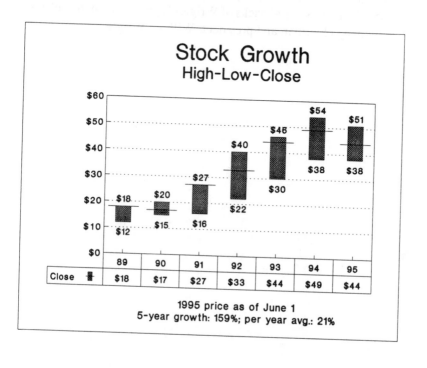

Stock Growth
High-Low-Close

Close	89	90	91	92	93	94	95
	$18	$17	$27	$33	$44	$49	$44

1995 price as of June 1
5-year growth: 159%; per year avg.: 21%

Franklin Resources, Inc.

777 Mariners Island Blvd.
San Mateo, CA 94404
415-312-3000

President and CEO: Charles B. Johnson

Earnings Growth	★ ★ ★ ★	Dividend Growth	★ ★ ★ ★
Stock Growth	★ ★ ★ ★	Consistency	★ ★ ★ ★
Dividend Yield	★	Shareholder Perks	★ ★
NYSE—BEN		**Total**	**19 points**

Over the past ten years, Franklin Resources has proved that it is not only adept at handling other people's assets, it's also pretty good at managing its own money.

The San Mateo, California, money management firm has seen its revenue grow more than twentyfold over the past ten years, from $37 million in 1994 to $850 million in 1994. It has had ten consecutive years of record sales and earnings.

In all, the company manages $118 billion in assets through its institutional clients and its broad line of mutual funds and other investment products. The company operates 101 mutual funds.

Best known of its subsidiaries is the Templeton group of mutual funds, acquired by Franklin Resources in 1992. The Templeton Funds, founded by investment legend John Templeton, is among the oldest and most well-respected family of funds in the business. The Templeton Growth Fund has been offered since 1954.

The Templeton Funds now boast assets of $42 billion.

The Franklin and Templeton funds are marketed nationwide through a network of brokers, financial planners and investment advisors. The firm also offers financial services in Canada, England, Germany, Japan, Australia, Hong Kong and parts of South America.

In addition to its investment management operations, the company owns the Franklin Bank (formerly the Pacific Union Bank & Trust Company), which has about $210 million in assets.

The firm also operates real estate and insurance services and a capital corporation that specializes in auto loans, although those services account for only about 3 percent of the company's total revenue.

Investment management fees provide the lion's share of Franklin's income—some 78 percent of total revenue. Founded in 1969, Franklin has 1,600 shareholders and 4,100 employees.

EARNINGS-PER-SHARE GROWTH ★ ★ ★ ★

Past 5 years: 200 percent (25 percent per year)
Past 10 years: 3,650 percent (43 percent per year)

STOCK GROWTH ★ ★ ★ ★

Past 10 years: 1018 percent (28 percent per year)
Dollar growth: $10,000 over 10 years (including reinvested dividends) would have grown to $130,000
Average annual compounded rate of return (including reinvested dividends): 29 percent

DIVIDEND YIELD ★

Average dividend yield in the past 3 years: 0.9 percent

DIVIDEND GROWTH ★ ★ ★ ★

Increased dividend: 10 consecutive years
Past 5-year increase: 113 percent (16 percent per year)

CONSISTENCY ★ ★ ★ ★

Increased earnings per share: 10 consecutive years
Increased sales: 10 consecutive years

SHAREHOLDER PERKS

Good dividend reinvestment and stock purchase plan: voluntary stock purchase plan allows contributions of $50 to $10,000 per quarter.

FRANKLIN RESOURCES AT A GLANCE

Fiscal year ended: Sept. 30
Revenue and net income in $ millions

	1989	1990	1991	1992	1993	1994	5-year Growth Avg. Annual (%)	5-year Growth Total (%)
Revenue ($)	225.2	251.3	301.0	371.0	640.7	826.9	30	270
Net income ($)	78.6	89.4	98.2	124.1	175.5	251.3	26	220
Earnings/share ($)	1.00	1.14	1.26	1.59	2.12	3.00	25	200
Div. per share ($)	.15	.20	.23	.26	.28	.32	16	113
Dividend yield (%)	1.5	1.5	1.3	1.0	0.7	1.0	—	—
Avg. PE ratio	19.9	11.7	14.5	18.2	23.2	12.5	—	—

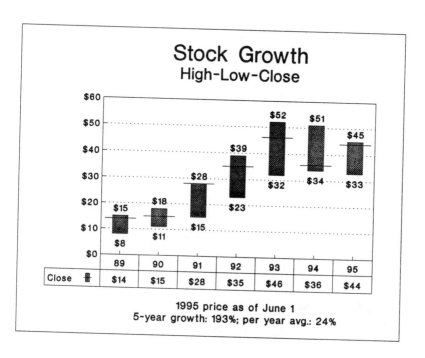

Stock Growth
High-Low-Close

	89	90	91	92	93	94	95
Close	$14	$15	$28	$35	$46	$36	$44

1995 price as of June 1
5-year growth: 193%; per year avg.: 24%

The Coca-Cola Co.

The Coca-Cola Company

One Coca-Cola Plaza, N.W.
Atlanta, GA 30313
404-676-2121

Chairman and CEO: Roberto C. Goizueta

Earnings Growth	★ ★ ★	Dividend Growth	★ ★ ★ ★
Stock Growth	★ ★ ★ ★	Consistency	★ ★ ★ ★
Dividend Yield	★ ★	Shareholder Perks	★ ★
NYSE—KO		**Total**	**19 points**

Coke has long been a favorite of thirsty drinkers from Topeka to Timbuktu. It's sold in nearly 200 countries. But now the 109-year-old American institution is pushing hard into two untapped mega-markets with potential beyond anything the company has seen before.

Coke's new markets are India and China, two countries that, combined, make up nearly half the world's population. The company is also venturing into markets in east-central Europe, such as Poland and Hungary.

In China, the company is penetrating the market with huge outdoor signs, sports sponsorships, television advertising and increased market presence.

In India, where Coca-Cola had a 16-year absence, the company has returned with a vengeance. In 1993, Coke formed a strategic alliance with Parle Exports, which has a 60-plant bottling network in India. Coke has invested more than $60 million in the Indian market, upgrading bottling plants, and setting up a vast marketing infrastructure.

Coca-Cola is the world's most recognized trademark. It sells more than 6 billion unit cases per year worldwide. Coke commands a 60 percent share of the worldwide cola market. Foreign sales account for about 65 percent of the Atlanta-based company's $16.2 billion in annual revenue and 79 percent of its total operating income.

In addition to Coke, the company also produces Diet Coke, Sprite, Nestea, Fanta, Hi-C fruit drinks, Tab, Fresca, Mello Yello, Ramblin' root beer, Mr. Pibb and Minute Maid. The company's new PowerAde and Aquarius noncarbonated drinks have enjoyed rapid growth since their introduction.

Soft drink sales account for about 87 percent of the company's net operating revenue and 96 percent of its operating profit.

The balance of its sales and earnings comes from its foods division, which is the market leader in packaged citrus juices including Minute Maid, Five Alive, Bright & Early, Hi-C and Bacardi tropical fruit mixers.

Volume sales continue to increase for Coca-Cola. Worldwide consumption of the company's soft drinks has climbed about 75 percent over the past decade.

In the United States, the per capita consumption rate of Coke products is about 303 eight-ounce servings per year. The leading per capita market is Mexico, where the consumption rate is 306 servings per person per year. Worldwide, on average, every man, woman and child in Coke's market drinks about 32 eight-ounce servings per year. Outside North America, some of the leading markets include Australia (250 servings per person), Norway (238 servings), Chile (205 servings), Germany (180 servings), Argentina (174 servings) and Spain (155 servings).

In terms of Coke's total gallon sales, the United States accounts for 31 percent, while Latin America makes up 24 percent and Europe accounts for 17 percent.

In the United States, Coke holds about a 40 percent share of the soft drink market. Founded in 1886, the Coca-Cola Company employs about 31,000 people and has 110,000 shareholders.

EARNINGS-PER-SHARE GROWTH ★ ★ ★

Past 5 years: 130 percent (18 percent per year)
Past 10 years: 395 percent (15 percent per year)

STOCK GROWTH

Past 10 years: 835 percent (25 percent per year)
Dollar growth: $10,000 over 10 years (including reinvested dividends)
would have grown to $115,000
Average annual compounded rate of return (including reinvested dividends): 27.5 percent

DIVIDEND YIELD

Average dividend yield in the past 3 years: 1.6 percent

DIVIDEND GROWTH

Increased dividend: More than 19 consecutive years
Past 5-year increase: 129 percent (18 percent per year)

CONSISTENCY ★ ★ ★ ★

Increased earnings per share: 19 consecutive years
Increased sales: 9 of past 10 years

SHAREHOLDER PERKS ★ ★

Good dividend reinvestment and stock purchase plan: voluntary stock
purchase plan allows contributions of $10 to $60,000 per year.

COCA-COLA AT A GLANCE

Fiscal year ended: Dec. 31
Revenue and net income in $ millions

	1989	1990	1991	1992	1993	1994	5-year Growth Avg. Annual (%)	5-year Growth Total (%)
Revenue ($)	8,622	10,236	11,572	13,074	13,957	16,172	14	88
Net income ($)	1,537	1,382	1,618	1,664	2,176	2,554	11	66
Earnings/share ($)	.86	1.02	1.21	1.43	1.68	1.98	18	130
Div. per share ($)	.34	.40	.48	.56	.68	.78	18	129
Dividend yield (%)	2.3	1.9	1.6	1.4	1.6	1.7	—	—
Avg. PE ratio	17.8	20.4	24.4	28.7	25.1	22.5	—	—

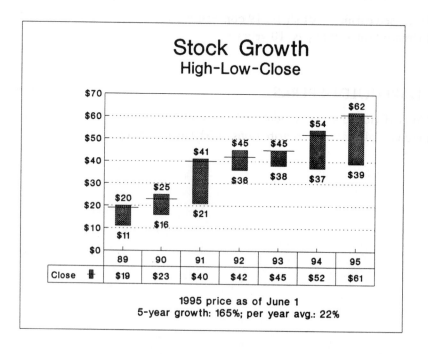

Stock Growth
High-Low-Close

	89	90	91	92	93	94	95
Close	$19	$23	$40	$42	$45	$52	$61

1995 price as of June 1
5-year growth: 165%; per year avg.: 22%

Albertson's Inc.

250 Parkcenter Blvd.
P. O. Box 20
Boise, ID 83726
208-385-6200

Chairman and CEO: Gary G. Michael
President and COO: John B. Carley

Earnings Growth	★ ★ ★	Dividend Growth	★ ★ ★ ★
Stock Growth	★ ★ ★ ★	Consistency	★ ★ ★ ★
Dividend Yield	★ ★	Shareholder Perks	★ ★
NYSE—ABS		**Total**	**19 points**

No grocery store chain in America has enjoyed greater success over the past quarter-century than Albertson's. The Boise-based grocer posted its 25th consecutive year of record sales and earnings in 1994, and through an aggressive program of expansion and acquisition, the firm has grown to become the fourth largest food-drug retail chain in America.

Through the years, Albertson's has been relentless in expanding both its store base and its store size. The company now has about 700 stores, most of which are large supermarkets of 15,000 to 35,000 square feet.

The company's five-year plan calls for the opening of an additional 295 stores, as well as the remodeling of 228 stores and the expansion of 30 stores.

In addition to its standard supermarkets, the company also has opened a number of combination food-drug stores that range in size from 35,000 to 75,000 square feet. It also operates a few no-frills warehouse style stores of up to 73,000 square feet that operate under the name Max Food and Drug.

Many of the larger stores provide not only the standard offering of grocery items but also include floral center, pharmacy, video rental, deli and full-service bakery.

Most of Albertson's stores are located in 17 western states, although the company has about 80 stores in Florida and 14 stores in Louisiana. Albertson's is strongest on the West Coast, where the company has 150 stores in California, 43 stores in Oregon and 65 stores in Washington.

In addition to its standard grocery offerings, many of Albertson's larger stores have five special service departments:

- **Pharmacy.** Grocery customers can also pick up prescription drugs at low-cost pharmacies in more than 200 Albertson's stores.
- **Lobby departments.** Most Albertson's stores offer a variety of special services for customers such as money orders, bus passes, lottery tickets, stamps, camera supplies, film developing and video rental.
- **Service deli.** Delicatessens in about 500 of its stores offer take-home foods, including meats, cheeses, fresh salads and fried chicken. Salad bars have been added in more than 200 Albertson's stores.
- **Service fish and meat departments.** Most of the larger Albertson's stores have specialty departments with a full array of fresh fish, shellfish, premium cuts of meat and semi-prepared items such as stuffed pork chops.
- **Bakeries.** The company offers a full range of baked goods in its in-store bakeries.

The company was founded in 1939 by the late Joe Albertson, who opened his first grocery in Boise, Idaho, in 1939. Although he retired from management in 1976, Albertson remained a director of the company's executive committee until his death in 1993 at age 86. Albertson's has 75,000 employees and 16,000 shareholders.

EARNINGS-PER-SHARE GROWTH   ★ ★ ★

Past 5 years: 116 percent (17 percent per year)
Past 10 years: 427 percent (18 percent per year)

STOCK GROWTH   ★ ★ ★ ★

Past 10 years: 742 percent (24 percent per year)
Dollar growth: $10,000 over 10 years (including reinvested dividends) would have grown to $97,000

Average annual compounded rate of return (including reinvested dividends): 25.5 percent

DIVIDEND YIELD ★ ★

Average dividend yield in the past 3 years: 1.5 percent

DIVIDEND GROWTH ★ ★ ★ ★

Increased dividend: 24 consecutive years
Past 5-year increase: 120 percent (17 percent per year)

CONSISTENCY ★ ★ ★ ★

Increased earnings per share: 25 consecutive years
Increased sales: 25 consecutive years

SHAREHOLDER PERKS ★ ★

Good dividend reinvestment and stock purchase plan: voluntary stock purchase plan allows contributions of $30 to $30,000 per quarter.

Shareholders who attend the annual meeting receive some of Albertson's private label groceries, including canned vegetables, napkins, paper towels and other household products.

ALBERTSON'S AT A GLANCE

Fiscal year ended: Jan. 31
Revenue and net income in $ millions

	1989	1990	1991	1992	1993	1994	5-year Growth Avg. Annual (%)	Total (%)
Revenue ($)	7,423	8,219	8,680	10,174	11,284	11,895	10	60
Net income ($)	197	234	258	269	340	400	15	103
Earnings/share ($)	.73	.87	.97	1.02	1.34	1.58	17	116
Div. per share ($)	.20	.24	.28	.32	.36	.44	17	120
Dividend yield (%)	1.6	1.5	1.3	1.4	1.4	1.6	—	—
Avg. PE ratio	17.0	18.2	21.7	22.2	19.8	17.7	—	—

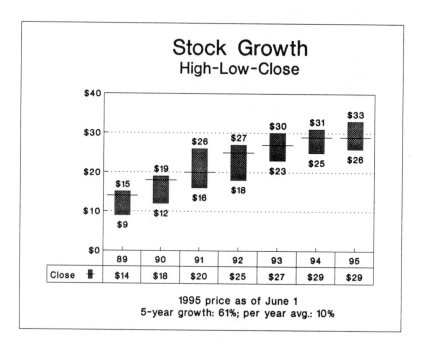

Stock Growth
High-Low-Close

1995 price as of June 1
5-year growth: 61%; per year avg.: 10%

UST, Inc.

100 West Putnam Ave.
Greenwich, CT 06830
203-661-1100

Chairman and CEO: Vincent A. Gierer, Jr.

Earnings Growth	★ ★ ★	Dividend Growth	★ ★ ★ ★
Stock Growth	★ ★ ★	Consistency	★ ★ ★ ★
Dividend Yield	★ ★ ★	Shareholder Perks	★ ★
NYSE—UST		**Total**	**19 points**

Tobacco lovers are smoking less, but chewing more—which is good news for UST, the nation's dominant smokeless tobacco producer.

The maker of Copenhagen, Skoal and Skoal Bandits saw its sales of moist, smokeless tobacco increase about 3 percent in 1994. The increased sales, along with new price hikes, enabled UST to achieve record sales and earnings per share for the 35th consecutive year.

That growth has come despite recent studies showing that smokeless tobacco can lead to cancer and other severe health problems.

The Greenwich, Connecticut, operation controls 85 percent of the United States smokeless tobacco market. It sells more than 600 million cans a year. And with the ban on radio and TV tobacco advertising, UST is not likely to face a serious challenge from other producers.

Tobacco products account for 87 percent of the company's $1.22 billion in annual revenue, and about 98.5 percent of operating income. In addition to its Skoal and Copenhagen brands, UST (formerly United States Tobacco) produces Red Seal, Rooster, Standard, Bruton, CC and Devoe dry tobaccos, as well as WB Cut chewing tobacco, Borkkum Riff, Amphora and Alsbo pipe tobaccos and Don Tomas and La Regenta cigars. Copenhagen is UST's oldest product, introduced in 1822.

The company also makes smoking accessories such as Dr. Grabow pre-smoked pipes, Mastercraft imported pipes and Dill's pipe cleaners.

In addition to tobacco, UST produces a line of wines (7 percent of revenue and 1 percent of operating earnings) through its International Wines and Spirits Ltd. subsidiary. Most of its wines are made in the state of Washington and sold under the labels of Chateau Ste. Michelle, Columbia Crest, Conn Creek, and Villa Mt. Eden.

The balance of UST's income (6 percent of revenue, less than 1 percent of operating earnings) comes from its "other" segment, which includes its international operations and its new home video subsidiary, Cabin Fever Entertainment. The firm recently released a 12-volume series of "Little Rascals" shows. UST has 3,700 employees and 13,600 shareholders.

EARNINGS-PER-SHARE GROWTH ★ ★ ★

Past 5 years: 128 percent (18 percent per year)
Past 10 years: 419 percent (18 percent per year)

STOCK GROWTH ★ ★ ★

Past 10 years: 560 percent (21 percent per year)
Dollar growth: $10,000 over 10 years (including reinvested dividends) would have grown to $93,000
Average annual compounded rate of return (including reinvested dividends): 25 percent

DIVIDEND YIELD ★ ★ ★

Average dividend yield in the past 3 years: 3.3 percent

DIVIDEND GROWTH ★ ★ ★ ★

Increased dividend: 24 consecutive years (has paid a dividend each year since 1912)
Past 5-year increase: 143 percent (19.5 percent per year)

CONSISTENCY ★ ★ ★ ★

Increased earnings per share: 35 consecutive years
Increased sales: 35 consecutive years

SHAREHOLDER PERKS ★ ★

Good dividend reinvestment and stock purchase plan: voluntary stock purchase plan allows contributions of $10 to $10,000 per month.

UST AT A GLANCE

Fiscal year ended: Dec. 31
Revenue and net income in $ millions

	1989	1990	1991	1992	1993	1994	5-year Growth Avg. Annual (%)	Total (%)
Revenue ($)	679.3	761.7	904.4	1,039.4	1,110.4	1,223.0	13	80
Net income ($)	190.5	223.3	265.9	312.6	349.0	387.5	15	100
Earnings/share ($)	.82	.98	1.18	1.41	1.71	1.87	18	128
Div. per share ($)	.46	.55	.66	.80	.96	1.12	19.5	143
Dividend yield (%)	3.0	3.0	2.0	2.5	3.5	4.0	—	—
Avg. PE ratio	15.7	15.2	19.8	21.6	17.7	14.9	—	—

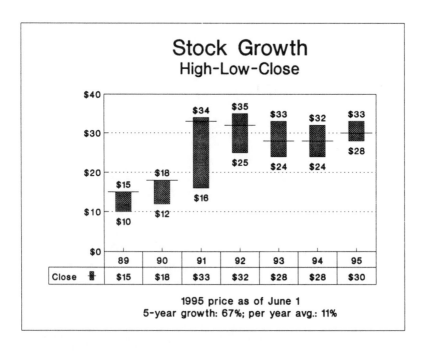

Stock Growth
High-Low-Close

	89	90	91	92	93	94	95
Close	$15	$18	$33	$32	$28	$28	$30

1995 price as of June 1
5-year growth: 67%; per year avg.: 11%

Medtronic, Inc.

Medtronic

7000 Central Ave. N.E.
Minneapolis, MN 55432
612-574-4000

Chairman: Winston R. Wallin
President and CEO: William W. George

Earnings Growth	★ ★ ★	Dividend Growth	★ ★ ★ ★
Stock Growth	★ ★ ★ ★	Consistency	★ ★ ★ ★
Dividend Yield	★	Shareholder Perks	★ ★
NYSE—MDT		**Total**	**18 points**

Steady as a heartbeat, Medtronic, the world's largest manufacturer of pacemakers and other implantable biomedical devices, has posted ten straight years of record sales, earnings and book value per share.

Even in the face of the price-cutting pressures of managed care, Medtronic has been able to sustain strong growth through aggressive cost control. The company has lowered manufacturing costs by adopting microprocessor technology for its pacemakers that simplifies their use and enhances their designs.

Medtronic pioneered the pacemaker 37 years ago when Dr. C. Walton Lillehei of the University of Minnesota Medical School identified a medical need for young heart block patients. Working with Earl Bakken, an electrical engineer, Dr. Lillehei developed the first wearable, external, battery-generated pulse generator.

Today, Medtronic's market-leading pacemakers are small, implantable pulse generators with extended battery life. The implantable pacemaker is among the biomedical devices that Medtronic makes to realize its mission to "alleviate pain, restore health and extend life."

Medtronic designs and manufactures pacing devices for patients whose heartbeats are irregular or too slow as well for patients whose hearts beat too rapidly. Medtronic's pacing devices can adjust electrical pulse intensity, duration, rate and other characteristics. The company's pacing business accounts for about 67 percent of its sales.

Cardiovascular products such as blood pumps, heart valves, oxygenators and catheters contribute about 23 percent of the company's sales. In addition to the product line, Medtronic provides such value-added services as physician education programs.

Medtronic's fast-growing neurological device segment is responsible for about 10 percent of sales. The company's neurological business offers therapies for treating pain, controlling movement disorders and providing patients a level of independence they could not normally achieve. For example, electrical stimulation of the spinal cord has been shown to be effective in helping people with chronic pain.

Medtronic has enjoyed strong growth in its international sales, which account for about 44 percent of total revenues. A well-stocked research and development pipeline has allowed Medtronic to launch a variety of new products in its international markets. Medtronic implements strategies tailored to each international market. In Japan, where the Minneapolis-based company has more than half the market share for pacing devices, it continues to increase the size of its sales force and its research and development activities.

About 62 percent of Medtronic's international sales were produced by its sales force while the balance of the products were sold through independent distributors in their respective countries. Medtronic has about 10,000 employees and 21,400 shareholders.

EARNINGS-PER-SHARE GROWTH ★ ★ ★

Past 5 years: 135 percent (19 percent per year)
Past 10 years: 339 percent (43 percent per year)

STOCK GROWTH ★ ★ ★ ★

Past 10 years: 1,559 percent (31.5 percent per year)

Dollar growth: $10,000 over 10 years (including reinvested dividends) would have grown to $170,000

Average annual compounded rate of return (including reinvested dividends): 33 percent

DIVIDEND YIELD

Average dividend yield in the past 3 years: 0.8 percent

DIVIDEND GROWTH ★ ★ ★ ★

Increased dividend: 17 consecutive years
Past 5-year increase: 127 percent (18 percent per year)

CONSISTENCY ★ ★ ★ ★

Increased earnings per share: 10 consecutive years
Increased sales: 10 consecutive years

SHAREHOLDER PERKS ★ ★

Good dividend reinvestment and stock purchase plan: voluntary stock purchase plan allows contributions of $25 to $4,000 per month

MEDTRONIC AT A GLANCE

Fiscal year ended: April 30
Revenue and net income in $ millions

	1989	1990	1991	1992	1993	1994	5-year Growth Avg. Annual (%)	Total (%)
Revenue ($)	765.8	865.9	1,021.4	1,176.9	1,382.2	1,390.9	13	82
Net income ($)	100.3	112.9	133.4	161.5	197.2	232.4	18	132
Earnings/share ($)	.86	.96	1.12	1.36	1.66	2.02	19	135
Div. per share ($)	.15	.18	.21	.24	.28	.34	18	127
Dividend yield (%)	1.3	1.1	0.7	0.7	0.9	0.9	—	—
Avg. PE ratio	11.5	14.8	19.0	26.4	25.2	18.0	—	—

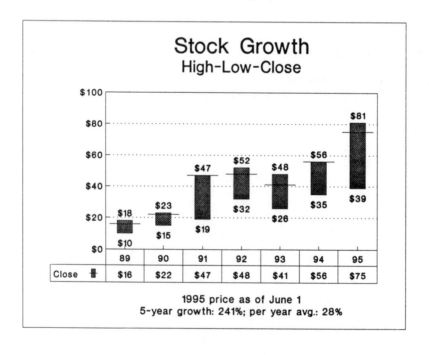

Stock Growth
High-Low-Close

	89	90	91	92	93	94	95
Close	$16	$22	$47	$48	$41	$56	$75

1995 price as of June 1
5-year growth: 241%; per year avg.: 28%

Merck & Company, Inc.

P. O. Box 2000
Rahway, NJ 07065
908-594-4000

Chairman: P. Roy Vagelos, M.D.
President and CEO: Raymond V. Gilmartin

Earnings Growth	★ ★	Dividend Growth	★ ★ ★ ★
Stock Growth	★ ★ ★	Consistency	★ ★ ★ ★
Dividend Yield	★ ★ ★	Shareholder Perks	★ ★
NYSE—MRK		**Total**	**18 points**

The quest for innovative new drugs can be an expensive proposition. Merck & Company, for instance, spends about $1.2 billion a year on research. But when you hit a winner, the rewards can be staggering. Vasotec, Merck's widely used heart and blood pressure medication, grosses about $2.2 billion a year.

The Rahway, New Jersey, operation is the world's largest pharmaceutical company. Its seven leading drugs all gross in excess of $500 million a year. Cholesterol medications Mevacor and Zocor each gross more than $1 billion a year. Merck's other leading drugs include Primaxin, an antibiotic; Prilosec and Pepcid, both of which are ulcer medications; and Ivermectin, an antiparasitic for animals.

The company's biggest market is cardiovascular medications, which account for 46 percent of Merck's $15 billion in annual revenue. Other leading drug groups include:

- Antibiotics (8 percent of sales), including Primaxin, Noroxin and Mefoxin;
- Anti-ulcerants (12 percent of sales), including Pepcid and Prilosec;
- Anti-inflammatories and analgesics (3 percent of sales), including Dolobid, Indocin and Clinoril;

- Ophthalmologicals (5 percent), including Timoptic;
- Vaccines (5 percent), including the M-M-RII (measles, mumps and rubella virus vaccine live) and hepatitis B vaccines;
- Other pharmaceuticals (4 percent), including anti-Parkinsonism products, psychotherapeutics and muscle relaxants;
- Other products through its Medco subsidiary (3 percent);
- Animal health and crop protection products (9 percent).

Merck also operates a specialty chemical products segment (5 percent of sales), producing applications for water treatment, paper manufacturing, oil field drilling, food processing, hard surface decontamination, skin care and wound management.

Merck has operations in about 20 countries, with sales in more than 100 countries. Foreign operations account for about 44 percent of total revenue.

The firm, which was founded in 1881, has 47,000 employees and 231,000 shareholders.

EARNINGS-PER-SHARE GROWTH

Past 5 years: 89 percent (14 percent per year)
Past 10 years: 543 percent (20.5 percent per year)

STOCK GROWTH ★ ★ ★

Past 10 years: 572 percent (21 percent per year)
Dollar growth: $10,000 over 10 years (including reinvested dividends) would have grown to $80,000
Average annual compounded rate of return (including reinvested dividends): 23 percent

DIVIDEND YIELD

Average dividend yield in the past 3 years: 2.8 percent

DIVIDEND GROWTH

Increased dividend: 11 consecutive years
Past 5-year increase: 107 percent (16 percent per year)

CONSISTENCY

Increased earnings per share: 13 consecutive years
Increased sales: 14 consecutive years

SHAREHOLDER PERKS ★ ★

Good dividend reinvestment and stock purchase plan: voluntary stock purchase plan allows contributions of $25 to $50,000 per year.

MERCK & COMPANY AT A GLANCE

Fiscal year ended: Dec. 31
Revenue and net income in $ millions

	1989	1990	1991	1992	1993	1994	5-year Growth Avg. Annual (%)	Total (%)
Revenue ($)	6,551	7,672	8,603	9,663	10,498	14,970	24	129
Net income ($)	1,495	1,781	2,121	2,447	2,687	2,997	15	100
Earnings/share ($)	1.26	1.52	1.83	2.12	2.33	2.38	14	89
Div. per share ($)	.55	.64	.77	.92	1.03	1.14	16	107
Dividend yield (%)	2.3	2.4	1.9	1.9	2.9	3.4	—	—
Avg. PE ratio	19	17	22	23	15	14	—	—

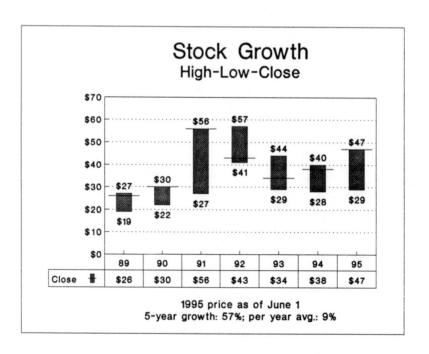

Stock Growth
High-Low-Close

	89	90	91	92	93	94	95
Close	$26	$30	$56	$43	$34	$38	$47

1995 price as of June 1
5-year growth: 57%; per year avg.: 9%

Schering-Plough Corp.

One Giralda Farms
Madison, NJ 07940
201-822-7000

Chairman and CEO: Robert P. Luciano
President: Richard J. Kogan

Earnings Growth	★ ★ ★	Dividend Growth	★ ★ ★
Stock Growth	★ ★ ★	Consistency	★ ★ ★ ★
Dividend Yield	★ ★ ★	Shareholder Perks	★ ★
NYSE—SGP		**Total**	**18 points**

From the nose to the toes, drugmaker Schering-Plough has a leading product to remedy pain and discomfort.

For hay fever sufferers Schering-Plough offers Claritin, which holds the number one position for new prescriptions in the plain antihistamine market. Launched in the United States in April 1993, Claritin recorded more than $130 million in sales by year's end, making it the company's largest and most successful product launch ever.

For the other end of the human body, Schering-Plough has Dr. Scholl's, which is the number one footcare company in North America. Capturing the top position in the athlete's foot market with a 25 percent share is Lotramin AF. Other leading footcare remedies are the antifungal Tinactin and Dr. Scholl's Bunion Guard.

With its Coppertone brand, Schering-Plough also leads in every segment of the United States sun care industry. Schering-Plough has been aggressively introducing new sunscreen products as medical evidence continues to mount on the dangers of exposure to the sun.

While Coppertone and Dr. Scholl are the products most familiar to consumers, Schering-Plough's line of pharmaceuticals is what powers the company's balance sheet. The company markets drugs for asthma and allergies, cancer and infectious diseases, skin ailments and cardiovascular disorders.

The company also has an animal health business and a vision care business operated under the Wesley-Jessen name. Its line of soft contact lenses is the second-leading United States brand.

The company has been particularly successful in converting its prescription drugs to over-the-counter status. Schering-Plough leads the pharmaceutical industry with eight conversions and is working on future candidates. It's a valuable skill in a cost-conscious medical era when more people are choosing to self-medicate through over-the-counter drugs.

Schering-Plough sells about half of its pharmaceuticals and health care products internationally. Sales have become tougher overseas because of intensified competition, but the company's broad product mix and aggressive marketing should keep it in the thick of the competition. The company has 21,600 employees and 32,200 shareholders.

EARNINGS-PER-SHARE GROWTH ★ ★ ★

Past 5 years: 130 percent (18 percent per year)
Past 10 years: 448 percent (18.5 percent per year)

STOCK GROWTH ★ ★ ★

Past 10 years: 494 percent (19.5 percent per year)
Dollar growth: $10,000 over 10 years (including reinvested dividends) would have grown to $74,000
Average annual compounded rate of return (including reinvested dividends): 22 percent

DIVIDEND YIELD ★ ★ ★

Average dividend yield in the past 3 years: 2.7 percent

DIVIDEND GROWTH

Increased dividend: 9 consecutive years
Past 5-year increase: 125 percent (18 percent per year)

CONSISTENCY

Increased earnings per share: 13 consecutive years
Increased sales: 15 consecutive years

SHAREHOLDER PERKS ★ ★

Good dividend reinvestment and stock purchase plan: voluntary stock purchase plan allows contributions of $25 to $36,000 per year.

Schering-Plough also hands out a tote bag packed with products to shareholders at its annual meetings. The bags include such products as Coppertone suntan lotion, Afrin nasal spray, Dr. Scholl's pads, Gyne-Lotramin and a wide variety of other over-the-counter products.

SCHERING-PLOUGH AT A GLANCE

Fiscal year ended: Dec. 31
Revenue and net income in $ millions

	1989	1990	1991	1992	1993	1994	5-year Growth Avg. Annual (%)	5-year Growth Total (%)
Revenue ($)	3,158	3,322	3,616	4,056	4,341	4,657	8	47
Net income ($)	471	565	646	720	825	922	14.5	96
Earnings/share ($)	1.05	1.25	1.51	1.80	2.12	2.41	18	130
Div. per share ($)	.44	.54	.64	.75	.87	.99	18	125
Dividend yield (%)	2.5	2.4	2.4	2.5	2.7	3.0	—	—
Avg. PE ratio	17	18	18	16	15	14	—	—

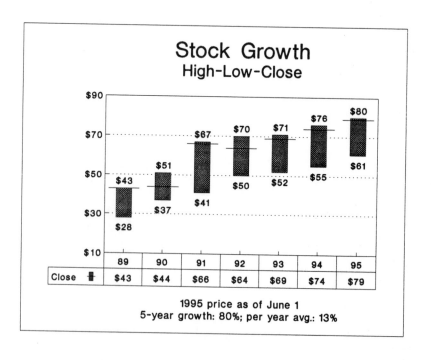

Stock Growth
High-Low-Close

	89	90	91	92	93	94	95
Close	$43	$44	$66	$64	$69	$74	$79

1995 price as of June 1
5-year growth: 80%; per year avg.: 13%

H&R Block, Inc.

H&R BLOCK®

4410 Main St.
Kansas City, MO 64111
816-753-6900

Chairman and CEO: Henry W. Bloch
President: Thomas M. Bloch

Earnings Growth	★ ★	Dividend Growth	★ ★ ★ ★
Stock Growth	★ ★ ★	Consistency	★ ★ ★ ★
Dividend Yield	★ ★ ★	Shareholder Perks	★ ★
NYSE—HRB		**Total**	**18 points**

Tax preparation has always been the backbone of H&R Block, but the company's greatest area of growth in recent years has come along the information superhighway.

CompuServe, the online computer information network, has been a subsidiary of H&R Block since 1980. With the new wave of computer users moving online, CompuServe has enjoyed a cyber-surge in popularity. Its revenue has grown 53 percent in the past two years and its earnings have nearly doubled. CompuServe now accounts for 35 percent of the company's $1.24 billion in total revenue.

The CompuServe online information service is available in about 100 countries, although most of its 1.8 million subscribers live in the United States. Europe is the fastest-growing market, doubling its subscriber base from 100,000 to 200,000 in the past year.

Thanks in part to the rapid growth of CompuServe, H&R Block has managed to overcome a rather stagnant period in the tax preparation market to maintain its string of 39 consecutive years of record sales. It has also enjoyed record earnings 38 of the past 39 years.

H&R Block prepares tax returns for about 13 million Americans each year. About 12 percent of all returns filed with the Internal Revenue Service are prepared by H&R Block. Outside the United States, the company prepares another 2 million returns in Canada, and has done a growing business in Europe, Australia and New Zealand.

In all, the company has 9,600 offices worldwide, including just over 4,500 company-owned branches and 5,040 franchised offices.

Block also offers some related services, including an "executive tax service," which it provides for about 513,000 clients with more complicated returns. About 7.6 million customers use its electronic filing program, which expedites the time it takes for taxpayers to receive their refunds. About 5.5 million customers use its "refund anticipation loan service," which provide on-the-spot advances for the amount of their calculated return, minus a transaction fee. H&R Block has about 3,600 permanent employees and 33,500 shareholders.

EARNINGS-PER-SHARE GROWTH ★ ★

Past 5 years: 98 percent (15 percent per year)
Past 10 years: 236 percent (13 percent per year)

STOCK GROWTH ★ ★ ★

Past 10 years: 447 percent (18.5 percent per year)
Dollar growth: $10,000 over 10 years (including reinvested dividends) would have grown to $72,000
Average annual compounded rate of return (including reinvested dividends): 22 percent

DIVIDEND YIELD ★ ★ ★

Average dividend yield in the past 3 years: 2.8 percent

DIVIDEND GROWTH ★ ★ ★ ★

Increased dividend: More than 19 consecutive years
Past 5-year increase: 118 percent (17 percent per year)

CONSISTENCY ★ ★ ★ ★

Increased earnings per share: 23 consecutive years
Increased sales: 39 consecutive years

SHAREHOLDER PERKS ★ ★

Good dividend reinvestment and stock purchase plan: voluntary stock
purchase plan allows contributions of $25 to $2,000 per month.

H&R BLOCK AT A GLANCE

Fiscal year ended: April 30
Revenue and net income in $ millions

	1989	1990	1991	1992	1993	1994	5-year Growth Avg. Annual (%)	Total (%)
Revenue ($)	690	820	925	986	1,074	1,239	13	80
Net income ($)	100	124	140	162	181	201	15	101
Earnings/share ($)	.95	1.15	1.31	1.49	1.68	1.88	15	98
Div. per share ($)	.50	.61	.75	.86	.97	1.09	17	118
Dividend yield (%)	3.7	3.5	2.7	2.7	2.7	3.0	—	—
Avg. PE ratio	14	16.5	22	21	22.5	22	—	—

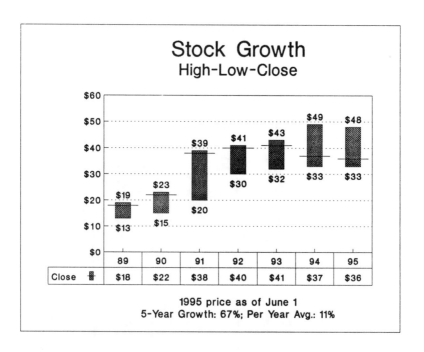

Stock Growth
High-Low-Close

Close	89	90	91	92	93	94	95
	$18	$22	$38	$40	$41	$37	$36

1995 price as of June 1
5-Year Growth: 67%; Per Year Avg.: 11%

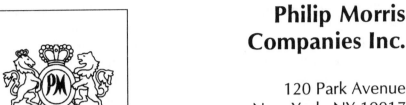

11
Philip Morris Companies Inc.

120 Park Avenue
New York, NY 10017
212-880-5000

Chairman: R. William Murray
President and CEO: Geoffrey Bible

Earnings Growth	★	Dividend Growth	★ ★ ★ ★
Stock Growth	★ ★ ★	Consistency	★ ★ ★
Dividend Yield	★ ★ ★ ★	Shareholder Perks	★ ★
NYSE—MO		**Total**	**17 points**

All around it is fire and fury—new, harsher government reports on the hazards of smoking; the threat of higher federal taxes on cigarettes; huge new lawsuits filed by state governments seeking to recover the health care costs of treating smokers; wide-sweeping bans on smoking in offices, airlines, restaurants and other establishments; and competitors cutting margins and flooding the cigarette market with discount brands.

How does the world's leading cigarette maker cope with the new wave of controversy?

The same way it has always coped with the controversy and competition of the tobacco industry—by racking up record sales and growing profits.

Philip Morris, the maker of Marlboro, Benson & Hedges, Merit and Virginia Slims, did have one bad year in 1993 when earnings tumbled as the company cut cigarette prices to combat the challenge of discount brands. But the company roared back in 1994, with a 34 percent increase in earnings per share. Its stock price, which had dropped from a high of $86 to a low of $45, roared back as well, edging as high as $75 by mid-1995.

Philip Morris markets its cigarettes around the world. It holds about a 7 percent share of the global cigarette market. Europe, Japan and the former Soviet Union are all booming markets for Philip Morris brands.

Marlboro is the country's and the world's largest selling cigarette, accounting for about 29 percent of the 500 billion cigarettes sold in the United States each year. Marlboro Lights, the leading "low tar" brand, accounts for another 10 percent of all U.S. sales. In all, Philip Morris' brands hold about a 45 percent share of the U.S. cigarette market.

Cigarette sales account for about 43 percent of the company's $65 billion in annual revenue and 62 percent of its operating profit.

The balance of the company's revenue comes from its food and beer groups. In all, the company puts more than 3,000 separate products on retailer's shelves. It is the largest consumer products producer in America and one of the largest in Europe, thanks to a series of recent acquisitions of European companies.

Among the company's wide array of recognizable brands are Kraft Foods, Oscar Mayer meats, Post cereals, Tang, Jell-O, Miracle Whip, Cool Whip and Kool-Aid. It also owns Maxwell House and Sanka coffees, Frusen Gladje and Breyers ice creams, Stove Top stuffing, Velveeta, Tombstone pizza and Parkay margarine.

The company's food group accounts for about 49 percent of sales and 33 percent of operating income.

Its beer group, led by Miller Beer, Molson and Icehouse, contributes 7 percent of revenue and 2 percent of operating income. The New York–based company has 161,000 employees and 100,000 shareholders.

EARNINGS-PER-SHARE GROWTH   ★

Past 5 years: 71 percent (11.5 percent per year)
Past 10 years: 414 percent (18 percent per year)

STOCK GROWTH   ★ ★ ★

Past 10 years: 509 percent (20 percent per year)
Dollar growth: $10,000 over 10 years (including reinvested dividends) would have grown to $88,000
Average annual compounded rate of return (including reinvested dividends): 24 percent

DIVIDEND YIELD

Average dividend yield in the past 3 years: 4.3 percent

DIVIDEND GROWTH

Increased dividend: 27 consecutive years
Past 5-year increase: 142 percent (19 percent per year)

CONSISTENCY ★ ★ ★

Increased earnings per share: 9 of past 10 years (and 39 of the past 40 years)
Increased sales: 40 consecutive years

SHAREHOLDER PERKS ★ ★

Good dividend reinvestment and stock purchase plan: voluntary stock purchase plan allows contributions of $10 to $60,000 per year.

PHILIP MORRIS AT A GLANCE

Fiscal year ended: Dec. 31
Revenue and net income in $ millions

	1989	1990	1991	1992	1993	1994	5-year Growth Avg. Annual (%)	5-year Growth Total (%)
Revenue ($)	44,080	51,169	56,458	59,131	60,901	65,125	8	48
Net income ($)	2,946	3,540	3,006	4,939	3,091	4,725	10	60
Earnings/share ($)	3.18	3.83	4.54	5.45	3.52	5.45	11.5	71
Div. per share ($)	1.25	1.55	1.91	2.35	2.60	3.03	19	142
Dividend yield (%)	3.5	3.5	2.8	3.0	4.7	5.1		
Avg. PE ratio	12	12	15	14	13.5	10		

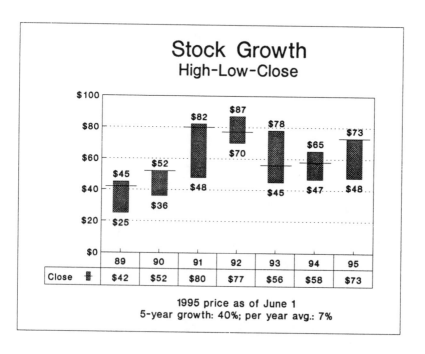

Stock Growth
High-Low-Close

Close	89	90	91	92	93	94	95
	$42	$52	$80	$77	$56	$58	$73

1995 price as of June 1
5-year growth: 40%; per year avg.: 7%

PepsiCo, Inc.

Purchase, NY 10577-1444
914-253-2000

Chairman and CEO: D. Wayne Calloway

Earnings Growth	★ ★	Dividend Growth	★ ★ ★ ★
Stock Growth	★ ★ ★	Consistency	★ ★ ★ ★
Dividend Yield	★ ★	Shareholder Perks	★ ★
NYSE—PEP		**Total**	**17 points**

Nothing like a cola to wash down your chips, chicken, tacos or pizza. PepsiCo offers the whole package. In addition to its namesake soft drink, PepsiCo's Frito-Lay division is the world's leading snack chip producer, while its Taco Bell, Pizza Hut and Kentucky Fried Chicken chains make the Purchase, New York, operation the world's leading restaurant system.

Occasionally the foods giant also likes to add a little controversy to the mix. In a recent advertising campaign for Pizza Hut's stuffed pizzas, the company featured pro basketball bad guy Dennis Rodman, multimillionaire Donald Trump and his ex-wife Ivana, and controversial conservative commentator Rush Limbaugh, whose portly proportions seem well-suited to a stuffed pizza ad.

PepsiCo has been making a concerted effort recently to expand its international operations. Foreign sales now account for about 33 percent of its total profits. Of the company's approximately 26,000 restaurants, about one-fourth are located outside the United States. The largest chain is Pizza Hut with 11,000 restaurants worldwide, including about 2,500 outside the United States. Next is Kentucky Fried Chicken with nearly 10,000 restaurants including 4,000 foreign outlets. Taco Bell has about 5,000 restaurants, more than 90 percent of which are in the United States.

In all, the company has restaurants in more than 70 countries worldwide. Two-thirds of its foreign restaurants are located in Japan, Canada, Australia and the United Kingdom.

The company is also focusing on foreign expansion of its soft drink market. The maker of Pepsi, Mountain Dew, All Sport, Mug Root Beer, Ocean Spray Cranberry Juice and Slice (and the marketer of 7-UP outside the United States) makes up about 19 percent of the international soft drink market (which falls well behind Coca-Cola's share). While Pepsi is sold in about 170 countries, its U.S. per capita soft drink consumption is more than ten times that of its foreign markets.

PepsiCo's most successful foreign segment is its Frito-Lay snack foods division, which draws about 39 percent of its revenue from the international market. PepsiCo is the maker of Lay's potato chips, Fritos, Doritos, Cheetos, Ruffles, Tostitos, Sun Chips and other snack chips. In the U.S. market, Frito-Lay products account for 53 percent of all snack chip sales.

Snack foods account for about 29 percent of the company's $28.5 billion in annual revenue, while soft drinks account for 34 percent and restaurants generate 37 percent of revenue. PepsiCo, which was founded in 1919, has 423,000 employees and 94,000 shareholders.

EARNINGS-PER-SHARE GROWTH   ★ ★

Past 5 years: 96 percent (14.5 percent per year)
Past 10 years: 484 percent (19 percent per year)

STOCK GROWTH   ★ ★ ★

Past 10 years: 562 percent (21 percent per year)
Dollar growth: $10,000 over 10 years (including reinvested dividends) would have grown to $80,000
Average annual compounded rate of return (including reinvested dividends): 23 percent

DIVIDEND YIELD

Average dividend yield in the past 3 years: 1.6 percent

DIVIDEND GROWTH

Increased dividend: More than 22 consecutive years
Past 5-year increase: 119 percent (17 percent per year)

CONSISTENCY ★ ★ ★ ★

Increased earnings per share: 11 consecutive years
Increased sales: More than 19 consecutive years

SHAREHOLDER PERKS ★ ★

Good dividend reinvestment and stock purchase plan: voluntary stock purchase plan allows contributions of $25 to $60,000 per year. Shareholders may also pick up sample products at the annual meeting.

PEPSICO AT A GLANCE

Fiscal year ended: Dec. 31
Revenue and net income in $ millions

	1989	1990	1991	1992	1993	1994	5-year Growth Avg. Annual (%)	Total (%)
Revenue ($)	15,049	17,515	19,292	21,970	25,021	28,472	14	89
Net income ($)	901	1,050	1,200	1,302	1,588	1,784	15	98
Earnings/share ($)	1.13	1.37	1.50	1.61	1.96	2.22	14.5	96
Div. per share ($)	.32	.38	.46	.51	.61	.70	17	119
Dividend yield (%)	1.8	1.6	1.5	1.4	1.6	1.9	—	—
Avg. PE ratio	16	18	20	23	20	16	—	—

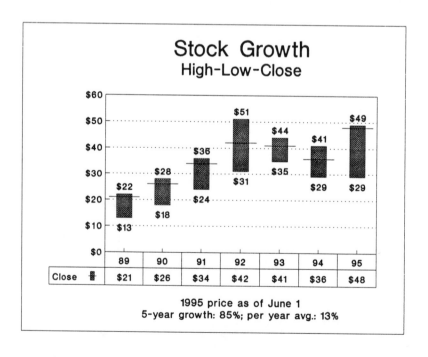

Stock Growth
High-Low-Close

	89	90	91	92	93	94	95
Close	$21	$26	$34	$42	$41	$36	$48

1995 price as of June 1
5-year growth: 85%; per year avg.: 13%

13

Norwest Corp.

Norwest Center
6th & Marquette
Minneapolis, MN 55479
612-667-1234

President and CEO: Richard M. Kovacevich

Earnings Growth	★ ★ ★ ★	Dividend Growth	★ ★ ★
Stock Growth	★ ★ ★	Consistency	★ ★
Dividend Yield	★ ★ ★	Shareholder Perks	★ ★
NYSE—NOB		**Total**	**17 points**

Norwest Corp. has become one of the nation's biggest banks by thinking small. "We're focused on the retail customer, small business and agriculture," says Norwest president and CEO Richard M. Kovacevich. "That's our emphasis."

The Minneapolis-based institution also takes a unique view of its branch bank system. "We view ourselves more as a retailer than a traditional bank," adds Kovacevich. "We deal with stores—not branches."

In Norwest's "stores," the focus is on "cross-selling"—selling customers multiple services such as savings, checking, CDs, consumer loans, mortgages, credit cards and investment services. A high percentage of Norwest's customers use several of its banking services.

Norwest has grown rapidly through a series of acquisitions. Its banking division now boasts about 620 branches in 15 states. The bank offers a wide range of traditional services, including community and corporate banking, trust, capital management and credit card services.

Along with the traditional banking operation, the company operates several related subsidiaries, including investment services, insurance and venture capital companies.

Norwest's mortgage division, which has offices in all 50 states, funded $24.9 billion in mortgages in 1994.

The company's consumer finance subsidiary, which offers installment loans and related services, has 1,042 offices in 46 states, Guam and all 10 Canadian provinces.

In all, Norwest has about 2,800 branches (or "stores" as the company refers to them). Its largest concentration is in its home state of Minnesota, with 311 offices, followed by California (187 offices), Colorado (156 offices), Arizona (154 offices), Indiana (116 offices) and Wisconsin (113 offices). Norwest also has 130 offices in Canada.

The company's banking segment is its most profitable, accounting for 63 percent of its $800 million in net income. Mortgage banking makes up 9 percent of income and consumer finance accounts for 28 percent. Founded in 1929, Norwest has 40,000 employees and 30,000 shareholders.

EARNINGS-PER-SHARE GROWTH   ★ ★ ★ ★

Past 5 years: 141 percent (19 percent per year)
Past 10 years: 653 percent (22 percent per year)

STOCK GROWTH   ★ ★ ★

Past 10 years: 478 percent (19 percent per year)
Dollar growth: $10,000 over 10 years (including reinvested dividends) would have grown to $75,000
Average annual compounded rate of return (including reinvested dividends): 22 percent

DIVIDEND YIELD   ★ ★ ★

Average dividend yield in the past 3 years: 2.8 percent

DIVIDEND GROWTH   ★ ★ ★

Increased dividend: 7 consecutive years
Past 5-year increase: 103 percent (15 percent per year)

CONSISTENCY

Increased earnings per share: 8 of the past 10 years

SHAREHOLDER PERKS ★ ★

Good dividend reinvestment and stock purchase plan: voluntary stock purchase plan allows contributions of $25 to $30,000 per quarter.

NORWEST AT A GLANCE

Fiscal year ended: Dec. 31
Revenue and net income in $ millions

	1989	1990	1991	1992	1993	1994	5-year Growth Avg. Annual (%)	Total (%)
Assets ($)	24,335	30,626	38,502	44,557	50,782	59,316	20	144
Net income ($)	284.5	169.4	418.3	394.0	613.1	800.4	23	181
Earnings/share ($)	1.00	.59	1.33	1.42	1.86	2.41	19	141
Div. per share ($)	.38	.42	.47	.54	.64	.77	15	103
Dividend yield (%)	3.8	4.4	3.3	2.8	2.6	3.1	—	—
Avg. PE ratio	8.0	7.1	9.9	11.2	11.9	10.4	—	—

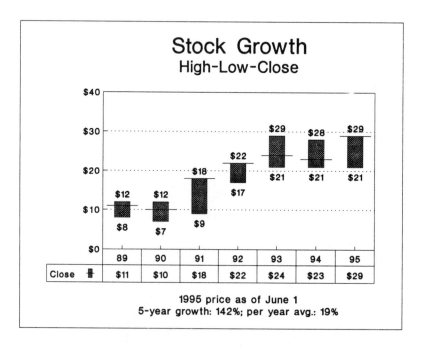

Stock Growth
High-Low-Close

	89	90	91	92	93	94	95
Close	$11	$10	$18	$22	$24	$23	$29

1995 price as of June 1
5-year growth: 142%; per year avg.: 19%

Wal-Mart Stores, Inc.

WAL★MART™

Bentonville, AR 72716
501-273-4000

Chairman: S. Robson Walton
President and CEO: David D. Glass

Earnings Growth	★ ★ ★ ★	Dividend Growth	★ ★ ★ ★
Stock Growth	★ ★ ★ ★	Consistency	★ ★ ★ ★
Dividend Yield	★	Shareholder Perks	
NYSE—WMT		**Total**	**17 points**

Wal-Mart's hottest new concept is the Supercenter, a combination discount store and grocery supermarket that covers a full four acres of floor space. First introduced in 1989, the Supercenters have been doubling in number each year. The total number of Supercenters went from 30 to 68 in 1994 and was expected to jump to about 140 by the end of 1995.

The Supercenters, which range in size from about 170,000 to 200,000 square feet, offer food, general merchandise and a wide range of services, including pharmacy, dry cleaning, portrait studios, photo finishing, hair salons and optical shops.

Wal-Mart is the worlds's largest retail chain, with total annual revenue of $67.3 billion. The company has about 2,000 Wal-Mart stores in 47 states. Wal-Mart also has about 420 Sam's Club warehouse stores and operates the McLane Company, the nation's largest distributor of food and non-food items to convenience stores.

Wal-Mart has also begun to establish a presence outside the United States. The company bought 122 Woolco stores in Canada in 1994 and has been building stores in Mexico through a joint venture with CIFRA SA, Mexico's largest retailer.

The company's product sales break down this way: soft goods (apparel, towels, sheets, etc.), 27 percent of sales; hard goods (hardware, housewares, auto supplies and small appliances), 26 percent; stationery and candy, 11 percent; sporting goods and toys, 9 percent; health and beauty aids, 8 percent; gifts, records and electronics, 8 percent; pharmaceuticals, 7 percent; shoes, 2 percent; jewelry, 2 percent.

Wal-Mart was founded in 1962 by Sam Walton, who ultimately became a legend of American business and the nation's richest man before his death in 1992. Walton entered the retailing business in 1945 when he opened a Ben Franklin variety store franchise in Newport, Arkansas. His first Wal-Mart store (called "Wal-Mart Discount City") was opened in Rogers, Arkansas, in 1962.

The Bentonville, Arkansas, retailer has posted 25 consecutive years of record earnings, dating back to 1969, the year the company went public.

Walton achieved his early success largely by locating stores in rural locations like Rogers where there was no competition from other discounters. The retailer's "everyday low prices" attracted throngs of shoppers wherever the new stores appeared. The company has been able to keep its prices low by buying its merchandise in large volume and turning it over quickly, incurring a minimum of overhead in the process.

Wal-Mart stores are now beginning to spring up in greater numbers in urban areas, where they compete toe-to-toe with Target, K mart and other discounters. While the competition is stiffer, the urban-based Wal-Marts have still proved very profitable. Wal-Mart has 528,000 employees and 260,000 shareholders.

EARNINGS-PER-SHARE GROWTH ★ ★ ★ ★

Past 5 years: 151 percent (20 percent per year)
Past 10 years: 883 percent (26 percent per year)

STOCK GROWTH ★ ★ ★ ★

Past 10 years: 603 percent (21.5 percent per year)
Dollar growth: $10,000 over 10 years (including reinvested dividends) would have grown to $73,000

Average annual compounded rate of return (including reinvested dividends): 22 percent

DIVIDEND YIELD ★

Average dividend yield in the past 3 years: 0.5 percent

DIVIDEND GROWTH ★ ★ ★ ★

Increased dividend: 17 consecutive years
Past 5-year increase: 167 percent (22 percent per year)

CONSISTENCY ★ ★ ★ ★

Increased earnings per share: 25 consecutive years (every year since going public in 1969)
Increased sales: 25 consecutive years

SHAREHOLDER PERKS

The company does not offer a dividend reinvestment plan. At the annual meeting, shareholders are often given Wal-Mart memorabilia such as hats, buttons and T-shirts.

WAL-MART AT A GLANCE

Fiscal year ended: Jan. 31
Revenue and net income in $ millions

	1989	1990	1991	1992	1993	1994	5-year Growth Avg. Annual (%)	Total (%)
Revenue ($)	25,810	32,601	43,886	55,483	67,344	82,493	26	219
Net income ($)	1,076	1,291	1,608	1,995	2,333	2,635	20	145
Earnings/share ($)	.47	.57	.70	.87	1.02	1.18	20	151
Div. per share ($)	.06	.07	.09	.11	.13	.16	22	167
Dividend yield (%)	0.5	0.5	0.3	0.3	0.5	0.7	—	—
Avg. PE ratio	21	24	33	33	27	21	—	—

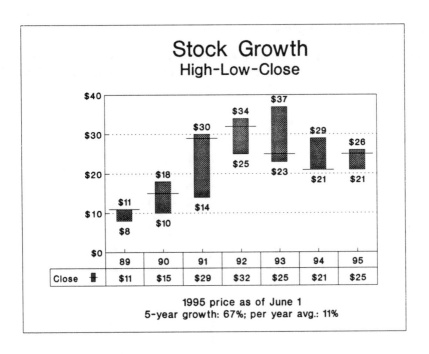

Stock Growth
High-Low-Close

	89	90	91	92	93	94	95
Close	$11	$15	$29	$32	$25	$21	$25

1995 price as of June 1
5-year growth: 67%; per year avg.: 11%

Abbott Laborato.

One Abbot Park Road
Abbott Park, IL 60064-3500
708-937-6100

Chairman and CEO: Duane L. Burnham
President and COO: Thomas R. Hodgson

Earnings Growth	★ ★	Dividend Growth	★ ★ ★ ★
Stock Growth	★ ★ ★	Consistency	★ ★ ★ ★
Dividend Yield	★ ★	Shareholder Perks	★ ★
NYSE—ABT		**Total**	**17 points**

A steady stream of medical advances has kept profits growing at Abbott Laboratories for more than 20 consecutive years. It's a trend that appears to be far from over.

Abbott, which has posted record sales, earnings and dividends every year since 1971, has introduced a new wave of highly touted drugs that are expected to propel earnings growth for years to come.

Abbott's brightest new star is clarithromycin (marketed under the brand names Biaxin, Klacid and Karicid), an antibiotic originally developed to treat respiratory infections. Clarithromycin, which grossed $650 million in sales in 1994, also received U.S. Food and Drug Administration clearance for use in treating a bacterial infection common in AIDS patients. The drug is also being tested as a treatment for peptic ulcers.

Abbott, a 107-year-old Chicago-area operation, may be most widely recognized for its diagnostic products. It is the world leader in blood screening equipment and was the first company to introduce an AIDS antibody test. It is also the world leader in tests for AIDS, hepatitis, sexually transmitted diseases, cancer, thyroid function, pregnancy, illicit drugs and drug monitoring.

Hospital and laboratory products account for about 48 percent of Abbott's $9.16 billion in annual revenue. Leading products include critical care monitoring instruments, intravenous and irrigation fluids (and the equipment to administer them), drug delivery devices and multiapplication diagnostic machines. Abbott is the world leader in anesthesia products and is a major manufacturer of urine drug sample testing systems for corporations and other organizations.

Abbott's pharmaceutical and nutritional products account for about 52 percent of its revenue. The company makes drugs for the treatment of anxiety, epilepsy and high blood pressure. It is a leading producer of antibiotics and it manufacturers a broad line of cardiovascular products, cough and cold formulas and vitamins.

While most of Abbott's products are specialized for the medical profession, the company produces a handful of consumer products such as Ensure nutritional supplement, Murine eye drops, Selsun Blue dandruff shampoo, Tronolane hemorrhoid medication and Isomil and Similac nutritional formulas for infants.

Abbott is also a leading producer of biological pesticides, plant growth regulators, herbicides and related agricultural products. The company recently introduced several anti-infective products for animals.

The firm boasts a strong international business, which accounts for about 36 percent of total revenue. It has operations in more than 130 countries.

Abbott Laboratories was founded in 1888 when Dr. Wallace C. Abbott began a sideline venture in his small Chicago apartment making pills from the alkaloid of plants.

EARNINGS-PER-SHARE GROWTH ★ ★

Past 5 years: 95 percent (14 percent per year)
Past 10 years: 345 percent (16 percent per year)

STOCK GROWTH ★ ★ ★

Past 10 years: 471 percent (19 percent per year)

Dollar growth: $10,000 over 10 years (including reinvested dividends) would have grown to $69,000

Average annual compounded rate of return (including reinvested dividends): 21 percent

DIVIDEND YIELD ★ ★

Average dividend yield in the past 3 years: 2.4 percent

DIVIDEND GROWTH ★ ★ ★ ★

Increased dividend: Every year since 1971
Past 5-year increase: 117 percent (17 percent per year)

CONSISTENCY ★ ★ ★ ★

Increased earnings per share: 24 consecutive years
Increased sales: 24 consecutive years

SHAREHOLDER PERKS ★ ★

Good dividend reinvestment and stock purchase plan: voluntary stock purchase plan allows contributions of $10 to $5,000 per quarter.

Shareholders who attend the annual meeting receive a sampling of Abbott's consumer products such as Selsun Blue, Murine, an ice pack and a bottle of vitamins.

ABBOTT LABORATORIES AT A GLANCE

Fiscal year ended: Dec. 31
Revenue and net income in $ millions

	1989	1990	1991	1992	1993	1994	5-year Growth Avg. Annual (%)	5-year Growth Total (%)
Revenue ($)	5,379.8	6,158.7	6,876.6	7,851.9	8,407.8	9,156.0	11	70
Net income ($)	859.8	965.8	1,088.7	1,239.1	1,399.1	1,516.7	12	76
Earnings/share ($)	.96	1.11	1.28	1.47	1.69	1.87	14	95
Div. per share ($)	.35	.42	.50	.60	.68	.76	17	117
Dividend yield (%)	2.4	2.2	1.9	2.0	2.5	2.6	—	—
Avg. PE ratio	15.3	17.2	20.5	21.6	15.9	15.9	—	—

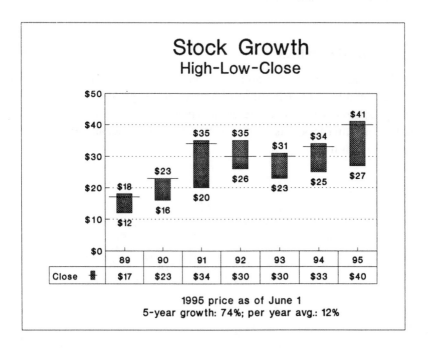

Stock Growth
High-Low-Close

	89	90	91	92	93	94	95
Close	$17	$23	$34	$30	$30	$33	$40

1995 price as of June 1
5-year growth: 74%; per year avg.: 12%

16
Walgreen Company

Walgreens

200 Wilmot Road
Deerfield, IL 60015
708-940-2500

Chairman and CEO: Charles R. Walgreen, III
President: L. Daniel Jorndt

Earnings Growth	★ ★	Dividend Growth	★ ★ ★ ★
Stock Growth	★ ★ ★	Consistency	★ ★ ★ ★
Dividend Yield	★ ★	Shareholder Perks	★ ★
NYSE—WAG		**Total**	**17 points**

It took Walgreen 83 years to grow from one store to 1,000, but the company needed only 10 more years—from 1984 to 1994—to add its next 1,000 stores. Even with 2,000 stores in 30 states, however, the Chicago-area retailer is far from the saturation point. The company expects to open its next 1,000 stores faster than ever—reaching the 3,000 mark by the year 2000.

Walgreen, which was founded in 1901 by Charles Walgreen, is the nation's largest and best-managed drug store chain. The company has posted 20 consecutive years of record sales and earnings.

Walgreen stores average about 10,000 square feet per store and carry a wide range of merchandise including clocks, calculators, jewelry, artwork, lunch buckets, wastebaskets, coffee makers, mixers, telephones, tape decks and TV sets along with the usual line of cosmetics, toiletries and tobacco. Many Walgreens also carry dairy products, frozen foods and a large selection of other grocery items.

The company's newest stores are 13,500 square feet and often include pharmacy waiting areas, consultation windows, fragrance departments, and one-hour photofinishing services.

Prescription drugs account for 41 percent of the company's $9.2 billion in annual revenue. Nonprescription drugs account for 13 percent; liquor and beverages, 9 percent; cosmetics and toiletries, 9 percent; tobacco products, 4 percent and general merchandise, 24 percent.

The company plans to open 200 new stores per year over the next five years. Its greatest concentration of stores is around its Chicago home base, with 313 stores in Illinois, 108 in Wisconsin and 94 in Indiana. Other leading areas are Florida, with 326 stores; Arizona, 110; California, 117; Texas, 182; Massachusetts, 67; Minnesota, 59; Missouri, 65; and Tennessee, 69.

The company's 2,000 stores are linked by satellite dish to Walgreen's home office, enabling the company to track inventory, monitor sales levels and provide prescription histories for Walgreen customers. Walgreen has 62,000 employees and 29,000 shareholders.

EARNINGS-PER-SHARE GROWTH   ★ ★

Past 5 years: 82 percent (13 percent per year)
Past 10 years: 240 percent (13 percent per year)

STOCK GROWTH   ★ ★ ★

Past 10 years: 400 percent (17.5 percent per year)
Dollar growth: $10,000 over 10 years (including reinvested dividends) would have grown to $57,000
Average annual compounded rate of return (including reinvested dividends): 19 percent

DIVIDEND YIELD   ★ ★

Average dividend yield in the past 3 years: 1.6 percent

DIVIDEND GROWTH

Increased dividend: More than 19 consecutive years
Past 5-year increase: 100 percent (15 percent per year)

CONSISTENCY

Increased earnings per share: 21 consecutive years
Increased sales: 21 consecutive years

SHAREHOLDER PERKS ★ ★

Good dividend reinvestment and stock purchase plan: voluntary stock purchase plan allows contributions of $10 to $5,000 eight times per year. Shareholders who attend the Walgreen annual meeting usually receive one or two Walgreen products, such as vitamins or other personal care products.

WALGREEN AT A GLANCE

Fiscal year ended: August 31
Revenue and net income in $ millions

	1989	1990	1991	1992	1993	1994	5-year Growth Avg. Annual (%)	Total (%)
Revenue ($)	5,380	6,047	6,733	7,475	8,295	9,235	12	72
Net income ($)	154	175	195	221	222	282	13	83
Earnings/share ($)	1.25	1.41	1.58	1.78	1.98	2.28	13	82
Div. per share ($)	.34	.40	.46	.52	.60	.68	15	100
Dividend yield (%)	1.8	1.8	1.6	1.5	1.5	1.7	—	—
Avg. PE ratio	15	16	18.5	19.5	20	17	—	—

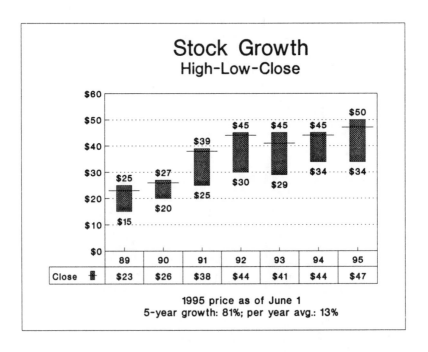

Stock Growth
High-Low-Close

Close	89	90	91	92	93	94	95
	$23	$26	$38	$44	$41	$44	$47

1995 price as of June 1
5-year growth: 81%; per year avg.: 13%

General Mills, Inc.

One General Mills Blvd.
P. O. Box 1113
Minneapolis, MN 55440
612-540-2311

Chairman and CEO: H. Brewster Atwater, Jr.
President: Stephen W. Sanger

Earnings Growth	★ ★	Dividend Growth	★ ★ ★ ★
Stock Growth	★ ★	Consistency	★ ★ ★
Dividend Yield	★ ★ ★	Shareholder Perks	★ ★ ★
NYSE—GIS		**Total**	**17 points**

Americans have been starting their day with the Big G since 1928. The maker of Cheerios, Wheaties, Trix, Kix and Lucky Charms, General Mills is the second-largest "ready-to-eat" cereal producer in America (and worldwide).

The Minneapolis-based operation also turns out a variety of other popular brand foods, such as Betty Crocker desserts, Hamburger Helper, Pop Secret microwave popcorn, Gold Medal flour, Bisquick, Yoplait yogurt, Fruit Roll-Ups, Fruit by the Foot, Gushers, Shark Bites and Berry Bears fruit candies.

But the driving force of the company's business continues to be its cereal division. Cheerios, for instance, is the leading brand in the cereal industry. Brand extensions Honey Nut Cheerios, introduced in 1979, and Apple Cinnamon Cheerios, launched in 1989, have also landed on the top ten list of the U.S. cereal market. Along with Multi-Grain Cheerios, the Cheerios family now accounts for nearly 10 percent of total sales in the U.S. ready-to-eat cereal market.

Among the company's other leading brands are Wheaties, Trix, Kix, Total, Berry Berry Kix, Cinnamon Toast Crunch, Triples, Cocoa Puffs,

Fiber One, Golden Grahams and Basic 4. General Mills' cereals hold a 29 percent share of the $8 billion U.S. ready-to-eat cereal market.

The company recently spun off its restaurant division into a separate company. The restaurant segment, which accounted for about 35 percent of the company's $8.5 billion in revenue in 1994, has about 1,100 restaurants including Red Lobster, The Olive Garden and China Coast.

Prior to the 1995 spin-off, General Mills had 126,000 employees and 34,000 shareholders. Foreign sales accounted for about 4 percent of the company's total revenue.

EARNINGS-PER-SHARE GROWTH   ★ ★

Past 5 years: 81 percent (13 percent per year)
Past 10 years: 182 percent (11 percent per year)

STOCK GROWTH   ★ ★

Past 10 years: 333 percent (16 percent per year)
Dollar growth: $10,000 over 10 years (including reinvested dividends) would have grown to $57,000
Average annual compounded rate of return (including reinvested dividends): 19 percent

DIVIDEND YIELD   ★ ★ ★

Average dividend yield in the past 3 years: 2.7 percent

DIVIDEND GROWTH   ★ ★ ★ ★

Increased dividend: 29 consecutive years
Past 5-year increase: 100 percent (15 percent per year)

CONSISTENCY   ★ ★ ★

Increased earnings per share: 9 consecutive years
Increased sales: 8 of past 10 years

SHAREHOLDER PERKS

Good dividend reinvestment and stock purchase plan: voluntary stock purchase plan allows contributions of $10 to $3,000 per quarter. The company occasionally sends out coupons for some of its products along with its quarterly reports.

It also offers holiday gift boxes in December at very attractive prices. Recently, for example, the boxes included nearly $50 worth of goods and coupons, including Betty Crocker's Southwest Cooking cookbook and packages of Multi-Grain Cheerios, a Breakfast pack cereal assortment, strawberry Gushers fruit snacks, Gold Medal blueberry muffin mix, mushroom and wild rice Hamburger Helper, cheddar flavor Potatoes Express, Betty Crocker Sunkist lemon bars, butter flavor Pop Secret and IncrediBites snacks. The cost to shareholders is about $20 per box.

GENERAL MILLS AT A GLANCE

Fiscal year ended: May 31
Revenue and net income in $ millions

	1989	1990	1991	1992	1993	1994	5-year Growth Avg. Annual (%)	Total (%)
Revenue ($)	5,620.6	6,448.3	7,153.2	7,777.8	8,134.6	8,516.9	9	51
Net income ($)	315.3	373.7	437.7	505.6	563.4	557.0	13	80
Earnings/share ($)	1.93	2.27	2.82	3.05	3.45	3.50	13	81
Div. per share ($)	.94	1.10	1.28	1.48	1.68	1.88	15	100
Dividend yield (%)	3.5	3.1	2.7	2.3	2.5	3.2	—	—
Avg. PE ratio	14.0	15.5	18.0	21.0	19.8	17.0	—	—

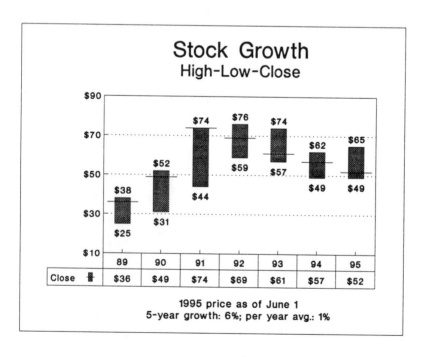

Stock Growth
High-Low-Close

	89	90	91	92	93	94	95
Close	$36	$49	$74	$69	$61	$57	$52

1995 price as of June 1
5-year growth: 6%; per year avg.: 1%

18

The Home Depot

2727 Paces Ferry Road N.W.
Atlanta, GA 30339
404-433-8211

Chairman and CEO: Bernard Marcus
President: Arthur M. Blank

Earnings Growth	★ ★ ★ ★	Dividend Growth	★ ★ ★
Stock Growth	★ ★ ★ ★	Consistency	★ ★ ★
Dividend Yield		Shareholder Perks	★ ★
NYSE—HD		**Total**	**16 points**

Do-it-yourselfers have found a home at Home Depot. Now with about 350 stores in 26 states and Canada, The Home Depot is the world's largest home improvement retailer. It is also, according to a survey conducted by *Fortune* magazine, America's "most admired" retailer.

Each of the company's cavernous warehouse-style outlets, which average about 100,000 square feet, stocks 40,000 to 50,000 home improvement products including nuts, bolts, brushes, boards, carpet, screens, saws, spades, power tools, appliances and lawn and garden supplies. The Atlanta-based operation has built its business by offering its vast selection of merchandise at low prices. Home Depot avoids special sales but routinely offers wholesale-type prices on all of its merchandise. In addition to the aisles and aisles of hardware, most stores also feature a small stage and bleachers for how-to clinics.

The company continues to test new features at some of its stores. Among its latest ventures is "Depot Diners," which are 1,200-square-foot restaurants near the front of the stores. The company has also added expanded garden centers at about 100 Home Depot stores.

One of the secrets to Home Depot's success is its well-trained sales force. Store employees are cross-trained in all departments and many have a background in the building industry. Customers with questions about home projects can usually learn all they need to know by talking with sales clerks. About 95 percent of the company's 60,000 employees are full-time, and the company offers above-average salary and benefits to keep its employees in the fold.

The Home Depot's primary customers are do-it-yourself homeowners, although many remodeling contractors and building maintenance professionals also buy supplies at Home Depot stores.

Of the company's $12.5 billion in annual revenue, 27.5 percent comes from plumbing, heating, lighting and electrical supplies, 34.2 percent from building materials, lumber, floor and wall coverings, 13 percent from hardware and tools, 14.5 percent from seasonal and specialty items, and 10.7 percent from paint and other products.

Ultimately Home Depot plans to have stores in all 50 states. It already has about a dozen stores in Canada and has announced plans to move into the Mexican market soon.

The Home Deport was founded in 1978 by Bernard Marcus (who still serves as the company's chairman and CEO), Arthur Blank (Home Depot president), and Kenneth G. Langone (a company board of directors member). The company has about 60,000 employees and 60,000 shareholders.

EARNINGS-PER-SHARE GROWTH ★ ★ ★ ★

Past 5 years: 313 percent (33 percent per year)
Past 10 years: 2,100 percent (37 percent per year)

STOCK GROWTH ★ ★ ★ ★

Past 10 years: 2,667 percent (39 percent per year)
Dollar growth: $10,000 over 10 years (including reinvested dividends) would have grown to $277,000
Average annual compounded rate of return (including reinvested dividends): 39 percent

DIVIDEND YIELD

Average dividend yield in the past 3 years: 0.3 percent

DIVIDEND GROWTH

Increased dividend: 7 consecutive years
Past 5-year increase: 650 percent (49 percent per year)

CONSISTENCY

Increased earnings per share: 9 of past 10 years
Increased sales: 14 consecutive years

SHAREHOLDER PERKS ★ ★

Good dividend reinvestment and stock purchase plan: voluntary stock
purchase plan allows contributions of $10 to $4,000 per month.

THE HOME DEPOT AT A GLANCE

Fiscal year ended: Jan. 31
Revenue and net income in $ millions

	1989	1990	1991	1992	1993	1994	5-year Growth Avg. Annual (%)	5-year Growth Total (%)
Revenue ($)	2,759	3,815	5,137	7,148	9,239	12,477	35	352
Net income ($)	111.9	163.4	249.1	362.9	457.4	604.5	40	440
Earnings/share ($)	.32	.45	.60	.82	1.01	1.32	33	313
Div. per share ($)	.02	.04	.05	.08	.11	.15	49	650
Dividend yield (%)	0.4	0.3	0.2	0.2	0.3	0.3	—	—
Avg. PE ratio	21.4	25.4	40.9	47.1	42.3	33.0	—	—

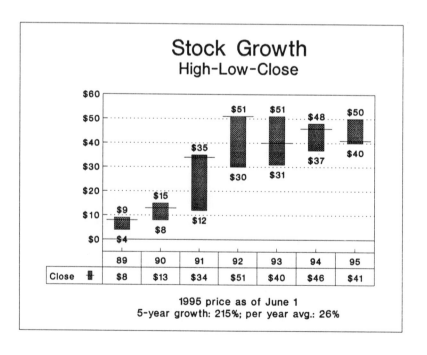

Stock Growth
High-Low-Close

Close	89	90	91	92	93	94	95
	$8	$13	$34	$51	$40	$46	$41

1995 price as of June 1
5-year growth: 215%; per year avg.: 26%

Crompton & Knowles Corp.

One Station Place, Metro Center
Stamford, CT 06902
203-353-5400

Chairman, President and CEO: Vincent A. Calarco

Earnings Growth	★ ★	Dividend Growth	★ ★ ★ ★
Stock Growth	★ ★ ★ ★	Consistency	★ ★
Dividend Yield	★ ★	Shareholder Perks	★ ★
NYSE—CNK		**Total**	**16 points**

How dull the world might be if not for Crompton & Knowles. The Stamford, Connecticut, manufacturer specializes in dyes, flavors, fragrances, food colorings, sweeteners, seasonings and coatings.

The company's dyes add color to clothing, carpeting, fabrics, upholstery, leather and paper products, while its flavorings, fragrances and coatings are used for beverages, prepared foods, pharmaceuticals, toiletries, perfumes and other cosmetics.

The firm's dyes are marketed to a variety of industries, including garment and upholstery manufacturers and paper, leather and ink industries for use on stationery, towels, shoes, apparel, luggage and other products. Specialty dyes account for 57 percent of the firm's $590 million in annual sales.

Crompton & Knowles manufactures flavorings and color additives for the food processing, bakery, beverage and pharmaceutical industries. Its fragrances are sold to manufacturers of personal care and household products. Flavors, colors and fragrances account for 16 percent of total revenue.

The other 27 percent of sales comes from its Davis-Standard division, which manufactures extrusion equipment for plastics and rubber, industrial blow molding equipment and related controls and equipment. Extrusion systems are used to mold plastics, resins and rubber into such products as sports equipment, plastic furniture, appliances, home siding, furniture trim and automotive parts.

Known originally as Crompton Loom Works, the company first opened for business in 1840. When Crompton joined with Knowles in 1898, the merged company became the world's largest manufacturer of fancy looms.

The company's loom business is long gone, but it continues to expand its presence in the fabrics industry. Crompton & Knowles sells its dyes and other specialty chemicals throughout the world. Foreign sales account for about 19 percent of total revenue. Crompton & Knowles has about 2,300 employees and 4,000 shareholders.

EARNINGS-PER-SHARE GROWTH ★ ★

Past 5 years: 100 percent (15 percent per year)
Past 10 years: 614 percent (22 percent per year)

STOCK GROWTH ★ ★ ★ ★

Past 10 years: 1,257 percent (30 percent per year)
Dollar growth: $10,000 over 10 years (including reinvested dividends) would have grown to $175,000
Average annual compounded rate of return (including reinvested dividends): 33 percent

DIVIDEND YIELD ★ ★

Average dividend yield in the past 3 years: 1.9 percent

DIVIDEND GROWTH ★ ★ ★ ★

Increased dividend: 18 consecutive years
Past 5-year increase: 207 percent (25 percent per year)

CONSISTENCY

Increased earnings per share: 8 of past 10 years
Increased sales: 8 of past 10 years

SHAREHOLDER PERKS ★ ★

Good dividend reinvestment and stock purchase plan: voluntary stock purchase plan allows contributions of $30 to $3,000 per quarter. (Participants must own at least 50 shares before enrolling.)

CROMPTON & KNOWLES AT A GLANCE

Fiscal year ended: Dec. 31
Revenue and net income in $ millions

	1989	1990	1991	1992	1993	1994	5-year Growth Avg. Annual (%)	Total (%)
Revenue ($)	355.8	390.0	450.2	517.7	558.3	589.8	11	66
Net income ($)	24.5	30.0	35.9	43.3	52.0	51	16	108
Earnings/share ($)	.50	.61	.73	.87	1.00	1.00	15	100
Div. per share ($)	.15	.20	.25	.31	.38	.46	25	207
Dividend yield (%)	2.6	2.1	1.7	1.6	1.7	2.8	—	—
Avg. PE ratio	11.1	15.0	20.4	22.6	22.0	19	—	—

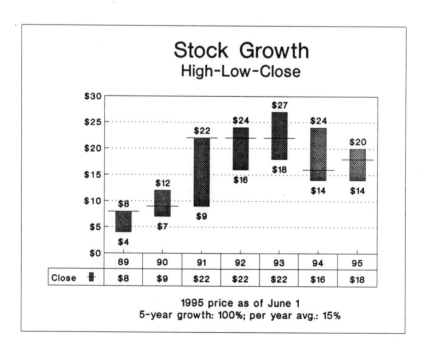

Stock Growth
High-Low-Close

Close	89	90	91	92	93	94	95
	$8	$9	$22	$22	$22	$16	$18

1995 price as of June 1
5-year growth: 100%; per year avg.: 15%

20

Federal Signal Corp.

1415 West 22nd St.
Oak Brook, IL 60521-9945
708-954-2000

Chairman, President and CEO:
Joseph J. Ross

Earnings Growth	★ ★	Dividend Growth	★ ★ ★
Stock Growth	★ ★ ★ ★	Consistency	★ ★ ★
Dividend Yield	★ ★	Shareholder Perks	★ ★
NYSE—FSS		**Total**	**16 points**

911 it's not, but Federal Signal Corp. is well-represented at fires, accidents and emergency situations across the country and around the world.

The Oak Brook, Illinois, operation is a leading manufacturer of fire trucks, ambulances, sirens, signals and communications equipment.

The company is well-diversified in other areas as well. It manufactures signs, specialized tools and a wide range of municipal sanitation equipment.

Federal Signal's largest division is its vehicle group which accounts for 52 percent of the company's $677 million in annual revenue. Along with its line of fire apparatus and fire trucks, airport rescue vehicles and ambulances, the company also makes air and mechanical street-sweeping equipment, municipal sewer and catch basin cleaner vehicles, vacuum street sweepers, catch basin cleaners and submersible pumping systems.

Federal Signal markets its products primarily to municipalities, airports, the military and fire and medical emergency services agencies.

The firm's other key divisions include:

- **Safety products** (20 percent of sales). Federal Signal makes warning, signaling and communications products, as well as parking, revenue and access control systems for airports, parking lots, toll roads and related applications. It is also a leading manufacturer of hazardous waste storage containers.

* **Tools** (18 percent of sales). The company produces carbide cutting tools, die components and precision parts for a wide range of manufacturers.
* **Signs** (10 percent of sales). The company builds and installs a variety of commercial signs, both illuminated and non-illuminated.

Founded in 1901, Federal Signal has enjoyed solid, consistent growth, including ten consecutive years of record sales and earnings. Its products are sold around the world. Foreign sales account for about 20 percent of the company's revenue. Federal Signal has about 4,800 employees and 8,000 shareholders.

EARNINGS-PER-SHARE GROWTH   ★ ★

Past 5 years: 104 percent (15 percent per year)
Past 10 years: 386 percent (17 percent per year)

STOCK GROWTH   ★ ★ ★ ★

Past 10 years: 588 percent (21 percent per year)
Dollar growth: $10,000 over 10 years (including reinvested dividends) would have grown to $90,000
Average annual compounded rate of return (including reinvested dividends): 24.5 percent

DIVIDEND YIELD   ★ ★

Average dividend yield in the past 3 years: 2.1 percent

DIVIDEND GROWTH   ★ ★ ★

Increased dividend: 7 consecutive years
Past 5-year increase: 121 percent (17 percent per year)

CONSISTENCY

Increased earnings per share: 9 of past 10 years
Increased sales: 10 consecutive years

SHAREHOLDER PERKS ★ ★

Good dividend reinvestment and stock purchase plan: voluntary stock purchase plan allows contributions of $25 to $3,000 per quarter.

FEDERAL SIGNAL AT A GLANCE

Fiscal year ended: Dec. 31
Revenue and net income in $ millions

	1989	1990	1991	1992	1993	1994	5-year Growth Avg. Annual (%)	5-year Growth Total (%)
Revenue ($)	398.4	439.4	466.9	518.2	565.2	677.2	11	70
Net income ($)	22.1	28.1	31.0	34.5	39.8	46.8	16	110
Earnings/share ($)	.50	.61	.67	.75	.86	1.02	15	104
Div. per share ($)	.19	.22	.27	.31	.36	.42	17	121
Dividend yield (%)	3.2	2.7	2.2	2.0	1.9	2.2	—	—
Avg. PE ratio	11.5	13.4	18.6	20.1	22	19	—	—

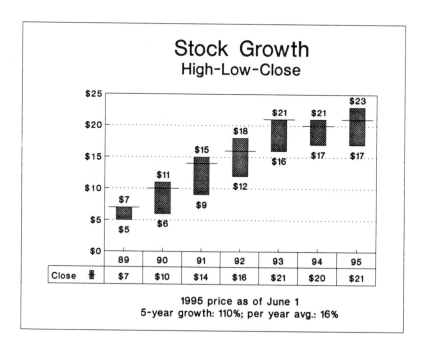

Stock Growth
High-Low-Close

	89	90	91	92	93	94	95
Close	$7	$10	$14	$16	$21	$20	$21

1995 price as of June 1
5-year growth: 110%; per year avg.: 16%

Johnson & Johnson

Johnson&Johnson

One Johnson & Johnson Plaza
New Brunswick, NJ 08933
908-524-0400

Chairman and CEO: Ralph S. Larsen

Earnings Growth	★ ★	Dividend Growth	★ ★ ★ ★
Stock Growth	★ ★ ★	Consistency	★ ★ ★
Dividend Yield	★ ★	Shareholder Perks	★ ★
NYSE—JNJ		**Total**	**16 points**

The nightly cleaning regimen for contact lens users could become a thing of the past if one of Johnson & Johnson's newest innovations succeeds in its market testing. The company has designed a new disposable contact lens you wear for one day and then throw away. The 1-Day Acuvue Disposable Lens is one of thousands of medical products produced by Johnson & Johnson, the nation's leading manufacturer of medical supplies.

The New Brunswick, New Jersey, manufacturer has manufacturing operations in 50 countries and sales in more than 150 countries. Approximately 50 percent of the firm's $15.7 billion in annual revenue is generated in foreign markets.

Johnson & Johnson is probably best known for its baby powders, lotions and related products. It is also the maker of Band-Aids, Tylenol, Mylanta antacid, Imodium A-D antidiarrheal medicine, Carefree panty shields, Stayfree and Sure and Natural sanitary protection products, Pediacare cold and allergy medications for children, Prevent and Reach toothbrushes, Serenity incontinence products and Piz Buin and Sundown sun

care products. Consumer products account for about 34 percent of the
company's annual revenue.

The company also has operations in other key segments:

- **Pharmaceutical products** (34 percent of revenue). The company's
  principal areas of treatment include allergy and asthma medications,
  antifungals, central nervous system medications, contraceptives, gas-
  trointestinal treatments and skin care formulas. Among its leading
  prescription drugs are Duragesic (a transdermal patch for chronic pain),
  Procrit (used to stimulate red blood cell production), Ergamisol (a colon
  cancer drug), Floxin (an antibacterial), and Hismanal (a sedating antihistamine).
- **Professional medical products** (33 percent of revenue). The company
  produces sutures, mechanical wound closure products, endoscopic products, dental products, diagnostic products, medical equipment and
  devices, ophthalmic products, surgical instruments, and medical supplies used by physicians, dentists, therapists, hospitals and clinics.

Johnson & Johnson has 82,000 employees and 70,000 shareholders.

EARNINGS-PER-SHARE GROWTH   ★ ★

Past 5 years: 93 percent (14 percent per year)
Past 10 years: 352 percent (16 percent per year)

STOCK GROWTH   ★ ★ ★

Past 10 years: 475 percent (19 percent per year)
Dollar growth: $10,000 over 10 years (including reinvested dividends)
would have grown to $69,000
Average annual compounded rate of return (including reinvested dividends): 21 percent

DIVIDEND YIELD

Average dividend yield in the past 3 years: 2.2 percent

DIVIDEND GROWTH

Increased dividend: 29 consecutive years
Past 5-year increase: 102 percent (15 percent per year)

CONSISTENCY

Increased earnings per share: 9 of past 10 years
Increased sales: 19 consecutive years

SHAREHOLDER PERKS ★ ★

Good dividend reinvestment and stock purchase plan: voluntary stock
purchase plan allows contributions of up to $50,000 per year.

JOHNSON & JOHNSON AT A GLANCE

Fiscal year ended: Dec. 31
Revenue and net income in $ millions

	1989	1990	1991	1992	1993	1994	5-year Growth Avg. Annual (%)	Total (%)
Revenue ($)	9,757	11,232	12,447	13,753	14,138	15,734	10	61
Net income ($)	1,082	1,143	1,461	1,625	1,787	2,006	13	85
Earnings/share ($)	1.62	1.72	2.19	2.46	2.74	3.12	14	93
Div. per share ($)	.56	.66	.77	.89	1.01	1.13	15	102
Dividend yield (%)	2.2	2.1	1.7	1.8	2.4	2.4	—	—
Avg. PE ratio	15.4	16.5	20.5	20.0	15.4	15.4	—	—

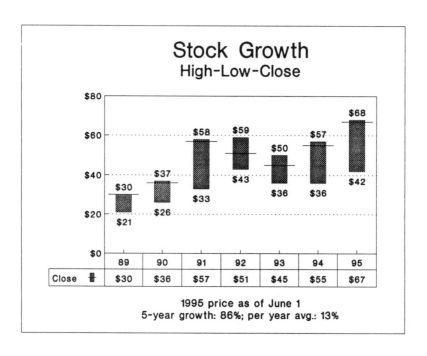

Stock Growth
High-Low-Close

Close ▉	89	90	91	92	93	94	95
	$30	$36	$57	$51	$45	$55	$67

1995 price as of June 1
5-year growth: 86%; per year avg.: 13%

22

Fifth Third Bancorp

38 Financial Square Plaza
Cincinnati, OH 45263
513-579-5300

President and CEO: George A. Schaefer Jr.

Earnings Growth	★ ★	Dividend Growth	★ ★ ★ ★
Stock Growth	★ ★	Consistency	★ ★ ★ ★
Dividend Yield	★ ★	Shareholder Perks	★ ★
NYSE—FITB		**Total**	**16 points**

In the banking business, where imposing, self-important names are the norm, Fifth Third Bancorp sounds decidedly modest. But there's been nothing modest about the regional bank holding company's financial performance in the 1990s. Salomon Brothers recently ranked Fifth Third first in overall profitability, productivity, credit quality and capital strength for the fifth consecutive year.

The Cincinnati-based institution has consistently ranked in the top 1 percent of all publicly trade companies based on dividend growth. Fifth Third has achieved that lofty distinction and steady growth over the past 20 years through aggressive new product development, increasing market share in existing markets and geographic expansion into new markets.

In August 1994, for example, Fifth Third acquired the Cumberland Federal Bancorporation and brought the Kentucky bank's $1 billion in assets and 45 branches under its ever-growing tent.

Fifth Third has made more than 25 mergers and acquisitions of other financial institutions in Ohio, Indiana, Kentucky and Florida. The company acquired its improbable-sounding name in the early part of the century through the merger of the Fifth National and Third National Banks of Ohio. The firm continues to bill itself as "the only bank you'll ever need."

Fifth Third has a reputation for quick response to credit problems, high credit standards, a strong sales culture and strict cost control measures. The bank is also noted for eagerness to extend loans to businesses and consumers in the local markets it serves.

The company has won customers over the years through its mix of convenience and personal service delivered along with a comprehensive package of banking services. In addition to its regular branch offices, the bank operates seven-day-a-week banking centers in Kroger, Finast and Marsh supermarkets. The bank pioneered the use of automatic teller machines more than 20 years ago and continues to operate the Jeanie system, one of the premier ATM networks.

About 30 percent of Fifth Third's loan portfolio is commercial loans, 23 percent consumer loans, 22 percent residential mortgages, 10 percent consumer leases, 7 percent commercial mortgages, 3 percent commercial leases and 3 percent construction loans. Fifth Third is the parent company of Midwest Payment Systems, the nation's largest third-party provider of electronic funds transfer services. The subsidiary processes about 75 million transactions per month. Fifth Third has about 6,000 employees and 14,000 shareholders.

EARNINGS-PER-SHARE GROWTH ★★

Past 5 years: 104 percent (15 percent per year)
Past 10 years: 296 percent (15 percent per year)

STOCK GROWTH ★★

Past 10 years: 310 percent (15 percent per year)
Dollar growth: $10,000 over 10 years (including reinvested dividends) would have grown to $52,000
Average annual compounded rate of return (including reinvested dividends): 18 percent

DIVIDEND YIELD

Average dividend yield in the past 3 years: 2.1 percent

DIVIDEND GROWTH   ★ ★ ★ ★

Increased dividend: More than 19 consecutive years
Past 5-year increase: 100 percent (15 percent per year)

CONSISTENCY   ★ ★ ★ ★

Increased earnings per share: 21 consecutive years

SHAREHOLDER PERKS   ★ ★

Good dividend reinvestment and stock purchase plan: voluntary stock purchase plan allows contributions of $25 to $2,500 per month.

FIFTH THIRD BANCORP AT A GLANCE

Fiscal year ended: Dec. 31
Revenue and net income in $ millions

	1989	1990	1991	1992	1993	1994	5-year Growth Avg. Annual (%)	5-year Growth Total (%)
Assets ($)	7,143	7,956	8,826	10,213	11,966	14,957	16	109
Net income ($)	113.3	121.0	143.0	172.0	206.2	244.5	17	116
Earnings/share ($)	1.86	1.97	2.31	2.76	3.29	3.80	15	104
Div. per share ($)	.60	.68	.78	.90	1.02	1.20	15	100
Dividend yield (%)	2.43	3.09	1.72	1.67	1.97	2.50	—	—
Avg. PE ratio	13.26	11.17	19.64	19.57	15.73	12.63	—	—

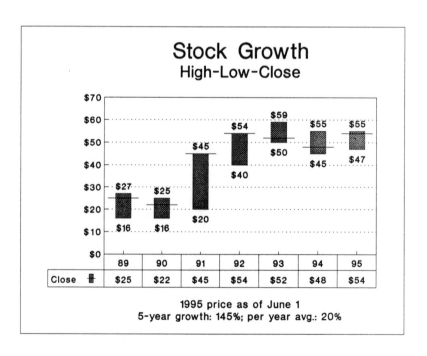

Stock Growth
High-Low-Close

	89	90	91	92	93	94	95
Close	$25	$22	$45	$54	$52	$48	$54

1995 price as of June 1
5-year growth: 145%; per year avg.: 20%

Bemis Company, Inc.

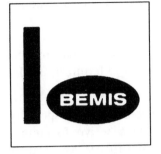

222 S. Ninth St., Suite 2300
Minneapolis, MN 55402-4099
612-376-3000

President and CEO: John H. Roe

Earnings Growth	★	Dividend Growth	★ ★ ★
Stock Growth	★ ★ ★	Consistency	★ ★ ★ ★
Dividend Yield	★ ★	Shareholder Perks	★ ★
NYSE—BMS		**Total**	**15 points**

If it's wrapped, bottled, bagged or boxed, there's a good chance Bemis produced the packaging. The Minneapolis-based operation manufactures the packaging for everything from foods to fertilizer and seeds to cement.

The company is also a leading manufacturer of on-site packaging equipment typically used in grocery stores to package meats, nuts, candy, fresh produce, pharmaceuticals and other products.

Founded in 1858 as a grain bag manufacturer, Bemis has sales offices and plants throughout the United States, Canada, Great Britain, Europe, Scandinavia, Australia and Mexico. About 16 percent of the company's $1.39 billion in annual revenue comes from its foreign operations.

Flexible packaging products account for 70 percent of the company's $1.39 billion in annual sales. Its flexible packaging products include:

- **Coated and laminated film packaging** (31 percent of the company's $1.39 billion in total sales). The company does resin manufacturing, extruding, coating, laminating, metallizing, printing and converting for perishable and frozen food packaging.
- **Polyethylene packaging products** (16 percent of sales). Bemis makes preformed bags, extruded products and printed roll packaging.
- **Industrial and consumer paper bags** (16 percent). Includes packaging for products such as seed, feed, flour, cement and chemicals and small

consumer-size packages for products such as sugar, flour, rice and pet food.

* **Packaging machinery** (11 percent of sales). Bemis manufactures packaging systems for a wide range of consumer and industrial products ranging from toilet tissue, candy and frozen foods to fertilizer, insulation, detergent and pharmaceuticals.

About 30 percent of the company's revenue comes from its specialty coated and graphics products. Bemis makes industrial adhesives for mounting and bonding, quality roll label and sheet print stock for packaging labels and a line of specialized laminates for graphics and photography.

Bemis has about 8,100 employees and 5,700 shareholders.

EARNINGS-PER-SHARE GROWTH ★

Past 5 years: 56 percent (9 percent per year)
Past 10 years: 338 percent (16 percent per year)

STOCK GROWTH ★ ★ ★

Past 10 years: 536 percent (20 percent per year)
Dollar growth: $10,000 over 10 years (including reinvested dividends) would have grown to $86,000
Average annual compounded rate of return (including reinvested dividends): 24 percent

DIVIDEND YIELD ★ ★

Average dividend yield in the past 3 years: 2.1 percent

DIVIDEND GROWTH ★ ★ ★

Increased dividend: 11 consecutive years
Past 5-year increase: 80 percent (13 percent per year)

CONSISTENCY   ★ ★ ★ ★

Increased earnings per share: 12 consecutive years
Increased sales: 12 consecutive years

SHAREHOLDER PERKS   ★ ★

Good dividend reinvestment and stock purchase plan: voluntary stock purchase plan allows contributions of $25 to $10,000 per quarter.

BEMIS AT A GLANCE

Fiscal year ended: Dec. 31
Revenue and net income in $ millions

	1989	1990	1991	1992	1993	1994	5-year Growth Avg. Annual (%)	Total (%)
Revenue ($)	1,076.7	1,128.2	1,141.6	1,181.3	1,203.5	1,390.5	5	29
Net income ($)	47.0	50.9	53.0	57.0	57.4	72.8	9	55
Earnings/share ($)	.90	.99	1.03	1.10	1.14	1.40	9	56
Div. per share ($)	.30	.36	.42	.46	.50	.54	13	80
Dividend yield (%)	2.6	2.1	2.2	2.2	2.0	2.3	—	—
Avg. PE ratio	17	16	17	22	27	17	—	—

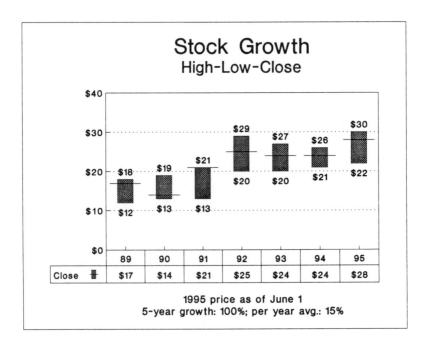

Stock Growth
High-Low-Close

	89	90	91	92	93	94	95
Close	$17	$14	$21	$25	$24	$24	$28

1995 price as of June 1
5-year growth: 100%; per year avg.: 15%

2.

Donaldson Company, Inc.

1400 West 94th Street
P. O. Box 1299
Minneapolis, MN 55440
612-887-3131

Chairman and CEO: William A. Hodder
President and COO: William G. Van Dyke

Earnings Growth	★ ★ ★	Dividend Growth	★ ★
Stock Growth	★ ★ ★ ★	Consistency	★ ★ ★
Dividend Yield	★	Shareholder Perks	★ ★
NYSE—DCI		**Total**	**15 points**

The world's growing obsession with cleaner water and cleaner air has been a boon to business for Donaldson Company. Donaldson makes filters and purifiers for trucks, turbines and a broad range of industrial and agricultural equipment.

The Minneapolis-based business has manufacturing operations in nine countries and sales offices in 13 nations in Europe, Asia and elsewhere around the world. About 34 percent of the company's $593.5 million in annual sales come from its foreign operations.

Donaldson makes filtration systems for a wide range of applications. Its biggest market is construction equipment filters, which accounts for about 24 percent of total revenue. Transportation equipment filters account for 19 percent, industrial dust collection equipment makes up 15 percent and gas turbine systems comprise 11 percent. The company also manufactures filters for defense, agriculture and other industries.

The company's leading products include:

- **Filtration and exhaust products.** Donaldson makes air cleaners and accessories, liquid filters and exhaust products such as mufflers for the construction, industrial, mining, agricultural and transportation market.

- **Dust collection.** The company makes dust, fume and mist collectors for manufacturing and assembly plants.
- **Gas turbine systems.** Donaldson manufactures static and pulse-clean air filter systems, replacement filters, exhaust silencers, chiller coils and anti-icing systems for turbine engines for use in the electric power generation and the oil and gas industries.
- **High-purity products.** The firm makes specialized air filtration systems for computer disk drives, aircraft and automotive cabins, industrial and hospital clean rooms, business machines, room air cleaners, personal respirators and air emission control.
- **Aftermarket.** The company makes a variety of filtration products for several aftermarket distributors including automotive jobbers, fleets, national buying groups, specialty installers and hydraulic distributors.

The company was founded in 1915 by Frank Donaldson, whose first filter was a tin can and Spanish moss air filter he made for a farmer's tractor. By the late 1920s, Donaldson had developed a spark-arresting muffler designed to cut the incidence of crop fires from engine sparks. From that beginning, the company expanded to the wide range of filter systems it offers today. Donaldson has 4,000 employees and 1,500 shareholders.

EARNINGS-PER-SHARE GROWTH ★ ★ ★

Past 5 years: 117 percent (17 percent per year)
Past 10 years: 303 percent (15 percent per year)

STOCK GROWTH ★ ★ ★ ★

Past 10 years: 614 percent (22 percent per year)
Dollar growth: $10,000 over 10 years (including reinvested dividends) would have grown to $86,000
Average annual compounded rate of return (including reinvested dividends): 24 percent

DIVIDEND YIELD ★

Average dividend yield in the past 3 years: 1.0 percent

DIVIDEND GROWTH

Increased dividend: 7 consecutive years
Past 5-year increase: 92 percent (14 percent per year)

CONSISTENCY

Increased earnings per share: 9 of past 10 years
Increased sales: 11 consecutive years

SHAREHOLDER PERKS ★ ★

Good dividend reinvestment and stock purchase plan: voluntary stock
purchase plan allows contributions of $10 to $1,000 per month.

DONALDSON AT A GLANCE

Fiscal year ended: July 31
Revenue and net income in $ millions

	1989	1990	1991	1992	1993	1994	5-year Growth Avg. Annual (%)	Total (%)
Revenue ($)	397.5	422.9	457.7	482.1	533.3	593.5	8	49
Net income ($)	16.8	21.0	24.1	25.8	28.2	32.0	14	90
Earnings/share ($)	.54	.72	.84	.92	1.01	1.17	17	117
Div. per share ($)	.13	.14	.15	.19	.20	.25	14	92
Dividend yield (%)	1.7	1.2	1.1	1.0	0.9	1.0	—	—
Avg. PE ratio	10.7	10.9	13.1	14.9	17.4	18.7	—	—

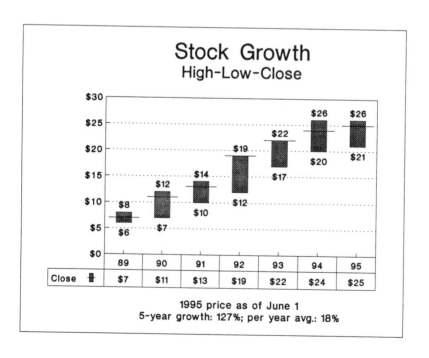

Stock Growth
High-Low-Close

	89	90	91	92	93	94	95
Close	$7	$11	$13	$19	$22	$24	$25

1995 price as of June 1
5-year growth: 127%; per year avg.: 18%

U. S. Healthcare, Inc.

980 Jolly Road
P. O. Box 1109
Blue Bell, PA 19422
215-628-4800

Principal Executive Officer:
Leonard Abramson

Earnings Growth	★ ★ ★ ★	Dividend Growth	★ ★ ★ ★
Stock Growth	★ ★ ★	Consistency	★ ★ ★
Dividend Yield	★	Shareholder Perks	
NASDAQ—USHC		**Total**	**15 points**

Medical cost containment has been a major political focus in the United States since the presidential election campaign of 1993. But it's been U.S. Healthcare's primary focus since its inception in 1981.

U.S. Healthcare has been one of the nation's fastest-growing health maintenance organizations (HMOs). Its membership grew 70 percent in the two-year period from 1992 to 1994, from 1.4 million members to 2 million members. Over the past decade, the company has enjoyed phenomenal earnings and sales growth. Earnings have grown 3,357 percent since 1984 and sales have grown 1,341 percent.

The Pennsylvania-based HMO provides health care services in its home state as well as in New Jersey, New York, Delaware, Connecticut, Massachusetts, New Hampshire and Maryland. In addition to the standard health care coverage, the company also offers other options such as dental, vision, prescription drug and employee assistance plans, as well as mental health and substance abuse benefits management.

Through its Corporate Health Administrators subsidiary, the company also provides services to self-insured employers, such as claims processing, patient management and access to participating health care providers in the U.S. Healthcare HMO network.

Other services of U.S. Healthcare include employee assistance and wellness programs, medical and return-to-work management for employees with job-related injuries, quality assessment and improvement programs, patient surveys and outcome tracking, and data analysis systems for providers and purchasers of health care services.

The company provides its medical coverage through independent physicians who work out of their own offices. U.S. Healthcare has 3,400 employees and 2,700 shareholders.

EARNINGS-PER-SHARE GROWTH ★ ★ ★ ★

Past 5 years: 1,343 percent (71 percent per year)
Past 10 years: 3,357 percent (42 percent per year)

STOCK GROWTH ★ ★ ★

Past 10 years: 539 percent (20 percent per year)
Dollar growth: $10,000 over 10 years (including reinvested dividends) would have grown to $70,000
Average annual compounded rate of return (including reinvested dividends): 21.5 percent

DIVIDEND YIELD ★

Average dividend yield in the past 3 years: 1.3 percent

DIVIDEND GROWTH ★ ★ ★ ★

Increased dividend: 10 consecutive years
Past 5-year increase: 1,200 percent (68 percent per year)

CONSISTENCY ★ ★ ★

Increased earnings per share: 9 of past 10 years
Increased sales: 11 consecutive years

SHAREHOLDER PERKS

The company offers no dividend reinvestment and stock purchase plan, nor does it provide any other shareholder perks.

U.S. HEALTHCARE AT A GLANCE

Fiscal year ended: Dec. 31
Revenue and net income in $ millions

	1989	1990	1991	1992	1993	1994	5-year Growth Avg. Annual (%)	Total (%)
Revenue ($)	1,000	1,330	1,708	2,189	2,645	2,974	24	197
Net income ($)	28	77	151	200	300	391	72	1,395
Earnings/share ($)	.18	.48	.93	1.23	1.84	2.42	71	1,343
Div. per share ($)	.06	.10	.16	.27	.39	.72	68	1,200
Dividend yield (%)	1.9	2.0	1.2	1.0	1.2	1.7	—	—
Avg. PE ratio	19	11	14.5	20	17.5	17	—	—

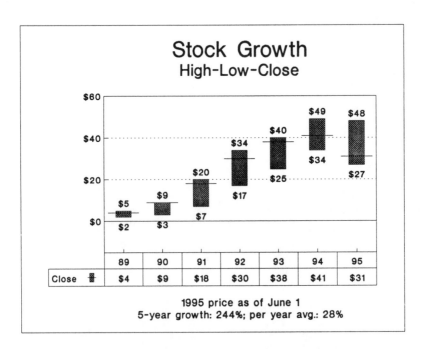

Stock Growth
High-Low-Close

	89	90	91	92	93	94	95
Close	$4	$9	$18	$30	$38	$41	$31

1995 price as of June 1
5-year growth: 244%; per year avg.: 28%

Cintas

6800 Cintas Blvc
P. O. Box 625737
Cincinnati, OH 45262-5737
513-459-1200

Chairman and CEO: Richard T. Farmer
President and COO: Robert J. Kohlhepp

Earnings Growth	★ ★ ★	Dividend Growth	★ ★ ★ ★
Stock Growth	★ ★ ★	Consistency	★ ★ ★ ★
Dividend Yield	★	Shareholder Perks	
NASDAQ—CTAS		**Total**	**15 points**

It's not the military, but Cintas still manages to put uniforms on a million Americans a day. The Cincinnati-based operation is one of the nation's leading suppliers of business uniforms.

For Cintas, the uniform business has produced uniform financial returns. The company has enjoyed 25 consecutive years of record sales and earnings.

Cintas operates 102 uniform rental centers in 96 cities and 33 states, plus four garment manufacturing plants and two distribution centers. The company's customer base extends from coast to coast.

The company's growth has come to a large degree through a continuing series of acquisitions. Cintas acquired 20 smaller uniform operations in 1993 and 1994 and made 24 acquisitions in the previous eight years. The company has become the largest public company in the uniform business.

Cintas also continues to expand its product line. It recently introduced a new line of flame-retardant garments and a complete line of industrial footwear.

Cintas divides its operations into two divisions. Its rental division is by far the largest, accounting for 89 percent of its $523 million in annual sales. Its uniform sales division accounts for the other 11 percent.

The company designs, manufactures and launders most of the uniforms it supplies to customers.

In addition to uniforms, the company also supplies rain gear, caps, gloves, long underwear, socks and work shoes. Founded in 1929, Cintas employees 8,600 people.

EARNINGS-PER-SHARE GROWTH ★ ★ ★

Past 5 years: 115 percent (16 percent per year)
Past 10 years: 460 percent (19 percent per year)

STOCK GROWTH ★ ★ ★

Past 10 years: 567 percent (21 percent per year)
Dollar growth: $10,000 over 10 years (including reinvested dividends) would have grown to $70,000
Average annual compounded rate of return (including reinvested dividends): 21.5 percent

DIVIDEND YIELD ★

Average dividend yield in the past 3 years: 0.5 percent

DIVIDEND GROWTH ★ ★ ★ ★

Increased dividend: 10 consecutive years
Past 5-year increase: 240 percent (28 percent per year)

CONSISTENCY ★ ★ ★ ★

Increased earnings per share: 25 consecutive years
Increased sales: 25 consecutive years

SHAREHOLDER PERKS

The company offers no dividend reinvestment and stock purchase plan, nor does it provide any other shareholder perks.

CINTAS AT A GLANCE

Fiscal year ended: May 31
Revenue and net income in $ millions

	1989	1990	1991	1992	1993	1994	5-year Growth Avg. Annual (%)	5-year Growth Total (%)
Revenue ($)	269	312	352	402	453	523	14	94
Net income ($)	23	28	31	39	45	52	21	126
Earnings/share ($)	.52	.62	.69	.85	.97	1.12	16	115
Div. per share ($)	.05	.07	.09	.11	.14	.17	28	240
Dividend yield (%)	0.5	0.6	0.6	0.4	0.5	0.6	—	—
Avg. PE ratio	21.4	22.2	23.0	32.6	28.1	26.0	—	—

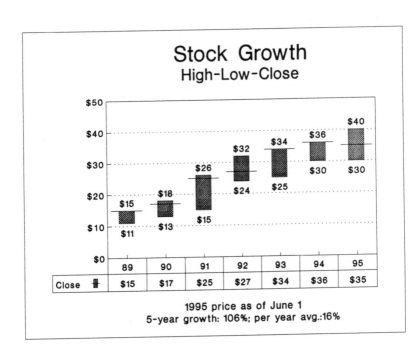

Stock Growth
High-Low-Close

	89	90	91	92	93	94	95
Close		$15	$17	$25	$27	$34	$36	$35

1995 price as of June 1
5-year growth: 106%; per year avg.:16%

27

Sara Lee Corp.

Three First National Plaza
Chicago, IL 60602-4260
312-726-2600

Chairman and CEO: John H. Bryan

Earnings Growth	★	Dividend Growth	★ ★ ★
Stock Growth	★ ★ ★	Consistency	★ ★ ★ ★
Dividend Yield	★ ★	Shareholder Perks	★ ★
NYSE—SLE		**Total**	**15 points**

It's called the Wonderbra, and it's been responsible for giving a boost not only to the women who wear it, but also to Sara Lee's bottom line. With its line of Playtex, Hanes and Bali intimate wear, Sara Lee is the nation's leading bra manufacturer with a 22 percent share—a figure that should be pushed up still higher by the burgeoning success of the Wonderbra.

In fact, according to Sara Lee's recent annual report, the product's early success—first in Britain and then in the United States market—has prompted the Chicago-based company to "develop an expanded line of figure-enhancing products under the Wonderbra name."

While Sara Lee is best known for its frozen desserts, the company's leading segment is its personal products division. With its Hanes, Playtex, L'eggs, Isotoner, Sheer Energy and other lines of hosiery, knits and intimate apparel, Sara Lee's personal products segment accounts for about 42 percent of the its $15.5 billion in annual revenue.

Sara Lee is the leading manufacturer of women's hosiery and brassieres, and the second leading manufacturer of men's and boys' underwear and printed T-shirts.

Sara Lee's other segments include:

- **Packaged meats and bakery** (35 percent of total revenue). Leading products include Sara Lee desserts, Ball Park Franks, Hillshire Farm,

Hygrade, Jimmy Dean, Mr. Turkey and Best's Kosher. Sara Lee is the nation's number one producer of frozen baked goods with a 21 percent share of the market. It is also the leading producer of packaged meats.

- **Household and personal care products** (10 percent of revenue). Based in Utrecht, the Netherlands, Sara Lee's household goods and personal care products division generates 90 percent of its sales revenue outside the United States. The company makes shoe care products (Kiwi, Esquire and Meltonian shoe polish), toiletries, over-the-counter medications, specialty detergents and insecticides.

- **Coffee and grocery products** (14 percent of sales). Sara Lee holds leading positions in coffee sales in several Scandinavian countries. Its brands include Chat Noir, Douwe Egbert, Maison du Cafe, Merrild and several other lines. It also owns Duyvis nuts. About 86 percent of the company's coffee and grocery products revenue is generated outside the United States.

Sara Lee has sales in about 120 countries. Foreign sales account for about 35 percent of total revenue.

Sara Lee was founded in 1939 when Nathan Cummings acquired the C.D. Kenny Company, a small Baltimore sugar, tea and coffee distributor. The company changed its named to Consolidated Grocers Corp. in 1945—a name that stuck until 1985 when the firm changed names again, this time to Sara Lee. The company now employees about 146,000 people and has 96,000 shareholders.

EARNINGS-PER-SHARE GROWTH ★

Past 5 years: 73 percent (12 percent per year)
Past 10 years: 259 percent (14 percent per year)

STOCK GROWTH ★ ★ ★

Past 10 years: 419 percent (18 percent per year)
Dollar growth: $10,000 over 10 years (including reinvested dividends) would have grown to $67,000
Average annual compounded rate of return (including reinvested dividends): 21 percent

DIVIDEND YIELD ★ ★

Average dividend yield in the past 3 years: 2.3 percent

DIVIDEND GROWTH ★ ★ ★

Increased dividend: 17 consecutive years
Past 5-year increase: 80 percent (13 percent per year)

CONSISTENCY ★ ★ ★ ★

Increased earnings per share: 19 consecutive years
Increased sales: 8 of past 10 years

SHAREHOLDER PERKS ★ ★

Good dividend reinvestment and stock purchase plan: voluntary stock
purchase plan allows contributions of $10 to $5,000 per quarter.

Each year at the annual meeting, Sara Lee shareholders receive a gift
box of Sara Lee products, including such items as coupons, bath soaps and
other company products.

Occasionally shareholders will receive coupons or product discounts.

SARA LEE AT A GLANCE

Fiscal year ended: June 30
Revenue and net income in $ millions

	1989	1990	1991	1992	1993	1994	5-year Growth Avg. Annual (%)	5-year Growth Total (%)
Revenue ($)	11,718	11,606	12,381	13,243	14,580	15,536	6	33
Net income ($)	410	470	535	621	704	729	12	78
Earnings/share ($)	.85	.96	1.08	1.24	1.40	1.47	12	73
Div. per share ($)	.35	.41	.46	.61	.56	.63	13	80
Dividend yield (%)	3.0	2.8	2.8	2.1	2.1	2.7	—	—
Avg. PE ratio	13.6	15.4	15.2	19.4	19.9	16.2	—	—

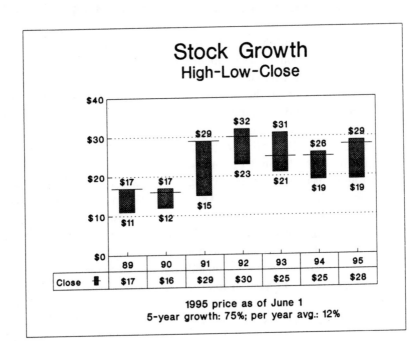

Stock Growth
High-Low-Close

	89	90	91	92	93	94	95
Close	$17	$16	$29	$30	$25	$25	$28

1995 price as of June 1
5-year growth: 75%; per year avg.: 12%

Colgate-Palmolive Company

300 Park Avenue
New York, NY 10022
212-310-2000

Chairman, President and CEO: Reuben Mark

Earnings Growth	★ ★	Dividend Growth	★ ★ ★
Stock Growth	★ ★	Consistency	★ ★ ★ ★
Dividend Yield	★ ★	Shareholder Perks	★ ★
NYSE—CL		**Total**	**15 points**

In households around the world, Colgate-Palmolive's leading brands can be found in just about every cupboard, cabinet and closet.

In the medicine cabinet, there's Colgate toothpaste, the world's leading oral health product. In the broom closet, there's Ajax, the number-one brand in household cleaning, and Murphy's, a well-established wood furniture and floor cleaner.

In the kitchen Palmolive soap is a mainstay, while in the laundry room Fab and Sta-soft are popular brands.

Colgate has successfully leveraged its brand names into worldwide brand marketing success stories. The New York–based operation has been accelerating the speed with which it launches new products worldwide. Not surprising, considering that the nation's second-largest maker of detergents, personal care products and household cleaners derives about two-thirds of its pretax profits from outside the United States.

Colgate is an old hand at international marketing. While many U.S. companies have only recently gotten religion about European and emerging markets, Colgate has been generating more than half its sales in foreign markets since 1960. Colgate, which has operated in Latin America since 1925, barely flinches in the face of hyperinflation or currency devaluations that seem to unnerve many other U.S. marketers.

Colgate's long-term commitment to foreign markets has paid off handsomely. Colgate commands half of the world's market share of toothpaste, 28 percent of the soap market and about 25 percent of the all-purpose cleaner market.

One of the keys to Colgate's international success has been the development of new products that can work in multiple markets. The new product development process begins with Colgate's Global Technology and Business Development Groups, which analyze consumer insights from targeted countries to create universal products.

To improve the odds of success, potential new products are test-marketed in lead countries that represent both developing and mature economies. For example, its Protex antibacterial soap was first introduced as bar soap nine years ago. Protex is now sold in 30 countries throughout Africa, Asia and Latin America and is available in many countries as a talcum powder and a shower gel.

Colgate's most profitable categories are oral care, personal care and pet dietary care. Six years ago, those categories accounted for 45 percent of total sales. Today they account for more than 60 percent of Colgate's $7.6 billion in annual revenue. Founded in Manhattan in 1806 as the Colgate Company, the nearly 200-year-old institution today has about 28,000 employees and subsidiaries in 57 countries. The company has about 40,300 shareholders.

EARNINGS-PER-SHARE GROWTH   ★ ★

Past 5 years: 93 percent (14 percent per year)
Past 10 years: 311 percent (15 percent per year)

STOCK GROWTH   ★ ★

Past 10 years: 386 percent (17 percent per year)
Dollar growth: $10,000 over 10 years (including reinvested dividends) would have grown to $62,000
Average annual compounded rate of return (including reinvested dividends): 20 percent

DIVIDEND YIELD   ★ ★

Average dividend yield in the past 3 years: 2.4 percent

DIVIDEND GROWTH   ★ ★ ★

Increased dividend: More than 17 consecutive years
Past 5-year increase: 97 percent (15 percent per year)

CONSISTENCY   ★ ★ ★ ★

Increased earnings per share: 10 consecutive years
Increased sales: 9 of past 10 years

SHAREHOLDER PERKS   ★ ★

Good dividend reinvestment and stock purchase plan: voluntary stock
purchase plan allows contributions of $20 per month up to $60,000 per
year. (Nominal cash-in fee.)

COLGATE-PALMOLIVE AT A GLANCE

Fiscal year ended: Dec. 31
Revenue and net income in $ millions

	1989	1990	1991	1992	1993	1994	5-year Growth Avg. Annual (%)	5-year Growth Total (%)
Revenue ($)	5,038.8	5,691.3	6,060.3	7,007.2	7,141.3	7,587.9	8.5	51
Net income ($)	280.0	321.0	367.9	477.0	548.1	580.2	16	107
Earnings/share ($)	1.98	2.28	2.57	2.98	3.38	3.82	14	93
Div. per share ($)	.78	.90	1.02	1.15	1.34	1.54	15	97
Dividend yield (%)	2.9	2.8	2.6	2.2	2.3	2.6	—	—
Avg. PE ratio	14	14	15	18	17	15	—	—

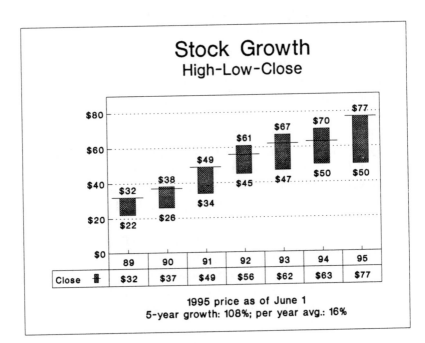

Stock Growth
High-Low-Close

	89	90	91	92	93	94	95
Close	$32	$37	$49	$56	$62	$63	$77

1995 price as of June 1
5-year growth: 108%; per year avg.: 16%

Sysco Corp.

1390 Enclave Parkway
Houston, TX 77077-2027
713-584-1390

Chairman and CEO:
John F. Woodhouse
President and COO: Bill M. Lindig

Earnings Growth	★ ★	Dividend Growth	★ ★ ★ ★
Stock Growth	★ ★ ★	Consistency	★ ★ ★ ★
Dividend Yield	★	Shareholder Perks	★
NYSE—SYY		**Total**	**15 points**

There's no question America is a nation of people who love to eat, and Sysco's the company that delivers the goods. The Houston operation is America's largest marketer and distributor of food service products, with operations in the nation's 150 largest cities (plus the Pacific coast of Canada). In all, Sysco delivers 165,000 cases of food a day.

Founded in 1969 through the merger of nine small food distributors, Sysco has grown rapidly through a series of acquisitions. In all, the company has acquired about 50 other food-related businesses.

Sysco serves essentially as a wholesale distributor of foods and related products. It does not produce its own products, but rather procures goods from several thousand independent sources, including both large name-brand food producers and independent private-label processors and packers.

In all, the company markets 150,000 individual items. Sysco's leading product segment is canned and dry products, which account for about 25 percent of the company's $10.9 billion annual revenue. Other significant contributors are fresh and frozen meats, 16 percent; frozen fruits, vegetables and bakery goods, 14 percent; dairy products, 16 percent; paper and disposables, 7 percent; and poultry, 9 percent. The company also han beverages, fresh produce and seafood as well as janitorial products and medical supplies.

Sysco services 245,000 restaurants, hotels, schools, health care facilities and other institutions. Restaurant sales account for about 60 percent of Sysco's annual revenue, while hospitals and nursing homes account for 13 percent, schools and colleges comprise 7 percent, hotels and motels generate 6 percent and other sources such as retail groceries account for 14 percent.

The company's 8,000 sales and service representatives also help food service clients with menu planning and inventory control, as well as contract services for installing kitchen equipment and beverage dispensers. The company has 23,000 employees and 20,000 shareholders.

EARNINGS-PER-SHARE GROWTH ★ ★

Past 5 years: 97 percent (15 percent per year)
Past 10 years: 337 percent (16 percent per year)

STOCK GROWTH ★ ★ ★

Past 10 years: 463 percent (19 percent per year)
Dollar growth: $10,000 over 10 years (including reinvested dividends) would have grown to $93,000
Average annual compounded rate of return (including reinvested dividends): 20 percent

DIVIDEND YIELD ★

Average dividend yield in the past 3 years: 1.1 percent

DIVIDEND GROWTH ★ ★ ★ ★

Increased dividend: 17 consecutive years
Past 5-year increase: 256 percent (28 percent per year)

CONSISTENCY ★ ★ ★ ★

Increased earnings per share: 18 consecutive years
Increased sales: 15 consecutive years

SHAREHOLDER PERKS ★

The company offers a dividend reinvestment plan but no stock purchase plan. Shareholders of record may have their dividends automatically reinvested in additional shares.

SYSCO AT A GLANCE

Fiscal year ended: June 30
Revenue and net income in $ millions

	1989	1990	1991	1992	1993	1994	5-year Growth Avg. Annual (%)	5-year Growth Total (%)
Revenue ($)	6,851	7,591	8,150	8,893	10,022	10,942	10	60
Net income ($)	107.9	132.5	153.8	172.2	201.8	216.8	15	100
Earnings/share ($)	.60	.73	.83	.93	1.08	1.18	15	97
Div. per share ($)	.09	.10	.12	.17	.26	.32	28	256
Dividend yield (%)	0.9	0.7	0.7	0.9	1.1	1.2	—	—
Avg. PE ratio	26.5	23.1	28.2	28.4	27.1	21.8	—	—

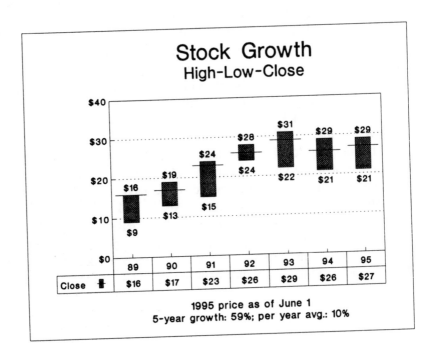

Stock Growth
High-Low-Close

	89	90	91	92	93	94	95
Close	$16	$17	$23	$26	$29	$26	$27

1995 price as of June 1
5-year growth: 59%; per year avg.: 10%

30

The Interpublic Group of Companies, Inc.

1271 Avenue of the Americas
New York, NY 10020
212-399-8000

Chairman, President and CEO: Philip H. Geier, Jr.

Earnings Growth	★	Dividend Growth	★ ★ ★
Stock Growth	★ ★ ★	Consistency	★ ★ ★ ★
Dividend Yield	★ ★	Shareholder Perks	★ ★
NYSE—IPG		**Total**	**15 points**

In the world of advertising, agencies are used to seeing clients come and go. In 1994, advertising mega-agency Interpublic Group lost one of its bigger clients when IBM took its business elsewhere. But with Coca-Cola, Unilever, General Motors and about 4,000 other clients still intact, Big Blue was hardly missed. Interpublic still managed to extend its string of success to 13 consecutive years of record earnings.

Interpublic is the world's second-largest organization of advertising agencies. Its lead agencies include McCann-Erickson, Lintas Worldwide, Dailey and Associates and the Lowe Group. In 1994, it acquired Amirati & Puris and Scali, McCabe.

The company does business through 345 offices in 90 countries. About 66 percent of its $1.96 billion in annual revenue and 71 percent of its operating income are generated outside the United States.

Among its clients are Levi-Strauss, Nestle, GMAC, Camel cigarettes, L'Oreal, Gillette, Mennen, Black & Decker, Delta faucets, Johnson & Johnson, Maybelline, Goodyear, Exxon, Casio and Del Monte fruits. Interpublic gave Chevrolet the "Heartbeat of America," deemed Coke "the Real Thing" and made UPS the "tightest ship in the shipping business."

In addition to creating advertisements, the agencies plan campaigns and place advertising on TV and radio and in magazines, newspapers and direct response mailers.

Interpublic traces its roots to 1902 when A. W. Erickson founded the Erickson agency. He later merged with an agency founded in 1911 by Harrison K. McCann. The firm was first incorporated in 1930 as McCann-Erickson, and has been operating under the name Interpublic Group since 1961. The New York–based agency has about 17,000 employees and 3,500 shareholders.

EARNINGS-PER-SHARE GROWTH ★

Past 5 years: 77 percent (12 percent per year)
Past 10 years: 265 percent (14 percent per year)

STOCK GROWTH ★ ★ ★

Past 10 years: 431 percent (18 percent per year)
Dollar growth: $10,000 over 10 years (including reinvested dividends) would have grown to $62,000
Average annual compounded rate of return (including reinvested dividends): 20 percent

DIVIDEND YIELD ★ ★

Average dividend yield in the past 3 years: 1.6 percent

DIVIDEND GROWTH ★ ★ ★

Increased dividend: 11 consecutive years
Past five-year increase: 72 percent (12 percent per year)

CONSISTENCY ★ ★ ★ ★

Increased earnings per share: 13 consecutive years
Increased sales: 9 of the past 10 years

SHAREHOLDER PERKS

Good dividend reinvestment and stock purchase plan: voluntary stock purchase plan allows contributions of $10 to $3,000 per month.

INTERPUBLIC GROUP AT A GLANCE

Fiscal year ended: Dec. 31
Revenue and net income in $ millions

	1989	1990	1991	1992	1993	1994	5-year Growth Avg. Annual (%)	5-year Growth Total (%)
Revenue ($)	1,256.9	1,368.2	1,677.5	1,856.0	1,793.9	1,984.2	10	60
Net income ($)	70	77	98	116	132	114	10	63
Earnings/share ($)	1.05	1.19	1.30	1.50	1.67	1.86	12	77
Div. per share ($)	.32	.37	.41	.45	.49	.55	12	72
Dividend yield (%)	2.1	2.3	1.8	1.5	1.6	1.7	—	—
Avg. PE ratio	14.6	13.6	17.2	20.1	17.9	17.2	—	—

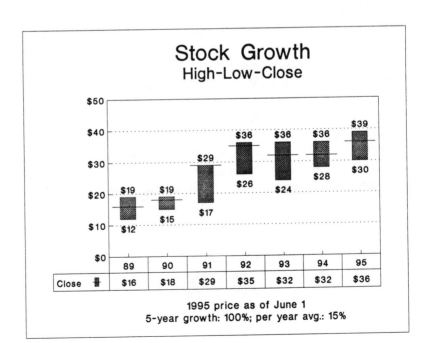

Stock Growth
High-Low-Close

	89	90	91	92	93	94	95
Close	$16	$18	$29	$35	$32	$32	$36

1995 price as of June 1
5-year growth: 100%; per year avg.: 15%

31

Electronic Data Systems (General Motors "E")

7171 Forest Lane
Dallas, TX 75320
214-604-6000

Chairman and CEO: Lester M. Alberthal Jr.

Earnings Growth	★ ★	Dividend Growth	★ ★ ★
Stock Growth	★ ★ ★	Consistency	★ ★ ★ ★
Dividend Yield	★	Shareholder Perks	★ ★
NYSE—GM "E"		**Total**	**15 points**

Life after Ross Perot has been bountiful for Electronic Data Systems (EDS), one of the largest players in the booming field of information technology services.

Revenues have grown nearly fourfold for the company since Perot sold EDS to General Motors (GM) for $2.6 billion in 1984. Once heavily reliant on its GM parent for its lifeblood, EDS has been gradually reducing its relationship with the auto maker. Today, only a little more than a third of EDS's business comes from GM.

EDS handles such tasks as benefits administration, dealer networks, engineering technologies and business information systems for GM. The automaker has announced plans to spin off EDS, a process expected to be completed sometime in 1996.

EDS's forte is running the computer networks of its corporate clients more efficiently than they can do it themselves. A major "outsourcer," EDS works assiduously to build a bond of trust with customers who unload their computing on the information technology specialist. For example, EDS has a ten-year, $3.2 billion contract with Xerox Corp. to run its telecommunications systems and computer networks. EDS not only assumes the customer's equipment but hires the customer's information services employees as well.

EDS can boast of some $32 billion of future business already on its books, which bodes well for future earnings performance. Although large outsourcing contracts have been EDS's traditional bread and butter, the company has been focusing more on the higher-margin, smaller contracts in the $50 million to $100 million range.

One of the company's hottest areas of growth is management consulting work. Launched in 1993 with about 450 consultants and about $60 million in revenue, EDS's management consultancy had 1,600 consultants by the end of 1994 and is expected to add between 500 and 1,000 more by the end of 1996.

Although a proposed merger with Sprint was scuttled in the spring of 1994, EDS remains committed to increasing its presence in the telecommunications field by striking partnerships with smaller providers. A third area of emphasis is multimedia, where EDS has become partners with Apple Computer to produce a compact disc–based shopping catalog.

Road warriors who enjoy the latest movies in their hotels can thank EDS, which has partnered with SpectraVision to beam digitized videos via satellite on demand.

About 25 percent of EDS's $9.96 billion in annual revenue is generated overseas. The company has vowed to double that figure by 2000 through aggressive marketing in Europe and Asia. The Dallas-based operation has 71,000 employees and about 393,000 shareholders.

EARNINGS-PER-SHARE GROWTH ★ ★

Past 5 years: 88 percent (14 percent per year)
Past 10 years: 969 percent (27 percent per year)

STOCK GROWTH ★ ★ ★

Past 10 years: 406 percent (17.5 percent per year)
Dollar growth: $10,000 over 10 years (including reinvested dividends) would have grown to $57,000
Average annual compounded rate of return (including reinvested dividends): 19 percent

DIVIDEND YIELD   ★

Average dividend yield in the past 3 years: 1.3 percent

DIVIDEND GROWTH   ★ ★ ★

Increased dividend: 9 consecutive years
Past 5-year increase: 100 percent (15 percent per year)

CONSISTENCY   ★ ★ ★ ★

Increased earnings per share: 12 consecutive years
Increased sales: 12 consecutive years

SHAREHOLDER PERKS   ★ ★

The company offers a dividend reinvestment and stock purchase plan.

EDS AT A GLANCE

Fiscal year ended: Dec. 31
Revenue and net income in $ millions

	1989	1990	1991	1992	1993	1994	5-year Growth Avg. Annual (%)	5-year Growth Total (%)
Revenue ($)	5,373	6,021	7,029	8,155	8,507	9,960	13	86
Net income ($)	435.3	469.9	563.0	635.5	724.0	821.9	14	89
Earnings/share ($)	.91	1.04	1.18	1.33	1.51	1.71	14	88
Div. per share ($)	.24	.28	.32	.36	.40	.48	15	100
Dividend yield (%)	1.9	1.7	1.3	1.2	1.3	1.4	—	—
Avg. PE ratio	14.0	15.5	20.6	22.1	20.0	20.3	—	—

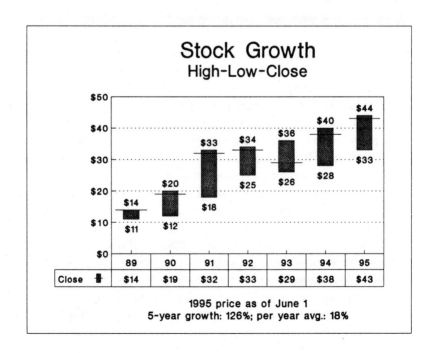

Stock Growth
High-Low-Close

	89	90	91	92	93	94	95
Close	$14	$19	$32	$33	$29	$38	$43

1995 price as of June 1
5-year growth: 126%; per year avg.: 18%

32

Rubbermaid, Inc.

1147 Akron Road
Wooster, OH 44691
216-264-6464

Chairman and CEO: Wolfgang R. Schmidt
President: Charles A. Carroll

Earnings Growth	★ ★	Dividend Growth	★ ★ ★ ★
Stock Growth	★ ★	Consistency	★ ★ ★ ★
Dividend Yield	★	Shareholder Perks	★ ★
NYSE—RBD		**Total**	**15 points**

Rubbermaid has built its business by taking garden-variety household, office, playroom and workshop products and recasting them in virtually indestructible plastic.

The Wooster, Ohio, operation has lent its rubbery touch to storage sheds, laundry hampers, cosmetic kits, file cabinets, tackle boxes, garden carts, patio furniture and a wide variety of toys.

The secret of Rubbermaid's success has been knowing how to pick the products that consumers and commercial customers want. The company uses a combination of sophisticated trend analysis, new technology and cross-functional teams to reduce new product development times and make it to store shelves ahead of the competition.

About 75 percent of Rubbermaid's $2.2 billion in annual revenue comes from the consumer segment, while the other 25 percent is generated by commercial customers such as factories and institutions.

Rubbermaid's formula for new product introductions works 90 percent of the time—a remarkable figure considering the alarmingly high new

product failure rate most manufacturers experience. Ru
afford to seize on the wrong trend because 33 percent of it
from products introduced in the past five years.

The company is just as aggressive about extending its brands to new markets. Rubbermaid has stepped up its new market penetration timetable from every 18 to 24 months to every 12 to 18 months.

The company attributes part of its new product success to its teamwork approach. Product development teams are encouraged to respond quickly to ever-changing trends—and can sometimes churn out new products in as little as 20 weeks.

Rubbermaid doesn't waste time test marketing. All products are rolled out on a full, nationwide basis. Rubbermaid does a strong business in the home and commercial office segment, with its line of desk accessories, floor mats, storage devices, copy stands and portable desktops. The company also took a step into the booming home health care market with its 1994 acquisition of Carex.

International sales make up about 11 percent of the company's revenues—a figure the company hopes to more than double by the turn of the century as it targets high-growth markets.

The company was founded in 1920 as a balloon manufacturer called the Wooster Rubber Company. In 1934 it began producing its first housewares products—rubber dustpans, drainboard mats and soap dishes, which were to become the driving force of the company's long tradition of growth. Rubbermaid has 13,000 employees and 31,000 shareholders.

EARNINGS-PER-SHARE GROWTH ★ ★

Past 5 years: 82 percent (13 percent per year)
Past 10 years: 306 percent (15 percent per year)

STOCK GROWTH ★ ★

Past 10 years: 365 percent (17 percent per year)
Dollar growth: $10,000 over 10 years (including reinvested dividends) would have grown to $53,000
Average annual compounded rate of return (including reinvested dividends): 18 percent

DIVIDEND YIELD

Average dividend yield in the past 3 years: 1.4 percent

DIVIDEND GROWTH

Increased dividend: 40 consecutive years
Past 5-year increase: 100 percent (15 percent per year)

CONSISTENCY

Increased earnings per share: 14 consecutive years
Increased sales: 43 consecutive years

SHAREHOLDER PERKS ★ ★

Good dividend reinvestment and stock purchase plan: voluntary stock purchase plan allows contributions of $50 to $5,000 per month.

Shareholders who attend the annual meeting usually receive a free Rubbermaid product such as a file case, a food tray or a food storage container. Shareholders may also shop in the company store on annual meeting day and take advantage of discounts on dozens of Rubbermaid products.

RUBBERMAID AT A GLANCE

Fiscal year ended: Dec. 31
Revenue and net income in $ millions

	1989	1990	1991	1992	1993	1994	5-year Growth Avg. Annual (%)	5-year Growth Total (%)
Revenue ($)	1,452	1,534	1,667	1,805	1,960	2,169	8	49
Net income ($)	125	144	163	164	211	228	13	82
Earnings/share ($)	.78	.90	1.02	1.15	1.32	1.42	13	82
Div. per share ($)	.23	.27	.31	.35	.41	.46	15	100
Dividend yield (%)	1.5	1.4	1.2	1.1	1.3	1.7	—	—
Avg. PE ratio	20	21	26	28	24	20	—	—

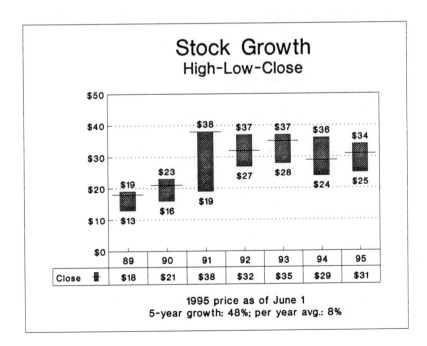

Stock Growth
High-Low-Close

	89	90	91	92	93	94	95
Close	$18	$21	$38	$32	$35	$29	$31

1995 price as of June 1
5-year growth: 48%; per year avg.: 8%

33
ConAgra, Inc.

One ConAgra Drive
Omaha, NE 68102-5001
402-595-4000

Chairman and CEO: Philip B. Fletcher

Earnings Growth	★	Dividend Growth	★ ★ ★ ★
Stock Growth	★ ★	Consistency	★ ★ ★ ★
Dividend Yield	★ ★	Shareholder Perks	★ ★
NYSE—CAG		**Total**	**15 points**

For 75 years, ConAgra has been putting food on America's dinner tables. In addition to its traditional fare of grains, meats and seafood, the Omaha operation has slowly acquired a vast spread of name-brand prepared foods.

Among the company's most recognized brands are Hunt's, Peter Pan, Orville Redenbacher's, Wesson, Morton, Chun King, Banquet, Armour, Country Pride, Eckrich and Healthy Choice. Other well-known brands include Swiss Miss, Manwich, La Choy, Patio, Decker, Butterball and Country Skillet.

ConAgra has been one of the nation's most consistent food companies, posting record earnings for 14 consecutive years. With annual revenue of $23.5 billion, it is the nation's second largest food processor.

The company's leading segment is its prepared foods division, which accounts for 77 percent of its revenue. In addition to its popular name-brand foods, the company also produces frozen potato products, delicatessen and food service products, pet accessories and Singer sewing accessories.

ConAgra operates in two other market segments:

- **Agricultural products and specialty retailing** (13 percent of revenue). The company sells a wide range of fertilizers, insecticides and crop protection chemicals. It also sells livestock health care products, animal feeds and nutrient additives for feeds.

ConAgra owns 107 Country General stores (operating under the names Country General, Wheelers, S & S, Sanvig's, Peavy Ranch, Home, and Anfinson's), and 97 fabric and craft stores (operating as Northwest Fabrics & Crafts and Rainbow Bay Crafts).
* **Trading and processing** (10 percent of revenue). ConAgra Flour Milling Company is a leader in the U.S. flour milling industry with 27 mills in 14 states. ConAgra's commodity trading business has offices in 15 nations, trading agricultural commodities and foodstuffs on the world market.

The company has 87,000 employees and 32,000 shareholders of record. In all, ConAgra has operations in 27 countries.

EARNINGS-PER-SHARE GROWTH ★

Past 5 years: 66 percent (11 percent per year)
Past 10 years: 293 percent (15 percent per year)

STOCK GROWTH ★ ★

Past 10 years: 307 percent (15 percent per year)
Dollar growth: $10,000 over 10 years (including reinvested dividends) would have grown to $48,000
Average annual compounded rate of return (including reinvested dividends): 17 percent

DIVIDEND YIELD ★ ★

Average dividend yield in the past 3 years: 2.2 percent

DIVIDEND GROWTH ★ ★ ★ ★

Increased dividend: 19 consecutive years
Past 5-year increase: 112 percent (16 percent per year)

CONSISTENCY

Increased earnings per share: 14 consecutive years
Increased sales: 14 consecutive years

SHAREHOLDER PERKS

Good dividend reinvestment and stock purchase plan: voluntary stock purchase plan allows contributions of $25 to $5,000 per quarter.

At its annual meetings, the company passes out a gift pack of some of its foods to its shareholders, and it sometimes sends out discount offers along with its quarterly earnings reports.

CONAGRA AT A GLANCE

Fiscal year ended: May 31
Revenue and net income in $ millions

	1989	1990	1991	1992	1993	1994	5-year Growth Avg. Annual (%)	5-year Growth Total (%)
Revenue ($)	11,340	15,501	19,505	21,219	21,519	23,512	16	107
Net income ($)	198	232	311	372	391	437	17	121
Earnings/share ($)	1.09	1.25	1.42	1.50	1.58	1.81	11	66
Div. per share ($)	.33	.39	.45	.52	.60	.70	16	112
Dividend yield (%)	2.4	2.2	1.8	1.7	2.3	2.7	—	—
Avg. PE ratio	12.6	14.2	17.6	19.8	18.1	14.5	—	—

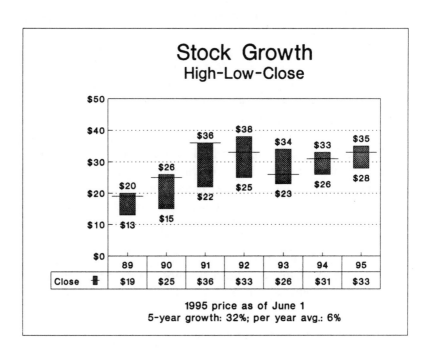

Stock Growth
High-Low-Close

Close	89	90	91	92	93	94	95
	$19	$25	$36	$33	$26	$31	$33

1995 price as of June 1
5-year growth: 32%; per year avg.: 6%

Pfizer, Inc.

235 East 42nd St.
New York, NY 10017
212-573-2323

Chairman and CEO: William C. Steere, Jr.

Earnings Growth	★ ★	Dividend Growth	★ ★ ★
Stock Growth	★ ★	Consistency	★ ★ ★
Dividend Yield	★ ★ ★	Shareholder Perks	★ ★
NYSE—PFE		**Total**	**15 points**

You may know Pfizer best for some of its smaller contributions to the human condition. Its Visine eye drops "get the red out," Plax mouth rinse loosens dental plaque, Barbasol Shaving Cream softens whiskers and Ben-Gay soothes aching muscles.

But consumer health care products make up just 5 percent of Pfizer's $8.3 billion in annual sales. Most of the New York–based company's revenue comes from pharmaceuticals and hospital products. The health care segment accounts for 84 percent of total revenue (pharmaceuticals make up 70 percent while hospital products account for 14 percent).

Within the pharmaceuticals segment, the leading product group is cardiovascular medications, led by Procardia XL, which grossed $1.18 billion in 1994. Other leading cardiovasculars are Norvasc and Cardura.

Anti-infectives account for 21 percent of total revenue, led by Diflucan, Unasyn and Zithromax. The company also does a solid business in the sale of anti-inflammatories, antidiabetes agents and central nervous system agents.

In the hospital products category, Pfizer's biggest subsidiary is Howmedica, a manufacturer of artificial hips, knees and other orthopedic implants. Howmedica accounts for about 8 percent of total revenue. Pfizer is also a manufacturer of angioplasty devices, electrosurgical devices, ultrasonic cutting devices and impotence and incontinence implants.

Pfizer's other key segments include:

- **Animal health** (7 percent of sales). The company makes a wide range of animal medications including antibiotics, anthelmintics and antibacterials. It also produces feed supplements.
- **Food science** (4 percent). The company produces food ingredients designed to add to the taste, freshness or nutritional balance of existing foods. Pfizer is currently researching new fat extenders, intense sweeteners, flavors, food protectants and high-temperature fat substitutes.

The company is well-entrenched internationally. About 50 percent of its revenue comes from foreign operations. Pfizer has 40,500 employees and 62,000 shareholders.

EARNINGS-PER-SHARE GROWTH ★ ★

Past 5 years: 108 percent (16 percent per year)
Past 10 years: 173 percent (10.5 percent per year)

STOCK GROWTH ★ ★

Past 10 years: 268 percent (14 percent per year)
Dollar growth: $10,000 over 10 years (including reinvested dividends) would have grown to $50,000
Average annual compounded rate of return (including reinvested dividends): 17 percent

DIVIDEND YIELD ★ ★ ★

Average dividend yield in the past 3 years: 2.5 percent

DIVIDEND GROWTH ★ ★ ★

Increased dividend: 27 consecutive years
Past 5-year increase: 71 percent (11 percent per year)

CONSISTENCY   ★ ★ ★

Increased earnings per share: 9 of past 10 years
Increased sales: 45 consecutive years

SHAREHOLDER PERKS

Good dividend reinvestment and stock purchase plan: voluntary stock purchase plan allows contributions of $25 to $10,000 per month.

PFIZER AT A GLANCE

Fiscal year ended: Dec. 31
Revenue and net income in $ millions

	1989	1990	1991	1992	1993	1994	5-year Growth Avg. Annual (%)	5-year Growth Total (%)
Revenue ($)	5,671.5	6,406	6,950	7,230.2	7,477.7	8,281.3	8	46
Net income ($)	681.1	801.2	722.1	810.9	657.5	1,298.4	14	91
Earnings/share ($)	1.01	1.19	1.36	1.63	1.84	2.10	16	108
Div. per share ($)	.55	.60	.66	.74	.84	.94	11	71
Dividend yield (%)	3.5	3.5	2.2	2.0	2.6	2.9	—	—
Avg. PE ratio	15	14	22	23	17.5	16	—	—

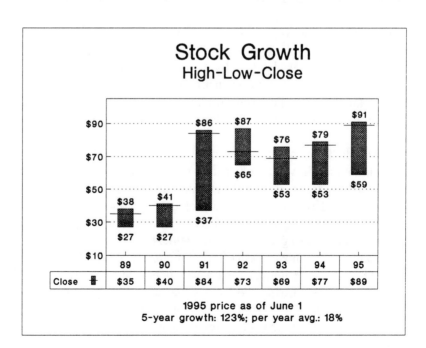

Stock Growth
High-Low-Close

	89	90	91	92	93	94	95
Close	$35	$40	$84	$73	$69	$77	$89

1995 price as of June 1
5-year growth: 123%; per year avg.: 18%

State Street Boston Corp.

225 Franklin St.
Boston, MA 02110
617-786-3000

Chairman and CEO: Marshall N. Carter

Earnings Growth	★ ★	Dividend Growth	★ ★ ★ ★
Stock Growth	★ ★	Consistency	★ ★ ★ ★
Dividend Yield	★	Shareholder Perks	★ ★
NYSE—STT		**Total**	**15 points**

State Street Boston Corp. is a banking organization that traces its roots back two centuries to the Union Bank, which opened in 1792. The company's scope of services has changed dramatically since then, as has its scope of operations. The Boston-based institution has offices in Canada, Hong Kong, Japan, Australia, New Zealand, Taiwan, the United Kingdom, France, Belgium, Luxembourg, Germany and several other overseas locations.

Although the company does offer many traditional banking services, its main source of revenue comes from the managing and servicing of assets for mutual funds, pension funds and other large asset pools. The company offers a broad range of services including accounting, recordkeeping, custody of securities, information services, investment management, foreign exchange trading and cash management.

State Street, which began offering mutual fund services in 1924, now has $683 billion of mutual fund assets under custody. It is the leading mutual fund custodian in the United States, servicing 37 percent of the registered funds. The company also provides services for nearly 200 collective investment funds registered outside the United States.

State Street is also a leader in the pension asset segment, servicing $574 billion in assets for North American customers and $66 billion in assets for customers outside North America. State Street is the nation's largest servicer of tax-exempt assets for corporations and public funds.

The company's $1.6 trillion in assets under custody breaks down this way: mutual funds and collective investment funds, 42 percent; master trust, master custody and global custody services, 41 percent; corporate trust, insurance and other related services, 13 percent; European services, 1.5 percent; and Asia-Pacific services, 3 percent. State Street has 11,000 employees and 6,000 shareholders.

EARNINGS-PER-SHARE GROWTH ★ ★

Past 5 years: 94 percent (14 percent per year)
Past 10 years: 347 percent (16 percent per year)

STOCK GROWTH ★ ★

Past 10 years: 310 percent (15 percent per year)
Dollar growth: $10,000 over 10 years (including reinvested dividends) would have grown to $44,000
Average annual compounded rate of return (including reinvested dividends): 17 percent

DIVIDEND YIELD ★

Average dividend yield in the past 3 years: 1.4 percent

DIVIDEND GROWTH ★ ★ ★ ★

Increased dividend: 16 consecutive years
Past 5-year increase: 100 percent (15 percent per year)

CONSISTENCY ★ ★ ★ ★

Increased earnings per share: 15 consecutive years

SHAREHOLDER PERKS ★ ★

Good dividend reinvestment and stock purchase plan: voluntary stock purchase plan allows contributions of $10 to $1,000 per month.

STATE STREET BOSTON AT A GLANCE

Fiscal year ended: Dec. 31
Revenue and net income in $ millions

	1989	1990	1991	1992	1993	1994	5-year Growth Avg. Annual (%)	Total (%)
Revenue ($)	657	749	852	987	1,160	1,360	16	107
Net income ($)	104	117	139	160	180	207	15	99
Earnings/share ($)	1.38	1.55	1.81	2.07	2.33	2.68	14	94
Div. per share ($)	.30	.34	.39	.45	.52	.60	15	100
Dividend yield (%)	1.8	1.9	1.6	1.3	1.4	1.6	—	—
Avg. PE ratio	12.0	11.4	13.5	17.3	16.1	13.7	—	—

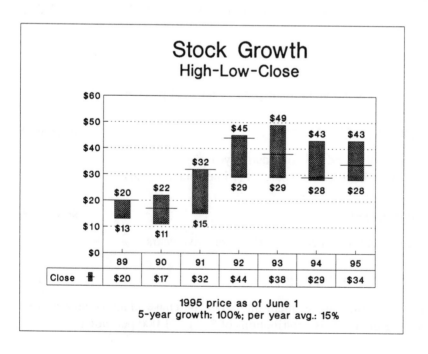

Stock Growth
High-Low-Close

	89	90	91	92	93	94	95
Close	$20	$17	$32	$44	$38	$29	$34

1995 price as of June 1
5-year growth: 100%; per year avg.: 15%

RPM, I.

2628 Pearl Road
P. O. Box 777
Medina, OH 44258
216-273-5090

Chairman and CEO: Thomas C. Sullivan
President: James A. Karman

Earnings Growth	★	Dividend Growth	★ ★ ★
Stock Growth	★ ★	Consistency	★ ★ ★ ★
Dividend Yield	★ ★ ★	Shareholder Perks	★ ★
NASDAQ—RPOW		**Total**	**15 points**

It's not just new product innovations that have made RPM the world's most consistent corporation. The Medina, Ohio, manufacturer has managed to post 47 consecutive years of record sales and earnings in large part because its management has become astute at acquiring solid companies with products that fit well within RPM's existing line of coatings and sealants.

The company has made dozens of acquisitions through the years, including two major buyouts in 1994. RPM acquired Rust-Oleum Corp., the nation's leading producer of consumer rust-preventive coatings. It also acquired Stonhard Corp., which is the worldwide leader in industrial and commercial polymer flooring and related products.

RPM was founded in 1947 by Frank C. Sullivan, who invented the Alumanation process for coating outdoor metal structures. While Alumanation continues to be the world's leading liquid aluminum coating solution, the process is now just a small part of RPM's total business.

The company owns 37 subsidiaries, all of which are involved in the manufacture of coatings, sealants and specialty chemicals (including corrosion protection, waterproofing and maintenance products, roofing materials, touch-up products for autos and furniture, and fabrics and wall coverings).

About 60 percent of the company's sales comes from the industrial market, while the other 40 percent comes from its line of consumer products.

RPM divides its business into the following market segments:

- **Corrosion control.** RPM produces a wide range of coatings and chemicals for power plants, oil rigs, railcars, tankers, smokestacks and other structures that are subject to harsh environments. Leading brands include Carboline, Plasite and Bitumastic.
- **Specialty chemicals.** The company makes fluorescent colorants and pigments, concrete additives that provide corrosion resistance and add strength to cement used in construction, additives for coatings and dyes, and coatings and cleaners for the textile trade. It produces furniture stains, fillers and polishes, auto refinishing products and auto corrosion control additives. Its leading lines include Day-Glo Color, Alox, Mohawk and American Emulsions.
- **Waterproofing and general maintenance.** The company makes coatings for metal structures such as buildings, bridges and industrial facilities; it also produces sheet roofing, sealants and deck coatings. Its leading lines include RPM Alumanation coating, Mameco sealants, Martin Mathys water-based coatings and Stonhard polymer floors, linings and wall systems.
- **Consumer hobby and leisure.** RPM's Testor subsidiary is America's leading producer of models, paints and accessory items for the model and hobby market. RPM's Craft House subsidiary markets a variety of crafts, including Paint-by-Numbers sets.
- **Consumer do-it-yourself.** The company sells a wide range of paints and coatings for the consumer market, including Zinsser shellac-based coatings, Bondax patch and repair products, Dynatron/Bondo, Talsol and Rust-Oleum.

RPM is among the industry leaders in the development of "environmentally sound" products such as water-based paints and primers, concrete additives, an ozone-safe airbrush propellant and an inorganic zinc corrosion control coating.

The company has sales in about 110 countries and manufacturing operations in 45 locations in the United States, Canada, Belgium, Luxembourg and the Netherlands. Foreign sales account for about 12 percent of total revenue.

RPM's coatings cover the Statue of Liberty, the Eiffel Tower and hundreds of bridges, ships, highways, factories, office towers, warehouses and other structures around the world. RPM has about 4,500 employees and 45,000 shareholders.

EARNINGS-PER-SHARE GROWTH ★

Past 5 years: 66 percent (11 percent per year)
Past 10 years: 200 percent (11.5 percent per year)

STOCK GROWTH ★ ★

Past 10 years: 251 percent (13 percent per year)
Dollar growth: $10,000 over 10 years (including reinvested dividends) would have grown to $45,000
Average annual compounded rate of return (including reinvested dividends): 16 percent

DIVIDEND YIELD ★ ★ ★

Average dividend yield in the past 3 years: 2.8 percent

DIVIDEND GROWTH ★ ★ ★

Increased dividend: 20 consecutive years
Past 5-year increase: 60 percent (10 percent per year)

CONSISTENCY ★ ★ ★ ★

Increased earnings per share: 47 consecutive years
Increased sales: 47 consecutive years

SHAREHOLDER PERKS

Good dividend reinvestment and stock purchase plan: voluntary stock purchase plan allows contributions of $25 to $5,000 per month.

RPM AT A GLANCE

Fiscal year ended: May 31
Revenue and net income in $ millions

	1989	1990	1991	1992	1993	1994	5-year Growth Avg. Annual (%)	Total (%)
Revenue ($)	493.2	571.7	619.6	680.1	768.4	815.6	11	65
Net income ($)	27.3	31.9	37.4	38.5	39.5	52.6	14	93
Earnings/share ($)	.56	.65	.72	.73	.79	.93	11	66
Div. per share ($)	.32	.35	.39	.44	.47	.51	10	59
Dividend yield (%)	3.4	3.5	3.1	2.8	2.7	2.8	—	—
Avg. PE ratio	17	16	18	21	24	19	—	—

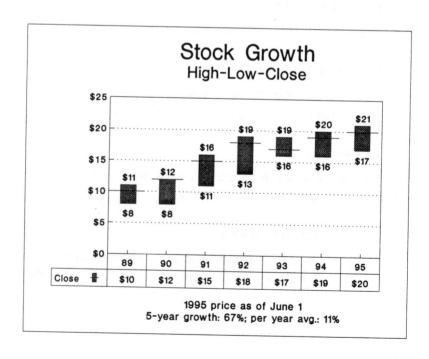

Stock Growth
High-Low-Close

	89	90	91	92	93	94	95
Close	$10	$12	$15	$18	$17	$19	$20

1995 price as of June 1
5-year growth: 67%; per year avg.: 11%

37
Pall Corp.

2200 Northern Blvd.
East Hills, NY 11548
516-484-5400

Chairman and CEO: Eric Krasnoff
President: Jeremy Hayward-Surry

Earnings Growth	★	Dividend Growth	★ ★ ★ ★
Stock Growth	★ ★	Consistency	★ ★ ★ ★
Dividend Yield	★ ★	Shareholder Perks	★ ★
NYSE—PLL		**Total**	**15 points**

Separating the wheat from the chaff with its specialized filters has made Pall Corp. an important supplier to the aerospace, biomedical, petroleum and pharmaceutical industries.

Pall's traditional strength lies in fluid clarification. It makes a broad range of filters to remove microscopic contaminants from liquids and gases. In recent years, Pall has expanded its strategy to also focus on "separation" technology, or the removal of large amounts of solids from liquids or gases.

Half of Pall's $701 million in revenue comes from sales to the health care industry, a segment of the economy that had been flat but is recovering. Pall filters remove contaminating viruses, bacteria and toxins from blood, anesthesia gases, pharmaceuticals and food and beverages. Pall is the leading supplier of filters for the fast-growing cold stabilization process, or as brewers call it, the "cold filtering" of beer.

Pall serves other industry segments:

- **Aeropower** (26 percent of sales). Pall filters remove contaminants from hydraulic and lubricating fluids that can ground a plane or idle an automotive assembly line. Although military aerospace sales have been falling, sales to the commercial aerospace sector have been encouraging.

- **Fluid processing** (24 percent of sales). Pall's products are used in oil refining, electric generation and computer circuitry production.

A global company with manufacturing, research and distribution facilities all over the world, Pall's international sales account for 57 percent of revenue. The company has 5,300 employees and 6,200 shareholders.

EARNINGS-PER-SHARE GROWTH

Past 5 years: 72 percent (12 percent per year)
Past 10 years: 197 percent (11 percent per year)

STOCK GROWTH ★ ★

Past 10 years: 262 percent (14 percent per year)
Dollar growth: $10,000 over 10 years (including reinvested dividends) would have grown to $42,000
Average annual compounded rate of return (including reinvested dividends): 15.5 percent

DIVIDEND YIELD ★ ★

Average dividend yield in the past 3 years: 1.6 percent

DIVIDEND GROWTH ★ ★ ★ ★

Increased dividend: 20 consecutive years
Past 5-year increase: 140 percent (19 percent per year)

CONSISTENCY ★ ★ ★ ★

Increased earnings per share: 23 consecutive years
Increased sales: 23 consecutive years

SHAREHOLDER PERKS

Good dividend reinvestment and stock purchase plan: voluntary stock purchase plan allows contributions of up to $60,000 per year.

PALL AT A GLANCE

Fiscal year ended: July 31
Revenue and net income in $ millions

	1989	1990	1991	1992	1993	1994	Avg. Annual (%)	Total (%)
							5-year Growth	
Revenue ($)	497.0	564.5	657.0	685.1	687.2	700.8	7	40
Net income ($)	57.7	66.2	79.9	92.7	78.3	98.9	11	70
Earnings/share ($)	.50	.57	.69	.79	.83	.86	12	72
Div. per share ($)	.15	.18	.21	.26	.31	.36	19	140
Dividend yield (%)	1.6	1.7	1.5	1.3	1.5	2.0	—	—
Avg. PE ratio	18	20	20	25	23.5	20	—	—

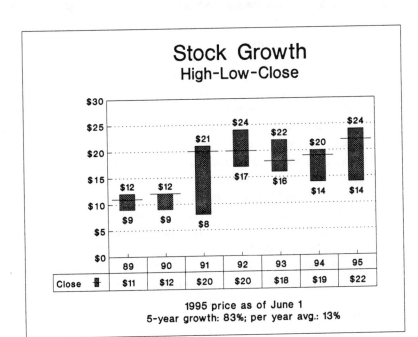

Stock Growth
High-Low-Close

Close		$11	$12	$20	$20	$18	$19	$22

1995 price as of June 1
5-year growth: 83%; per year avg.: 13%

38

Synovus Financial Corp.

One Arsenal Place
901 Front Avenue, Suite 301
P. O. Box 120
Columbus, GA 31902-0120
706-649-2387

Chairman and CEO: James H. Blanchard
President and CEO: Stephen L. Burts, Jr.

Earnings Growth	★ ★	Dividend Growth	★ ★ ★ ★
Stock Growth	★	Consistency	★ ★ ★ ★
Dividend Yield	★ ★	Shareholder Perks	★ ★
NYSE—SNV		**Total**	**15 points**

Like a number of fast-growth megabanks, Synovus Financial Corp. can credit its rapid growth to a series of mergers and buyouts.

But rather than turning its new acquisitions into branch banks that operate under the same name, Synovus preserves each bank's original name and keeps the management and board of directors intact. Only the back office duties such as auditing and data processing are rolled into the home office operations to cut costs.

Synovus has acquired 22 banks in the past five years and owns a total of 32 banks. Most are in smaller cities and towns throughout Georgia, Alabama, Florida and South Carolina. The company's flagship system is the Columbus, Georgia, Bank and Trust Company.

The company's unique hands-off management strategy has worked well. Synovus has posted 12 consecutive years of record earnings.

The company wrapped up its largest merger ever in the spring of 1995 when it acquired NBSC Corp., a Columbia, South Carolina–based bank with 43 offices throughout South Carolina. In addition to its banking operations, Synovus is the parent company of Total System Services, Inc., the world's second-largest processor of bank card transactions. (Synovus owns an 80.8 percent stake in the company.)

Total System Services provides bank card and private label card data processing services for customers issuing Visa, MasterCard and Diner's Club credit cards along with corporate cards, private label cards and automated teller machine cards. Among its leading customers are BankAmerica and NationsBank. Synovus has about 5,000 employees and 16,000 shareholders.

EARNINGS-PER-SHARE GROWTH ★ ★

Past 5 years: 93 percent (14 percent per year)
Past 10 years: 291 percent (15 percent per year)

STOCK GROWTH ★

Past 10 years: 233 percent (13 percent per year)
Dollar growth: $10,000 over 10 years (including reinvested dividends) would have grown to $41,000
Average annual compounded rate of return (including reinvested dividends): 15 percent

DIVIDEND YIELD ★ ★

Average dividend yield in the past 3 years: 2.2 percent

DIVIDEND GROWTH ★ ★ ★ ★

Increased dividend: 15 consecutive years
Past 5-year increase: 105 percent (16 percent per year)

CONSISTENCY ★ ★ ★ ★

Increased earnings per share: 12 consecutive years

SHAREHOLDER PERKS ★ ★

Good dividend reinvestment and stock purchase plan: voluntary stock purchase plan allows contributions of up to $2,500 per month.

SYNOVUS AT A GLANCE

Fiscal year ended: Dec. 31
Revenue and net income in $ millions

	1989	1990	1991	1992	1993	1994	5-year Growth Avg. Annual (%)	Total (%)
Revenue ($)	201.8	282.1	346.8	406.7	455.1	523.4	21	160
Net income ($)	31.4	35.1	40.5	61.2	74.1	86.4	23	180
Earnings/share ($)	.67	.70	.75	.92	1.11	1.29	14	93
Div. per share ($)	.22	.25	.27	.31	.37	.45	16	105
Dividend yield (%)	2.1	2.5	2.3	2.0	2.0	2.5	—	—
Avg. PE ratio	14.6	14.8	14.4	15.4	16.1	13.9	—	—

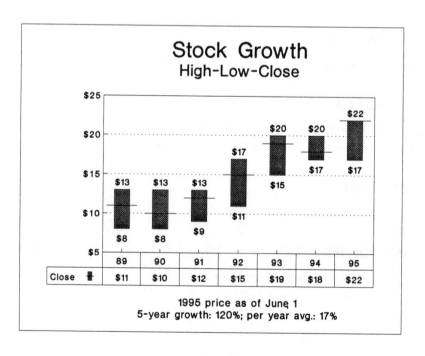

Stock Growth
High-Low-Close

	89	90	91	92	93	94	95
Close	$11	$10	$12	$15	$19	$18	$22

1995 price as of June 1
5-year growth: 120%; per year avg.: 17%

39

Hershey Foods Corp.

100 Crystal A Drive
P. O. Box 810
Hershey, PA 17033
717-534-6799

Chairman and CEO: Kenneth L. Wolfe
President and COO: Joseph P. Viviano

Earnings Growth	★	Dividend Growth	★ ★ ★
Stock Growth	★ ★	Consistency	★ ★ ★
Dividend Yield	★ ★ ★	Shareholder Perks	★ ★ ★
NYSE—HSY		**Total**	**15 points**

Known most for its chocolates, Hershey Foods puts a wide range of other sweets on the market as well. In fact, it is the nation's leading confectionery producer, with a 35 percent share of the $10 billion U.S. candy market.

America's sweet tooth has been good for business for the 102-year-old Pennsylvania company, which has posted record profits 15 of the past 16 years.

Through brand extension and a series of acquisitions, Hershey has assembled a long line of confectionery favorites: Peter Paul Almond Joy, Mounds Bars, Caramello, Cadbury's Creme Eggs, Hershey's Big Block, Special Dark, Golden Almond, Golden Almond Nuggets, Kit Kat, Krackel, Rolo caramels and Hershey's Kisses.

Other well-known brands include Skor, Mr. Goodbar, Reese's Peanut Butter Cups, Reese's Pieces, Fifth Avenue, Twizzlers, Bar None, Hershey's chocolate bar with almonds, York peppermint Pattie, Symphony, and the perennial favorite, Hershey's milk chocolate bar. The company also produces Luden's cough drops and Mellomints.

Hershey is one of four key players in the confectionery market. Their key competitors include Mars, a private company which holds about a 26 percent share, and Nestle USA and E.J. Brach, each of which holds about a 9 percent share.

In addition to its candies, Hershey offers a line of chocolate mixes including Hershey's cocoa, chocolate milk mix, baking chocolate, chocolate syrup, fudge topping, chocolate chips and premium chunks and chocolate flavor puddings.

The company also operates a burgeoning pasta division. Leading brands are Ronzoni, American Beauty, San Giorgio, Light'n Fluffy and Skinner.

Hershey's products are sold in 60 countries worldwide. Its international operations account for about 13 percent of its $3.6 billion in annual revenue. Founded in 1893 by Milton Hershey, the company has 14,300 employees and 33,000 shareholders.

EARNINGS-PER-SHARE GROWTH ★

Past 5 years: 60 percent (10 percent per year)
Past 10 years: 162 percent (10 percent per year)

STOCK GROWTH ★ ★

Past 10 years: 251 percent (13 percent per year)
Dollar growth: $10,000 over 10 years (including reinvested dividends) would have grown to $39,000
Average annual compounded rate of return (including reinvested dividends): 14.5 percent

DIVIDEND YIELD ★ ★ ★

Average dividend yield in the past 3 years: 2.5 percent

DIVIDEND GROWTH ★ ★ ★

Increased dividend: 20 consecutive years
Past 5-year increase: 69 percent (11 percent per year)

CONSISTENCY

Increased earnings per share: 9 of past 10 years
Increased sales: 9 of past 10 years

SHAREHOLDER PERKS ★ ★ ★

Good dividend reinvestment and stock purchase plan: voluntary stock purchase plan allows contributions of $50 to $20,000 per year.

Hershey makes Christmas shopping a lot easier for shareholders with chocolate-loving friends. Hershey's Chocolate World visitor's center mails its Christmas gift catalog to any shareholder requesting it and maintains a mailing list for annual receipt of the catalog. Shareholders may purchase special gift packages from the catalog and have them wrapped and mailed directly to their friends.

Shareholders who attend the annual meeting are treated to a free packet of Hershey's candies and pasta. At a recent meeting, shareholders received San Giorgio spaghetti, Mr. Goodbar, Special Dark and Symphony chocolate bars, a Mounds bar, Helps cough suppressant tablets, strawberry Twizzlers candy, a coupon for free Hershey's puddings, a coupon for Reese's Peanut Butter Cups and a pasta cookbook.

HERSHEY AT A GLANCE

Fiscal year ended: Dec. 31
Revenue and net income in $ millions

	1989	1990	1991	1992	1993	1994	5-year Growth Avg. Annual (%)	5-year Growth Total (%)
Revenue ($)	2,421.0	2,715.6	2,899.2	3,219.8	3,488.2	3,606.3	8.5	50
Net income ($)	171.1	215.9	220.0	243.0	257	264	9	54
Earnings/share ($)	1.90	2.39	2.43	2.69	2.86	3.04	10	60
Div. per share ($)	.74	.84	.94	1.03	1.14	1.25	11	69
Dividend yield (%)	2.4	2.4	2.3	2.4	2.3	2.7	—	—
Avg. PE ratio	16.2	16.1	16.7	16.0	17.6	15.2	—	—

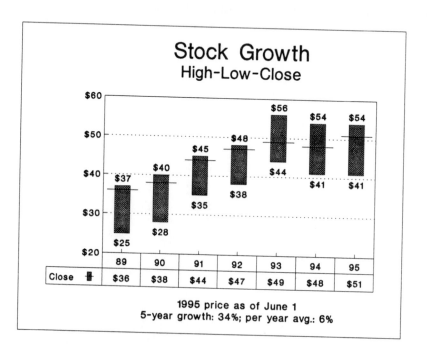

Stock Growth
High-Low-Close

	89	90	91	92	93	94	95
Close	$36	$38	$44	$47	$49	$48	$51

1995 price as of June 1
5-year growth: 34%; per year avg.: 6%

40

Newell Co.

29 East Stephenson St.
Freeport, IL 61032
815-235-4171

Chairman: Daniel C. Ferguson
CEO: William P. Scovey
President: Thomas A. Ferguson, Jr.

Earnings Growth	★	Dividend Growth	★ ★
Stock Growth	★ ★ ★ ★	Consistency	★ ★ ★
Dividend Yield	★ ★	Shareholder Perks	★ ★
NYSE—NWL		**Total**	**14 points**

Newell has built its business supplying many of America's largest retailers with housewares, hardware and office products. Now, with its 1994 acquisition of Corning's European consumer products business, Newell has taken a major step into the international arena. If the company's foreign operations achieve the same type of growth as its United States business, Newell may soon be a force to reckon with in the international market.

The Freeport, Illinois, manufacturer has been one of the nation's fastest-growing companies over the past quarter century. Twenty-five years ago Newell was a modest drapery hardware manufacturer with sales of $20 million a year. In 1994, the company grossed $2.1 billion in sales. Over the past ten years, its earnings per share have grown more than sixfold.

Newell concentrates primarily on selling its goods in mass volume to large discount retailers such as Wal-Mart, K mart, Target, Home Depot, Office Depot, True Value and other mass merchandisers.

Many of its goods are custom-labeled for its clients (such as "True Value" paint brushes or "Target" cookware). Among its leading brands are Anchor Hocking glassware, Amerock hardware, Mirro cookware, and EZ Paintr paint applicators.

Newell breaks its operations into four segments: housewares (33 percent of revenue), home furnishings (31 percent), office products (18 percent), and hardware (17 percent). Newell has 15,000 employees and 3,500 stockholders.

EARNINGS-PER-SHARE GROWTH ★

Past 5 years: 74 percent (12 percent per year)
Past 10 years: 520 percent (18 percent per year)

STOCK GROWTH ★ ★ ★ ★

Past 10 years: 921 percent (26 percent per year)
Dollar growth: $10,000 over 10 years (including reinvested dividends) would have grown to $120,000
Average annual compounded rate of return (including reinvested dividends): 28 percent

DIVIDEND YIELD ★ ★

Average dividend yield in the past 3 years: 1.7 percent

DIVIDEND GROWTH ★ ★

Increased dividend: 9 of past 10 years
Past 5-year increase: 86 percent (13 percent per year)

CONSISTENCY ★ ★ ★

Increased earnings per share: 9 of past 10 years
Increased sales: 9 of past 10 years

SHAREHOLDER PERKS ★ ★

Good dividend reinvestment and stock purchase plan: voluntary stock purchase plan allows contributions of $10 to $30,000 per year.

The company often hands out a special gift to shareholders at the annual meeting. At a recent meeting, shareholders received some stationery and office products associated with its Stewart Hall subsidiary.

NEWELL AT A GLANCE

Fiscal year ended: Dec. 31
Revenue and net income in $ millions

	1989	1990	1991	1992	1993	1994	5-year Growth Avg. Annual (%)	Total (%)
Revenue ($)	1,247	1,204	1,259	1,452	1,645	2,075	11	66
Net income ($)	106	126	136	163	165	196	13	85
Earnings/share ($)	.71	.84	.89	1.05	1.05	1.24	12	75
Div. per share ($)	.21	.25	.30	.30	.35	.39	13	86
Dividend yield (%)	2.2	1.9	1.7	1.4	1.9	1.8	—	—
Avg. PE ratio	13.5	15.7	19.4	20.5	17.5	17.3	—	—

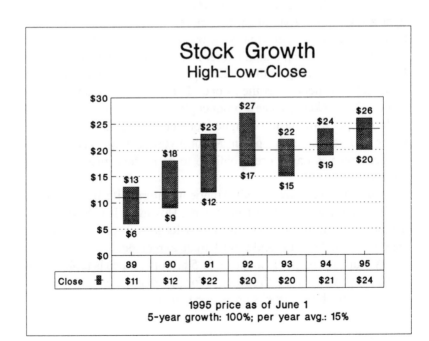

Stock Growth
High-Low-Close

	89	90	91	92	93	94	95
Close	$11	$12	$22	$20	$20	$21	$24

1995 price as of June 1
5-year growth: 100%; per year avg.: 15%

Cooper Tire & Rubber Co.

Lima and Western Avenues
Findlay, OH 45389
419-423-1321

Chairman and CEO: Patrick W. Rooney

Earnings Growth	★ ★ ★	Dividend Growth	★ ★ ★ ★
Stock Growth	★ ★ ★ ★	Consistency	★ ★
Dividend Yield	★	Shareholder Perks	
NYSE—CTB		**Total**	**14 points**

As the auto industry goes, so go the fortunes of Cooper Tire. More cars and light trucks on the road mean that more motorists will soon be shopping for replacement tires, and that's the bread and butter of Cooper's business.

The Finlay, Ohio, manufacturer is the world's ninth largest tire maker. Its tires are sold only in the replacement market, primarily through independent tire dealers under the Cooper, Falls Mastercraft and Starfire brand names. Cooper keeps its new product pipeline filled with innovations such as the Cooper Rainmaster, designed for wet-weather driving by channeling water and reducing the potential for hydroplaning. The most popular replacement passenger tires continue to be performance-type, all-season radials.

Cooper emphasizes its all-American nature with its "Put Your Trust in American Hands" advertising theme. However, it is beginning to look beyond the nation's borders to market its tires, a prospect aided by the passage of the NAFTA and GATT trade agreements.

About 85 percent of Cooper's $1.5 billion in sales is replacement tires. Some 60 percent of the tire sales is for passenger cars and the remaining 40 percent for buses, trucks and other vehicles.

The other 15 percent of revenue comes from the company's line of industrial rubber products such as body and window sealing systems, hoses and vibration control devices. About half of the industrial rubber products are purchased by General Motors. Cooper has 7,600 employees and 8,100 shareholders.

EARNINGS-PER-SHARE GROWTH ★ ★ ★

Past 5 years: 117 percent (17 percent per year)
Past 10 years: 413 percent (18 percent per year)

STOCK GROWTH ★ ★ ★ ★

Past 10 years: 991 percent (27 percent per year)
Dollar growth: $10,000 over 10 years (including reinvested dividends) would have grown to $120,000
Average annual compounded rate of return (including reinvested dividends): 28 percent

DIVIDEND YIELD ★

Average dividend yield in the past 3 years: 0.7 percent

DIVIDEND GROWTH ★ ★ ★ ★

Increased dividend: 8 consecutive years
Past 5-year increase: 156 percent (21 percent per year)

CONSISTENCY ★ ★

Increased earnings per share: 8 of past 10 years
Increased sales: 9 consecutive years

SHAREHOLDER PERKS

The company offers no dividend reinvestment plan, nor does it offer any other shareholder perks.

COOPER TIRE & RUBBER AT A GLANCE

Fiscal year ended: Dec. 31
Revenue and net income in $ millions

	1989	1990	1991	1992	1993	1994	5-year Growth Avg. Annual (%)	5-year Growth Total (%)
Revenue ($)	866.8	895.9	1,001.1	1,174.7	1,193.6	1,403.2	10	62
Net income ($)	58.2	66.5	79.4	108.2	102.2	128.5	17	121
Earnings/share ($)	.71	.81	.96	1.30	1.22	1.54	17	117
Div. per share ($)	.09	.11	.13	.17	.20	.23	21	156
Dividend yield (%)	1.2	1.3	.08	0.6	0.7	0.9	—	—
Avg. PE ratio	11	10	18	22	24	17	—	—

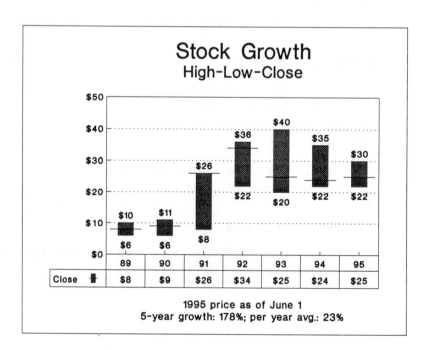

Stock Growth
High-Low-Close

	89	90	91	92	93	94	95
Close	$8	$9	$26	$34	$25	$24	$25

1995 price as of June 1
5-year growth: 178%; per year avg.: 23%

42
Intel Corp.

2200 Mission College Blvd.
P. O. Box 58119
Santa Clara, CA 95052-8119
408-765-8080

Chairman: Gordon E. Moore
President and CEO: Andrew S. Grove

Earnings Growth	★ ★ ★ ★	Dividend Growth	★ ★ ★
Stock Growth	★ ★ ★ ★	Consistency	★
Dividend Yield		Shareholder Perks	★ ★
NASDAQ—INTC		**Total**	**14 points**

It is the brains of the personal computer. The microprocessor chip processes system data and controls input, output, peripheral and memory devices in the PC. With its Pentium and 486 chips, Intel is the dominant player in the worldwide microprocessor market.

Founded in 1968, the Santa Clara, California, company has been the world leader in the microchip market since the mid-1980s, after designing the original microprocessor for the IBM PC. It has maintained its lead by first turning out its popular 286 chip, followed by the 386, then the 486 and finally the Pentium generation of chips. Worldwide, more than 105 million PCs are based on Intel architecture, compared with fewer than 20 million PCs based on other architectures.

Intel's primary customers are manufacturers of microcomputers.

The U.S. market accounts for about 51 percent of Intel's $11.5 billion in annual revenue. Its other leading markets are Europe (27 percent of revenue), Asia-Pacific (14 percent), and Japan (8 percent).

In addition to its standard microprocessing chips, Intel produces a line of related products, including:

- **Micro controllers.** Intel produces a wide range of single-chip computers (also called "embedded controllers") used to control the operation of communications systems, automobile control applications, robotics, electronic instrumentation, keyboards, home video machines and other high-tech products.
- **Computer modules and boards.** These are sold to manufacturers who integrate them into their products.
- **Network and communications products.** Intel's products help computers communicate with one another and provide access to online services.
- **Personal conferencing products.** PC users can install Intel software and cards that allow two users to view and manipulate the same documents simultaneously.
- **Parallel supercomputers.** The company's high-performance computer systems use multiple microprocessors to speed up the processing function and solve complex computational problems.
- **Semiconductor products.** Intel's flash memory products provide easily reprogrammable memory for cellular phones, computers and other systems.

Intel has about 31,000 employees and 32,500 shareholders.

EARNINGS-PER-SHARE GROWTH   ★ ★ ★ ★

Past 5 years: 397 percent (38 percent per year)
Past 10 years: 1,051 percent (28 percent per year)

STOCK GROWTH   ★ ★ ★ ★

Past 10 years: 867 percent (25 percent per year)
Dollar growth: $10,000 over 10 years (including reinvested dividends) would have grown to $97,000
Average annual compounded rate of return (including reinvested dividends): 25 percent

DIVIDEND YIELD

Average dividend yield in the past 3 years: 0.3 percent

DIVIDEND GROWTH   ★ ★ ★

Increased dividend: 3 consecutive years
Past 5-year increase (Intel has only offered a dividend for three years): 360
percent (36 percent per year)

CONSISTENCY   ★

Increased earnings per share: 7 of past 10 years
Increased sales: 8 consecutive year

SHAREHOLDER PERKS   ★ ★

Good dividend reinvestment and stock purchase plan: voluntary stock
purchase plan allows contributions of $25 to $15,000 per quarter.

INTEL AT A GLANCE

Fiscal year ended: Dec. 31
Revenue and net income in $ millions

	1989	1990	1991	1992	1993	1994	5-year Growth Avg. Annual (%)	5-year Growth Total (%)
Revenue ($)	3,127	3,921	4,779	5,844	8,782	11,521	30	268
Net income ($)	444	650	819	1,067	2,295	2,288	39	415
Earnings/share ($)	1.18	1.60	1.96	2.49	5.20	5.87	38	397
Div. per share ($)	–	–	–	.5	.20	.23	36	360
Dividend yield (%)	–	–	–	0.2	0.3	0.3	—	—
Avg. PE ratio	12.6	12.3	12.2	12.3	11.3	10.7	—	—

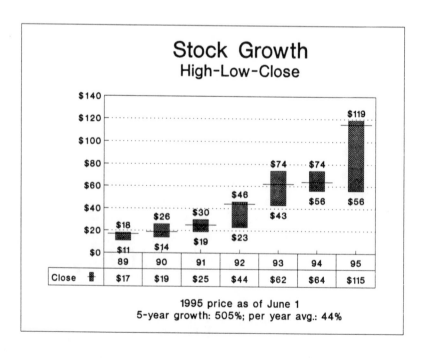

Stock Growth
High-Low-Close

	89	90	91	92	93	94	95
Close	$17	$19	$25	$44	$62	$64	$115

1995 price as of June 1
5-year growth: 505%; per year avg.: 44%

CPC International, Inc.

International Plaza
P. O. Box 8000
Englewood Cliffs, NJ 07632-9976
201-894-4000

Chairman, President and CEO:
Charles R. Shoemate

Earnings Growth	★	Dividend Growth	★ ★
Stock Growth	★ ★ ★	Consistency	★ ★ ★
Dividend Yield	★ ★ ★	Shareholder Perks	★ ★
NYSE—CPC		**Total**	**14 points**

Talk about spreading the mayo—Hellmann's mayonnaise maker CPC International continues to spread its mayonnaise and other food products around the world. It recently introduced Hellmann's in Russia, Hungary, Poland and Israel, and it opened a Knorr chicken bouillon production plant in South China.

Of the company's $7.4 billion in annual sales in 1994, 61 percent was generated outside of North America. In all, the company does business in about 60 countries on five continents.

CPC has been one of the most consistent U.S. foods companies, with nine consecutive years of record earnings. CPC's largest division is its consumer foods group, which accounts for 84 percent of total revenue. Along with Hellmann's, which is the world's top-selling mayonnaise, and Knorr foods, the company's leading brands include Jiffy peanut butter, Mazola corn oil, Argo cornstarch, Henri's salad dressings, Mueller's macaroni and Karo corn syrup.

Soups, sauces, bouillons and related products make up CPC's largest foods group in terms of sales, accounting for 32 percent of total revenue. Dressings (including Hellmann's) account for 21 percent, starches and syrups make up 6.5 percent, specialty baking products add 6 percent, bread spreads contribute 5 percent, and pasta, desserts, baking aids and other products combine for 13 percent.

CPC's other key business is corn refining, which accounts for 16.5 percent of total revenue. It has corn refining or distribution operations in 17 countries. CPC has 39,000 employees and about 32,000 shareholders.

EARNINGS-PER-SHARE GROWTH   ★

Past 5 years: 50 percent (8.5 percent per year)
Past 10 years: 217 percent (12 percent per year)

STOCK GROWTH   ★ ★ ★

Past 10 years: 413 percent (18 percent per year)
Dollar growth: $10,000 over 10 years (including reinvested dividends) would have grown to $68,000
Average annual compounded rate of return (including reinvested dividends): 21 percent

DIVIDEND YIELD   ★ ★ ★

Average dividend yield in the past 3 years: 2.8 percent

DIVIDEND GROWTH   ★ ★

Increased dividend: 9 consecutive years
Past 5-year increase: 60 percent (10 percent per year)

CONSISTENCY   ★ ★ ★

Increased earnings per share: 9 consecutive years
Increased sales: 8 of past 10 years

SHAREHOLDER PERKS   ★ ★

Good dividend reinvestment and stock purchase plan: voluntary stock purchase plan allows contributions of a minimum of $10 per month and a maximum of $12,000 per year.

CPC INTERNATIONAL AT A GLANCE

Fiscal year ended: Dec. 31
Revenue and net income in $ millions

	1989	1990	1991	1992	1993	1994	5-year Growth Avg. Annual (%)	5-year Growth Total (%)
Revenue ($)	5,103	5,781	6,189	6,599	6,738	7,425	8	46
Net income ($)	328	374	404	431	454	482	8	47
Earnings/share ($)	2.11	2.41	2.61	2.78	2.95	3.17	8.5	50
Div. per share ($)	.87	1.00	1.10	1.20	1.28	1.38	10	60
Dividend yield (%)	2.9	2.7	2.6	2.6	2.9	2.8	—	—
Avg. PE ratio	14.5	15.4	16.2	16.4	15.2	15.7	—	—

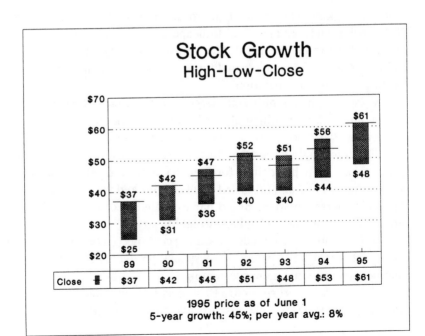

Stock Growth
High-Low-Close

	89	90	91	92	93	94	95
Close	$37	$42	$45	$51	$48	$53	$61

1995 price as of June 1
5-year growth: 45%; per year avg.: 8%

44

Valspar Corp.

1101 Third Street South
Minneapolis, MN 55415
612-332-7371

Chairman: C. Angus Wurtele
Vice Chairman: Robert E. Pajor
President and CEO: Richard M. Rompala

The Valspar Corporation

Earnings Growth	★ ★	Dividend Growth	★ ★ ★ ★
Stock Growth	★ ★ ★	Consistency	★ ★ ★ ★
Dividend Yield	★	Shareholder Perks	
NYSE—VAL		**Total**	**14 points**

Valspar is taking a broad-brush approach to the marketing of its growing line of paints and coatings. The Minneapolis-based manufacturer is spreading its colors around the world. The company recently opened sales offices in Hong Kong and Singapore and forged a joint venture in China for a new coatings production operation.

Valspar is the nation's sixth largest manufacturer of paints and coatings, with 20 plants throughout North America. It has annual sales of $724 million and has enjoyed 20 consecutive years of record earnings.

The company's largest and fastest-growing division is the consumer paints group, which accounts for 31 percent of total sales. The company sells a line of latex and oil-based paints, stains and varnishes primarily to the do-it-yourself market. Brand names include Colony, Valspar, Enterprise, Magicolor, BPS, McCloskey and Masury.

Its other divisions include packaging coatings (25 percent of revenue), industrial coatings (23 percent) and special products (21 percent) such as marine and heavy maintenance coatings.

Valspar traces its origins to a Boston paint shop called Color and Paint, which opened in 1806. That business eventually became Valentine & Co., which introduced a line of Valspar quick-drying varnishes and stains in 1906. Valspar was touted as "the varnish that won't turn white." Its claim to fame was a boiling-water test that Valspar-varnished woods could endure with no apparent ill effects. The company has 2,000 shareholders and 2,500 employees.

EARNINGS-PER-SHARE GROWTH ★ ★

Past 5 years: 100 percent (15 percent per year)
Past 10 years: 333 percent (16 percent per year)

STOCK GROWTH ★ ★ ★

Past 10 years: 473 percent (19 percent per year)
Dollar growth: $10,000 over 10 years (including reinvested dividends) would have grown to $64,000
Average annual compounded rate of return (including reinvested dividends): 20.5 percent

DIVIDEND YIELD ★

Average dividend yield in the past 3 years: 1.3 percent

DIVIDEND GROWTH ★ ★ ★ ★

Increased dividend: 16 consecutive years
Past 5-year increase: 136 percent (19 percent per year)

CONSISTENCY ★ ★ ★ ★

Increased earnings per share: 20 consecutive years
Increased sales: 8 consecutive years

SHAREHOLDER PERKS

Valspar provides no dividend reinvestment plan, nor does it offer any other special perks for its shareholders.

VALSPAR AT A GLANCE

Fiscal year ended: Oct. 31
Revenue and net income in $ millions

	1989	1990	1991	1992	1993	1994	5-year Growth Avg. Annual (%)	Total (%)
Revenue ($)	526.9	571.4	632.6	683.5	693.7	786.9	8	49
Net income ($)	23	27	28	34	40	45	14.5	96
Earnings/share ($)	1.04	1.22	1.27	1.57	1.85	2.08	15	100
Div. per share ($)	.22	.26	.30	.36	.44	.52	19	136
Dividend yield (%)	1.6	1.5	1.5	1.2	1.2	1.5	—	—
Avg. PE ratio	13	14	16	20	19	18	—	—

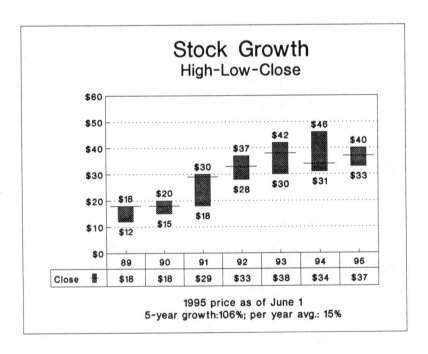

Stock Growth
High-Low-Close

1995 price as of June 1
5-year growth:106%; per year avg.: 15%

Kellogg Company

One Kellogg Square
Battle Creek, MI 49016-3599
616-961-2000

Chairman, President and CEO:
Arnold G. Langbo

Earnings Growth	★ ★	Dividend Growth	★ ★ ★
Stock Growth	★ ★	Consistency	★ ★ ★
Dividend Yield	★ ★	Shareholder Perks	★ ★
NYSE—K		**Total**	**14 points**

For many years, Kellogg has been forging new markets around the world, attempting to convert foreign consumers from their traditional breakfast fare to the American-style ready-to-eat cereals. The company's success has come slowly but steadily. Kellogg now dominates the foreign cold cereal market, holding a whopping 52 percent share outside the United States.

Foreign sales account for 40 percent of the company's $6.56 billion in annual sales. Kellogg products are now produced in 18 countries and sold in 160 countries. Kellogg's growing success on the international front has helped it achieve one of the most consistent records of growth in American industry. The Battle Creek, Michigan, operation has posted 50 consecutive years of record sales and 38 years of increased dividends. It has had record earnings per share 42 of the past 43 years.

In the United States, the company holds a 37 percent share of the cold cereals market. Among its leading cereals are Corn Flakes, Rice Krispies, Bran Flakes, All-Bran, Frosted Flakes, Froot Loops, Frosted Mini-Wheats, Nutri-Grain, Nut & Honey Crunch, Special K, Apple Jacks, Cocoa Krispies, Fruity Marshmallow Krispies, Mueslix, Product 19 and Crispix.

About 20 percent of the company's revenue is generated by its convenience foods other than cereal, including Mrs. Smith's frozen pies, Eggo frozen waffles, Nutri-Grain Bars and Pop Tarts.

The company was founded by W. K. Kellogg, who first test-marketed his toasted flake cereals in the late 1880s on the patients of the Battle Creek Sanitarium. The cereal was such a hit with patients that many of them wrote to the sanitarium after their release to ask where they might buy more of Kellogg's flakes.

Mr. Kellogg, recognizing a classic marketing opportunity when he saw one, founded the Battle Creek Toasted Corn Flake Company in 1906.

While W. K. Kellogg will be remembered most for his pioneering efforts in the development of cold cereals, it was his shrewd, aggressive marketing efforts that set his company apart from the competition. A full-page ad in the Ladies' Home Journal shortly after the company opened in 1906 helped propel Corn Flakes sales to 2,900 cases a day. By 1911, Kellogg's advertising budget had swelled to more than $1 million a year. And in 1912, the company erected the world's largest sign in Times Square in New York City—an 80-foot high, 100-foot wide "Kellogg's."

Kellogg introduced 40% Bran Flakes in 1915 and All-Bran in 1916. Rice Krispies first began to snap, crackle and pop on American breakfast tables in 1928. The company has 16,000 employees and 23,000 shareholders.

EARNINGS-PER-SHARE GROWTH ★ ★

Past 5 years: 82 percent (13 percent per year)
Past 10 years: 271 percent (14 percent per year)

STOCK GROWTH ★ ★

Past 10 years: 360 percent (16.5 percent per year)
Dollar growth: $10,000 over 10 years (including reinvested dividends) would have grown to $57,000
Average annual compounded rate of return (including reinvested dividends): 19 percent

DIVIDEND YIELD   ★ ★

Average dividend yield in the past 3 years: 2.3 percent

DIVIDEND GROWTH   ★ ★ ★

Increased dividend: 38 consecutive years
Past 5-year increase: 63 percent (10 percent per year)

CONSISTENCY   ★ ★ ★

Increased earnings per share: 9 of past 10 years
Increased sales: 50 consecutive years

SHAREHOLDER PERKS   ★ ★

Good dividend reinvestment and stock purchase plan: voluntary stock
purchase plan allows contributions of $25 to $25,000 per year.

All new shareholders of record receive a welcome kit with brochures
and reports on the company along with a pair of coupons for free grocery
products such as cereal, frozen waffles or one of Kellogg's newer products.
Those attending the annual meetings in Battle Creek also receive product
samples and discount coupons. The company sometimes hands out special
gifts such as decorative Kellogg's plates.

KELLOGG AT A GLANCE

Fiscal year ended: Dec. 31
Revenue and net income in $ millions

	1989	1990	1991	1992	1993	1994	5-year Growth Avg. Annual (%)	5-year Growth Total (%)
Revenue ($)	4,652	5,181	5,787	6,191	6,295	6,562	7	41
Net income ($)	422.1	502.8	606.0	682.8	680.7	705.4	11	70
Earnings/share ($)	1.73	2.08	2.51	2.86	2.94	3.15	13	82
Div. per share ($)	.86	.96	1.08	1.20	1.32	1.40	10	63
Dividend yield (%)	2.5	2.5	1.6	1.8	2.3	2.6	—	—
Avg. PE ratio	20.0	16.0	19.5	23.2	19.4	17.2	—	—

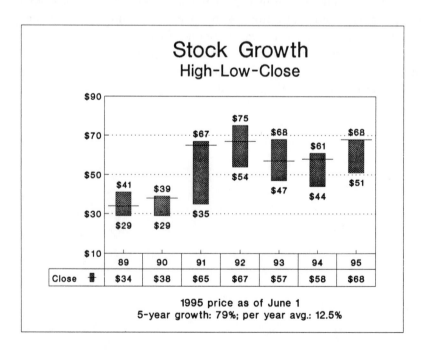

Stock Growth
High-Low-Close

	89	90	91	92	93	94	95
Close	$34	$38	$65	$67	$57	$58	$68

1995 price as of June 1
5-year growth: 79%; per year avg.: 12.5%

Automatic Data Processing

One ADP Boulevard
Roseland, NJ 07068
201-994-5000

Chairman and CEO: Josh S. Weston
President: Arthur F. Weinbach

Earnings Growth	★ ★	Dividend Growth	★ ★ ★ ★
Stock Growth	★ ★ ★	Consistency	★ ★ ★ ★
Dividend Yield	★	Shareholder Perks	
NYSE—AUD		**Total**	**14 points**

Doling out the paychecks of 17 million wage earners, issuing 32 million W-2 forms to employees and processing 20 percent of the transactions of the New York Stock Exchange keeps the profits flowing at Automatic Data Processing (ADP).

The nation's largest payroll and tax filing processor, ADP has rung up 132 consecutive quarters of double-digit earnings-per-share growth—a string of record-setting quarters unmatched by any publicly held company. The 46-year-old company is credited with pioneering "outsourcing," in which companies farm out tasks that don't directly relate to their core competencies.

ADP's largest and oldest business is Employer Services, which generates 58 percent of the company's $2.5 billion in annual revenue. The division provides payroll and employment-related services to about 275,000 employers, ranging from "mom and pop" businesses to industrial behemoths. To help differentiate itself from its smaller payroll services competitors, ADP has aggressively introduced new services such as its client-site payroll processing software. The product is designed for employers who prefer enhanced control and lower costs and who don't mind payroll preparation burdens.

The division has bolstered customer service by equipping its reorganized sales force with laptop computers that provide detailed territory information, multimedia demonstrations and instant sales activity reporting.

ADP's other segments include:

- **Brokerage services** (25 percent of revenue). ADP's second-largest unit provides data services, recordkeeping, order entry, proxy processing and other services for the financial services industry. ADP is the leading U.S. provider of retail equity information, with 87,000 front-office terminals in nearly 600 firms around the world.
- **Dealer services** (14 percent of revenue). The company provides some 20 software applications to more than 9,500 auto and truck dealers in North America and Europe. Driven by strong growth in the auto industry, dealer services is ADP's fastest-growing unit.

  Auto dealers use ADP's on-site systems to manage their accounting, factory communications, inventory, sales and service activities. To help auto dealers eliminate paperwork, ADP systems can digitize and store records that can be retrieved from workstations for viewing, faxing or printing.
- **Auto collision and general accounting** (3 percent). The company provides auto collision estimates for insurers and repair shops.

ADP has 22,000 employees and about 22,600 shareholders.

EARNINGS-PER-SHARE GROWTH ★ ★

Past 5 years: 86 percent (13 percent per year)
Past 10 years: 333 percent (16 percent per year)

STOCK GROWTH ★ ★ ★

Past 10 years: 420 percent (18 percent per year)
Dollar growth: $10,000 over 10 years (including reinvested dividends) would have grown to $58,000
Average annual compounded rate of return (including reinvested dividends): 19 percent

DIVIDEND YIELD

Average dividend yield in the past 3 years: 1.0 percent

DIVIDEND GROWTH   ★ ★ ★ ★

Increased dividend: 21 consecutive years
Past 5-year increase: 100 percent (15 percent per year)

CONSISTENCY   ★ ★ ★ ★

Increased earnings per share: 45 consecutive years
Increased sales: 45 consecutive years

SHAREHOLDER PERKS

The company provides no dividend reinvestment and stock purchase plan,
nor does it offer any other perks for its shareholders.

ADP AT A GLANCE

Fiscal year ended: June 30
Revenue and net income in $ millions

	1989	1990	1991	1992	1993	1994	5-year Growth Avg. Annual (%)	Total (%)
Revenue ($)	1,678	1,714	1,772	1,941	2,223	2,469	8	47
Net income ($)	188	218	228	256	294	329	12	75
Earnings/share ($)	1.26	1.44	1.63	1.84	2.08	2.34	13	86
Div. per share ($)	.27	.31	.36	.42	.48	.54	15	100
Dividend yield (%)	1.5	1.3	1.3	1.0	1.0	1.0	—	—
Avg. PE ratio	17	18	22	26	25	23	—	—

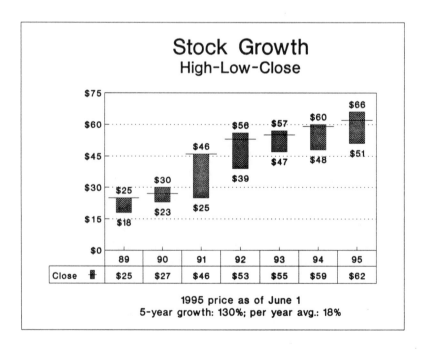

Stock Growth
High-Low-Close

	89	90	91	92	93	94	95
Close	$25	$27	$46	$53	$55	$59	$62

1995 price as of June 1
5-year growth: 130%; per year avg.: 18%

47

The Sherwin-Williams Company

101 Prospect Ave., N.W.
Cleveland, OH 44115-1075
216-566-2000

Chairman and CEO: John G. Breen
President: Thomas A. Commes

Earnings Growth	★	Dividend Growth	★ ★ ★
Stock Growth	★ ★	Consistency	★ ★ ★ ★
Dividend Yield	★ ★	Shareholder Perks	★ ★
NYSE—SHW		**Total**	**14 points**

Sherwin-Williams paints first adorned homes and barns in northern Ohio shortly after the Civil War, in 1866. Now the Cleveland-based company's paint "covers the earth," with sales in 36 foreign countries. Sherwin-Williams recently signed sales agreements in India, Belgium and the People's Republic of China.

Sherwin-Williams is the nation's largest producer of paints and varnishes, with paint stores in 48 states. Among its leading brands are Dutch Boy, Kem-Tone, Sherwin-Williams, Martin-Senour, Curinol, Acme, Pro-Mar, Perma-Clad, Western Automotive, Standox, Krylon, Color Works, Rust Tough, Rubberset and Dupli-Color. The company recently introduced a new "Ever Clean" line of paints that has been selling briskly.

The company's coatings segment accounts for 36 percent of its $3.1 billion in annual revenue. The coatings segment has four key divisions (plus a separate transportation division): coatings, consumer brands, automotive and specialty.

The company's largest segment is its paint store operations, which account for 64 percent of total revenue. The company's 2,046 stores offer paints, wall coverings, floor coverings, window treatments, spray equipment, brushes, scrapers, rollers and related products. The stores are geared to the do-it-yourself customer, professional painters, industrial and commercial maintenance customers, and small to mid-sized manufacturers. Sherwin-Williams has 17,000 employees and 12,000 shareholders.

EARNINGS-PER-SHARE GROWTH ★

Past 5 years: 71 percent (11.5 percent per year)
Past 10 years: 207 percent (12 percent per year)

STOCK GROWTH ★ ★

Past 10 years: 294 percent (15 percent per year)
Dollar growth: $10,000 over 10 years (including reinvested dividends) would have grown to $48,000
Average annual compounded rate of return (including reinvested dividends): 17 percent

DIVIDEND YIELD ★ ★

Average dividend yield in the past 3 years: 1.6 percent

DIVIDEND GROWTH ★ ★ ★

Increased dividend: 17 consecutive years
Past 5-year increase: 60 percent (10 percent per year)

CONSISTENCY ★ ★ ★ ★

Increased earnings per share: 17 consecutive years
Increased sales: 8 straight years

SHAREHOLDER PERKS ★ ★

Good dividend reinvestment and stock purchase plan: voluntary stock purchase plan allows contributions of $10 to $2,000 per month.

SHERWIN-WILLIAMS AT A GLANCE

Fiscal year ended: Dec. 31
Revenue and net income in $ millions

	1989	1990	1991	1992	1993	1994	5-year Growth Avg. Annual (%)	5-year Growth Total (%)
Revenue ($)	2,123	2,267	2,541	2,748	2,949	3,100	8	46
Net income ($)	109	123	128	145	165	187	11.5	71
Earnings/share ($)	1.26	1.41	1.45	1.63	1.85	2.15	11.5	71
Div. per share ($)	.35	.38	.42	.44	.50	.56	10	60
Dividend yield (%)	2.3	2.1	1.8	1.5	1.5	1.7	—	—
Avg. PE ratio	12	13	16	18	18	15	—	—

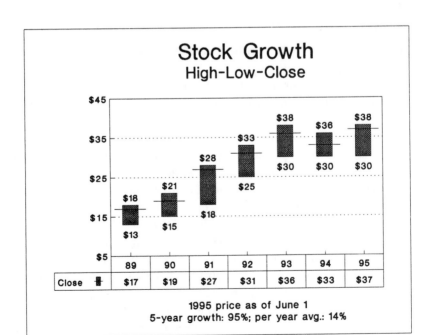

Stock Growth
High-Low-Close

	89	90	91	92	93	94	95
Close	$17	$19	$27	$31	$36	$33	$37

1995 price as of June 1
5-year growth: 95%; per year avg.: 14%

48

Warner-Lambert Company

WARNER LAMBERT

201 Tabor Road
Morris Plains, NJ 07950-2693
201-540-2000

Chairman and CEO: Melvin R. Goodes
President: Lodewijk J. R. de Vink

Earnings Growth	★	Dividend Growth	★ ★ ★
Stock Growth	★ ★	Consistency	★ ★ ★
Dividend Yield	★ ★ ★	Shareholder Perks	★ ★
NYSE—WLA		**Total**	**14 points**

A shave, a chew—or a pill for what ails you. Warner-Lambert offers a diverse range of products for use in and around the mouths of consumers.

The Morris Plains, New Jersey, manufacturer is among the world leaders in sales of chewing gum, breath fresheners (such as Certs and Listerine), cough drops and razors. It also manufactures a broad range of other over-the-counter and prescription medications.

Sales of chewing gum and other confectionery products account for 21 percent of the company's $6.4 billion in annual revenue. Among the company's leading brands are Trident, Dentyne, Freshen-Up, Chewels, Bubblicious, Chiclets, Clorets, Beemans, Blackjack and Clove brands.

Warner-Lambert acquired razor-maker Wilkinson Sword Blade in 1993 to go along with its Schick subsidiary. Schick and Wilkinson are both key players in the U.S. razor market, while Schick is a market leader in Japan and Wilkinson has a strong presence in Europe.

Consumer health care products account for 46 percent of the company's revenue. In addition to razors, Warner-Lambert makes a long list of familiar consumer over-the-counter health aids, including Rolaids, Certs, Listerine, Listermint, Halls throat lozenges, Sinutab and Efferdent.

Warner-Lambert's other key segment is pharmaceutical products, which accounts for 32 percent of its total revenue. Its Warner-Chilcott Laboratories produces more than 200 generic pharmaceutical products.

Warner-Lambert does business in more than 130 countries. Some 23,500 of the company's 35,000 employees work outside the United States, and 54 percent of Warner's revenue comes from foreign markets. The company has 46,000 shareholders.

EARNINGS-PER-SHARE GROWTH ★

Past 5 years: 70 percent (11 percent per year)
Past 10 years: 267 percent (10 percent per year)

STOCK GROWTH ★ ★

Past 10 years: 282 percent (14 percent per year)
Dollar growth: $10,000 over 10 years (including reinvested dividends) would have grown to $48,000
Average annual compounded rate of return (including reinvested dividends): 17 percent

DIVIDEND YIELD ★ ★ ★

Average dividend yield in the past 3 years: 3.2 percent

DIVIDEND GROWTH ★ ★ ★

Increased dividend: More than 19 consecutive years
Past 5-year increase: 91 percent (14 percent per year)

CONSISTENCY ★ ★ ★

Increased earnings per share: 9 of past 10 years
Increased sales: 8 straight years

SHAREHOLDER PERKS ★ ★

Good dividend reinvestment and stock purchase plan: voluntary stock purchase plan allows contributions of $10 to $60,000 per year.

WARNER-LAMBERT AT A GLANCE

Fiscal year ended: Dec. 31
Revenue and net income in $ millions

	1989	1990	1991	1992	1993	1994	5-year Growth Avg. Annual (%)	5-year Growth Total (%)
Revenue ($)	4,196	4,687	5,059	5,598	5,794	6,417	9	53
Net income ($)	413	485	559	644	654	694	11	68
Earnings/share ($)	3.05	3.61	4.16	4.78	4.78	5.17	11	70
Div. per share ($)	1.28	1.52	1.76	2.04	2.28	2.44	14	91
Dividend yield (%)	2.2	2.3	2.3	3.0	3.4	3.2	—	—
Avg. PE ratio	18	18	17	14	14	14	—	—

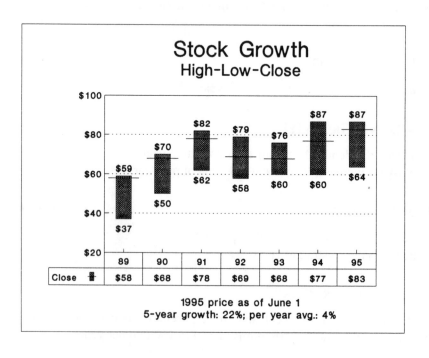

Stock Growth
High-Low-Close

	89	90	91	92	93	94	95
Close	$58	$68	$78	$69	$68	$77	$83

1995 price as of June 1
5-year growth: 22%; per year avg.: 4%

General Electric Company

3135 Easton Turnpike
Fairfield, CT 06431
203-373-2459

Chairman and CEO: John F. Welch, Jr.

Earnings Growth	★	Dividend Growth	★ ★ ★
Stock Growth	★	Consistency	★ ★ ★ ★
Dividend Yield	★ ★ ★	Shareholder Perks	★ ★
NYSE—GE		**Total**	**14 points**

Despite its immense size—with annual sales revenue of $60 billion in 1994—General Electric is still operating with the nimbleness of an emerging growth company. The Fairfield, Connecticut-based operation continues to expand its various market niches, and has seen its earnings per share jump 175 percent over the past 10 years.

The electronics and broadcasting giant breaks its business into several key segments. Its largest manufacturing segment is its industrial division, which accounts for 12 percent of revenue. The company manufactures factory automation products, motors, electrical equipment, transportation systems (including locomotives and transit propulsion equipment), light bulbs and other types of lighting products. GE's other leading divisions include:

- **GE Financial Services** (37 percent of revenue). GE owns a number of financial and insurance subsidiaries. Its largest division is GE Capital, a financing institution that specializes in revolving credit, credit cards and inventory financing for retail merchants.

- **Power systems** (11 percent of revenue). The company builds power generators (primarily steam-turbine generators) and transmitters for worldwide utility, industrial and government customers.
- **Aircraft engines** (11 percent of revenue). GE is a leading manufacturer of jet engines and engine parts for short, medium, intermediate and long-range commercial aircraft and military aircraft and helicopters.
- **Major appliances** (9 percent of revenue). The company is known for its GE, Hotpoint and Monogram appliances including refrigerators, ranges, microwaves, freezers, dishwashers, clothes washers and dryers and room air conditioners.
- **Materials** (8 percent of revenue). The company makes high-performance plastics for such uses as automobile bumpers, computer casings and other office equipment. It also produces silicones, superabrasives and laminates.
- **Technical products and service**s (7 percent of revenue). The company manufactures a variety of medical instruments including scanners, x-rays, nuclear imaging, ultrasound and other diagnostic equipment. It also manufactures communications systems.
- **Broadcasting** (5 percent of revenue). GE owns the National Broadcasting Company (NBC), which serves more than 200 affiliated stations throughout the U.S. NBC also owns the cable channel CNBC, as well as television stations in Chicago, Denver, Los Angeles, Miami, New York and Washington, D.C.

GE traces its roots back to the Edison Electric Company, which was founded in 1878 by Thomas Edison. The company has about 220,000 employees and 470,000 shareholders.

EARNINGS-PER-SHARE GROWTH ★

Past 5 years: 59 percent (10 percent per year)
Past 10 years: 175 percent (11 percent per year)

STOCK GROWTH

Past 10 years: 240 percent (13 percent per year)
Dollar growth: $10,000 over 10 years (including reinvested dividends) would have grown to $44,000

Average annual compounded rate of return (including reinvested dividends): 16 percent

DIVIDEND YIELD   ★ ★ ★

Average dividend yield in the past 3 years: 3 percent

DIVIDEND GROWTH   ★ ★ ★

Increased dividend: 19 consecutive years
Past 5-year increase: 75 percent (12 percent per year)

CONSISTENCY   ★ ★ ★ ★

Increased earnings per share: 19 consecutive years
Increased sales: 9 of past 10 years

SHAREHOLDER PERKS   ★ ★

Good dividend reinvestment and stock purchase plan: voluntary stock purchase plan allows contributions of $10 to $10,000 per quarter.

GENERAL ELECTRIC AT A GLANCE

Fiscal year ended: Dec. 31
Revenue and net income in $ millions

	1989	1990	1991	1992	1993	1994	5-year Growth Avg. Annual (%)	Total (%)
Revenue ($)	49,100	49,700	51,200	53,100	55,700	60,100	4	20
Net income ($)	3,939	3,889	3,984	4,305	4,424	4,726	4	20
Earnings/share ($)	2.18	2.19	2.29	2.41	3.03	3.46	10	59
Div. per share ($)	.85	.96	1.04	1.16	1.31	1.49	12	75
Dividend yield (%)	2.6	3.3	2.7	2.7	2.5	3.0	—	—
Avg. PE ratio	12.2	12.9	13.7	15.5	15.5	14.3	—	—

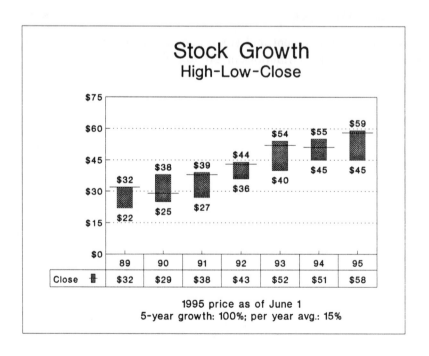

Stock Growth
High-Low-Close

	89	90	91	92	93	94	95
Close	$32	$29	$38	$43	$52	$51	$58

1995 price as of June 1
5-year growth: 100%; per year avg.: 15%

50

SunTrust Banks, Inc.

SUNTRUST

25 Park Place, N.E.
P. O. Box 4418
Atlanta, GA 30302
404-588-7711

Chairman and CEO: James B. Williams
President: L. Phillip Humann

Earnings Growth	★	Dividend Growth	★ ★ ★
Stock Growth	★	Consistency	★ ★ ★ ★
Dividend Yield	★ ★ ★	Shareholder Perks	★ ★
NYSE—STI		**Total**	**14 points**

There's no question that much of the success of SunTrust Banks the past few years can be attributed to its solid management and sound banking practices. But the Atlanta-based institution must credit part of its strong recent growth to an investment it picked up back in 1919.

When The Coca-Cola Company went public in 1919, it gave 5,000 shares (worth $110,000) of its stock as part of the underwriting fee to the two underwriters, J.P. Morgan Bank and the Trust Company of Georgia (now SunTrust Banks). J.P. Morgan sold its stock, but SunTrust held onto its original shares.

After years of stock splits, that original 5,000 shares has grown to 24 million shares. And its original $110,000 investment is now worth about $1 billion. Over the past 10 years, Coca-Cola has been one of the fastest-growing stocks on the New York Stock Exchange, posting a total return of nearly 1,000 percent. Even when the banking business is in a funk, SunTrust continues to ride high on the strength of its Coca-Cola stock.

SunTrust operates 658 bank offices in Georgia, Florida, Tennessee and Alabama. The company took on its present identity as SunTrust Banks in 1985 with the merger of Sun Banks of Florida and Trust Company of Georgia. It has grown rapidly through a series of acquisitions throughout its four-state operating area.

SunTrust is the third-largest bank holding company in the Southeast.

The company's Florida operations account for 49 percent of the $572 million in net income generated by the firm's banking segment in 1994, while its Georgia banks generated 37 percent of net income and its combined Tennessee and Alabama operations accounted for 14 percent.

EARNINGS-PER-SHARE GROWTH ★

Past 5 years: 69 percent (11 percent per year)
Past 10 years: 239 percent (13 percent per year)

STOCK GROWTH ★

Past 10 years: 237 percent (13 percent per year)
Dollar growth: $10,000 over 10 years (including reinvested dividends) would have grown to $45,000
Average annual compounded rate of return (including reinvested dividends): 16 percent

DIVIDEND YIELD ★ ★ ★

Average dividend yield in the past 3 years: 2.6 percent

DIVIDEND GROWTH ★ ★ ★

Increased dividend: More than 17 consecutive years
Past 5-year increase: 69 percent (11 percent per year)

CONSISTENCY ★ ★ ★ ★

Increased earnings per share: 15 consecutive years

SHAREHOLDER PERKS ★ ★

Good dividend reinvestment and stock purchase plan: voluntary stock purchase plan allows contributions of $10 to $60,000 per year.

SUNTRUST BANKS AT A GLANCE

Fiscal year ended: Dec. 31
Revenue and net income in $ millions

	1989	1990	1991	1992	1993	1994	5-year Growth Avg. Annual (%)	5-year Growth Total (%)
Revenue ($)	1,587.9	1,657.8	1,796.2	2,001.1	2,109.0	2,181.9	7	40
Net income ($)	343.3	355.2	377.3	404.4	473.7	522.7	8.5	50
Earnings/share ($)	2.59	2.72	2.88	3.13	3.77	4.37	11	69
Div. per share ($)	.78	.86	.94	1.03	1.16	1.32	11	69
Dividend yield (%)	3.4	4.1	2.5	2.4	2.6	2.8	—	—
Avg. PE ratio	8.9	7.6	10.6	12.0	11.9	10.9	—	—

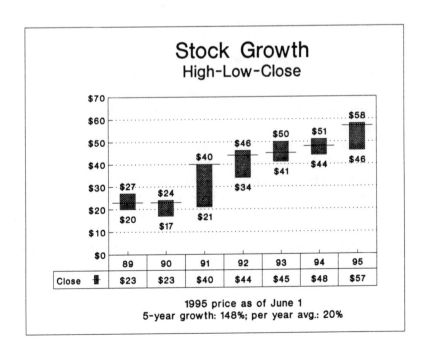

Stock Growth
High-Low-Close

Close	89	90	91	92	93	94	95
	$23	$23	$40	$44	$45	$48	$57

1995 price as of June 1
5-year growth: 148%; per year avg.: 20%

Anheuser-Busch Companies, Inc.

One Busch Place
St. Louis, MO 63118
314-577-2000

Chairman, CEO and President: August A. Busch III

Earnings Growth		Dividend Growth	★ ★ ★
Stock Growth	★	Consistency	★ ★ ★ ★
Dividend Yield	★ ★ ★	Shareholder Perks	★ ★ ★
NYSE—BUD		**Total**	**14 points**

This Bud's for you . . . and him . . . and her . . . and them . . . and millions of beer drinkers across America. Anheuser-Busch sells about 87 million barrels of beer a year. It is the world's largest brewer and now boasts the top-selling regular beer (Budweiser), the top-selling light beer (Bud Light) and the top-selling nonalcoholic beer (O'Doul's). The St. Louis–based brewer controls a whopping 44 percent share of the U.S. beer market. Beer sales account for about 75 percent of the company's $12.1 billion in annual revenue.

Among the company's other leading brands are Michelob, Busch, Bud Dry, Ice Draft, Natural Light and King Cobra. The company also imports two European-brewed beers, Carlsberg and Elephant Malt Liquor. Internationally, the company markets beer in more than 60 countries.

Busch's brewing business is fully integrated. It operates 13 breweries in the United States, owns a beverage can manufacturer, a barley processing plant, a label printing operation and a refrigerated railcar transportation subsidiary.

The company does business in two other segments:

- **Food Products** (18 percent of revenue). Campbell Taggart, the country's second-largest bakery operation, has 41 bakeries and several other related production facilities. It markets its baked goods under several regional labels including Grant's Farm, Colonial, Rainbo, Kilpatrick's, Ironkids, Break Cake and Earth Grains. The company also supplies sandwich buns to some of the major fast-food chains. The firm's Eagle Snacks subsidiary produces peanuts, pretzels, potato chips and other snack food products.
- **Family entertainment** (6 percent of revenue). Busch Entertainment is the nation's second-largest theme park operator. Its theme parks include two Busch Gardens parks (in Tampa, Florida, and Williamsburg, Virginia); Adventure Island in Tampa; Sesame Place in Langhorne, Pennsylvania; Cypress Gardens in Winter Haven, Florida; Baseball City Sports Complex near Orlando; and four Sea World parks. Anheuser-Busch also owns the St. Louis Cardinals National League baseball team.

Anheuser-Busch traces its roots to a small St. Louis brewery started in 1852. After a few years of lackluster results, the original owner, George Schneider, sold out the struggling operation to an investment group headed by St. Louis soap tycoon Eberhard Anheuser. Anheuser ultimately turned the business over to his son-in-law, a portly, gregarious man by the name of Adolphus Busch.

Mr. Busch, who converted the small brewery into a national force, is generally recognized as the founder of Anheuser-Busch. Budweiser, which Mr. Busch helped develop in 1876, was one of the first beers to achieve widespread distribution. Michelob, the company's "premium" beer, was first brought to market in 1896. When Adolphus Busch died in 1913, his son August A. Busch assumed control of the business. The reins have since been passed through two more generations of the Busch family. August A. Busch III, 57, now directs the company as its chairman of the board, president and CEO. Anheuser-Busch has 43,000 employees and 68,000 shareholders.

EARNINGS-PER-SHARE GROWTH

Past 5 years: 45 percent (8 percent per year)
Past 10 years: 213 percent (12 percent per year)

STOCK GROWTH

Past 10 years: 241 percent (13 percent per year)
Dollar growth: $10,000 over 10 years (including reinvested dividends) would have grown to $41,000
Average annual compounded rate of return (including reinvested dividends): 15 percent

DIVIDEND YIELD

Average dividend yield in the past 3 years: 2.6 percent

DIVIDEND GROWTH

Increased dividend: 22 consecutive years
Past 5-year increase: 90 percent (14 percent per year)

CONSISTENCY

Increased earnings per share: 18 consecutive years
Increased sales: 18 consecutive years

SHAREHOLDER PERKS

Good dividend reinvestment and stock purchase plan: voluntary stock purchase plan allows contributions of $25 to $5,000 per month.

New shareholders of record are sent a letter of welcome, a fact book on the company and a pamphlet on its dividend reinvestment plan.

The company makes a point of moving its annual meetings around the country. In recent years, meetings have been staged in Tampa and Orlando, Florida; Williamsburg, Virginia; and Fort Collins, Colorado. Those who attend get a chance to sample all of the company's brews.

Shareholders are also entitled to a discount on admission to the company's amusement parks.

ANHEUSER-BUSCH AT A GLANCE

Fiscal year ended: Dec. 31
Revenue and net income in $ millions

	1989	1990	1991	1992	1993	1994	5-year Growth Avg. Annual (%)	5-year Growth Total (%)
Revenue ($)	9,481	10,743	10,996	11,394	11,505	12,054	5	27
Net income ($)	767.2	842.4	939.8	917.5	980.6	1,032.1	6	35
Earnings/share ($)	2.68	2.96	3.26	3.48	2.17	3.88	8	45
Div. per share ($)	.80	.94	1.06	1.20	1.36	1.52	14	90
Dividend yield (%)	2.1	2.2	1.7	2.1	2.8	3.0	—	—
Avg. PE ratio	14.4	13.4	15.6	16.1	14.2	13.3	—	—

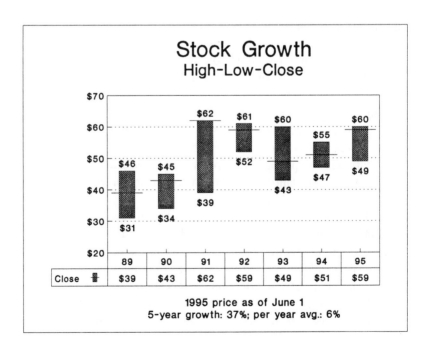

Stock Growth
High-Low-Close

	89	90	91	92	93	94	95
Close	$39	$43	$62	$59	$49	$51	$59

1995 price as of June 1
5-year growth: 37%; per year avg.: 6%

Bristol-Myers Squibb

345 Park Ave.
New York, NY 10154-0037
212-546-4000

Chairman: Richard L. Gelb
President and CEO:
Charles A. Heimbold, Jr.

Earnings Growth	★	Dividend Growth	★ ★
Stock Growth		Consistency	★ ★ ★ ★
Dividend Yield	★ ★ ★ ★	Shareholder Perks	★ ★ ★
NYSE—BMY		**Total**	**14 points**

Bristol-Myers Squibb pours about $1 billion a year into medical research, uncovering new treatments for everything from infections and cancer to high blood pressure and high cholesterol. But the research doesn't always end when the drugs go on the market.

For instance, the company is still doing research on one of its top-selling pharmaceuticals, Pravachol, which is a chloresterol-lowering agent. The company's new tests have shown that the drug can reduce the risk of heart attacks in high-risk patients by about 62 percent. While the new application is still pending approval by the Food and Drug Administration, it could add substantially to the $640 million a year in sales already generated by Pravachol.

Pharmaceuticals are the leading source of revenue for Bristol-Myers Squibb, accounting for 58 percent of the company's $12 billion in annual revenue. The company produces a broad range of anticancer agents and diagnostic products, plus drugs for the treatment of cardiovascular ailments, high cholesterol, infections, congestion and nervous disorders.

Bristol-Myers' 1989 merger with Squibb made it the nation's second-largest pharmaceuticals manufacturer (behind Johnson & Johnson). The company is probably best known for its consumer products, including toiletries, beauty aids and nonprescription medications.

Toiletries and beauty aids account for 11 percent of total revenue. Leading brands include Clairol, Vitalis, Nice 'n Easy, Loving Care, Ban deodorant, Final Net and Keri lotion.

The company's nonprescription medicines—including Bufferin, Comtrex, Excedrin, Nuprin, No Doz and other consumer lines—account for 17 percent of total revenue.

Its other market segment is medical devices, which account for 14 percent of annual sales. Among the company's leading medical devices are orthopedic implants such as artificial hips, knees and shoulders, implantable hearing devices, compression garments for burn treatments, powered surgical instruments and related devices.

Bristol-Myers Squibb does a strong international business, with sales in more than 100 countries. Foreign sales account for about 41 percent of the company's total revenue. The company has 50,000 employees and 138,000 shareholders.

EARNINGS-PER-SHARE GROWTH   ★

Past 5 years: 73 percent (12 percent per year)
Past 10 years: 150 percent (10 percent per year)

STOCK GROWTH

Past 10 years: 117 percent (8 percent per year)
Dollar growth: $10,000 over 10 years (including reinvested dividends) would have grown to $30,000
Average annual compounded rate of return (including reinvested dividends): 11.5 percent

DIVIDEND YIELD   ★ ★ ★ ★

Average dividend yield in the past 3 years: 4.6 percent

DIVIDEND GROWTH ★ ★

Increased dividend: 22 consecutive years
Past 5-year increase: 46 percent (8 percent per year)

CONSISTENCY ★ ★ ★ ★

Increased earnings per share: 10 consecutive years
Increased sales: 8 of past 10 years

SHAREHOLDER PERKS ★ ★ ★

Good dividend reinvestment and stock purchase plan: voluntary stock purchase plan allows contributions of $10 to $2,500 per month.

The company also sends all of its new shareholders of record a welcome packet of its consumer products, including, for example, small bottles of Excedrin, Bufferin, Nuprin, Clairol and Ban deodorant.

BRISTOL-MYERS SQUIBB AT A GLANCE

Fiscal year ended: Dec. 31
Revenue and net income in $ millions

| | | | | | | | 5-year Growth | |
| | | | | | | | Avg. Annual (%) | Total (%) |
	1989	1990	1991	1992	1993	1994		
Revenue ($)	9,189	9,741	10,571	11,156	11,413	11,984	5.5	30
Net income ($)	1,440	1,748	2,056	2,108	2,269	2,330	10	62
Earnings/share ($)	2.64	3.22	3.82	4.07	4.40	4.58	12	73
Div. per share ($)	2.00	2.12	2.40	2.76	2.88	2.92	8	46
Dividend yield (%)	4.0	3.6	3.0	3.8	4.9	5.2	—	—
Avg. PE ratio	18.1	17.8	20.1	17.6	13.3	12.2	—	—

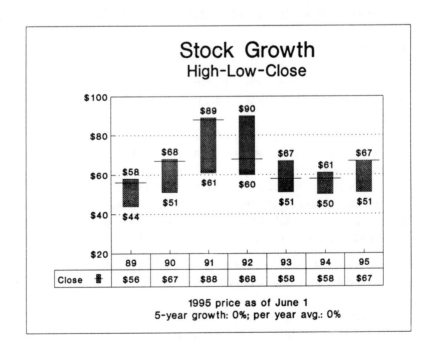

Stock Growth
High-Low-Close

| Close | $56 | $67 | $88 | $68 | $58 | $58 | $67 |

1995 price as of June 1
5-year growth: 0%; per year avg.: 0%

Stryker Corp.

stryker

2725 Fairfield Road
Kalamazoo, MI 49002
616-385-2600

Chairman, President and CEO: John W. Brown

Earnings Growth	★ ★ ★ ★	Dividend Growth	★
Stock Growth	★ ★ ★ ★	Consistency	★ ★ ★ ★
Dividend Yield		Shareholder Perks	
NASDAQ—STRY		**Total**	**13 points**

Titanium hips and cobalt knees. They may not be as good as the originals, but Stryker's line of artificial limbs gives renewed mobility to thousands of injured and arthritis-riddled patients. The Kalamazoo operation is one of the world's leading manufacturers of reconstructive products and powered surgical instruments.

In addition to its knee and hip replacements, Stryker also manufactures spinal implant systems used to treat degenerative spinal diseases and related ailments.

Surgical products account for 80 percent of Stryker's $682 million in annual sales. The company markets its products in more than 100 countries. Foreign operations and exports make up 48 percent of total revenue.

Stryker's other surgical products include:

- **Powered surgical tools.** The company makes powered drills, saws, fixation and reaming equipment and other surgical instruments. It also makes "micro" powered tools for more delicate operations such as spinal surgery, neurosurgery and plastic surgery.
- **Endoscopic systems.** Stryker makes medical video cameras, light sources, laparoscope and related products used in less-invasive surgery

such as arthroscopy. Stryker's high definition medical video system can be inserted into a patient's joint area to give surgeons a broadcast-quality image of the interior of the joint.

The other 20 percent of the company's revenue comes from medical products. Stryker makes a line of specialty stretchers and beds and other patient-handling equipment.

The company was founded in 1941 by Dr. Homer H. Stryker, a prominent orthopedic surgeon and the inventor of several leading orthopedic products. Stryker has 3,200 employees and 4,000 shareholders.

EARNINGS-PER-SHARE GROWTH ★ ★ ★ ★

Past 5 years: 266 percent (29.5 percent per year)
Past 10 years: 838 percent (25 percent per year)

STOCK GROWTH ★ ★ ★ ★

Past 10 years: 1,194 percent (29 percent per year)
Dollar growth: $10,000 over 10 years (including reinvested dividends) would have grown to $130,000
Average annual compounded rate of return (including reinvested dividends): 29 percent

DIVIDEND YIELD

Average dividend yield in the past 3 years: 0.2 percent

DIVIDEND GROWTH ★

Increased dividend: 3 consecutive years
Past 5-year increase: 60 percent (10 percent per year)

CONSISTENCY ★ ★ ★ ★

Increased earnings per share: More than 17 consecutive years
Increased sales: More than 17 consecutive years

SHAREHOLDER PERKS

Stryker does not offer a dividend reinvestment plan, nor does it provide any other shareholder perks.

STRYKER AT A GLANCE

Fiscal year ended: Dec. 31
Revenue and net income in $ millions

	1989	1990	1991	1992	1993	1994	5-year Growth Avg. Annual (%)	Total (%)
Revenue ($)	225,860	280,634	364,825	477,054	557,335	681,920	25	202
Net income ($)	19	33.5	33	48	60	72	30	276
Earnings/share ($)	.41	.71	.70	1.00	1.25	1.50	29.5	266
Div. per share ($)	–	–	.05	.06	.07	.08	10	60
Dividend yield (%)	–	–	–	0.1	0.3	0.3	–	–
Avg. PE ratio	23	26	39	37	22	20	–	–

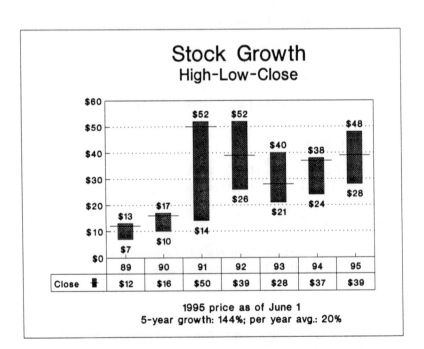

Stock Growth
High-Low-Close

	89	90	91	92	93	94	95
Close	$12	$16	$50	$39	$28	$37	$39

1995 price as of June 1
5-year growth: 144%; per year avg.: 20%

Shaw Industries, Inc.

❋ Shaw Industries, Inc.

616 E. Walnut Ave.
P. O. Box 2128
Dalton, GA 30722-2128
706-278-3812

Chairman: J. C. Shaw
President and CEO: Robert E. Shaw

Earnings Growth	★ ★	Dividend Growth	★ ★ ★ ★
Stock Growth	★ ★ ★ ★	Consistency	★ ★
Dividend Yield	★	Shareholder Perks	
NYSE—SHX		**Total**	**13 points**

Now that Shaw Industries has rolled out the carpet across America, the company is pushing hard to expand its foothold in the worldwide carpet market.

The Dalton, Georgia–based manufacturer has become the world's largest carpet maker. After building a strong base in the United States, Shaw began expanding abroad in 1993. Through a series of acquisitions, Shaw quickly became the largest carpet maker in both Great Britain and Australia. In 1994, Shaw established a presence in Latin and South America through a joint venture with Grupo Industrial Alfa, S.A., a major Mexican carpet manufacturer. Foreign sales account for about 8 percent of Shaw's $2.6 billion in annual revenue.

In the U.S. carpet market, Shaw is the dominant player, with a 35 to 40 percent market share. Through years of acquisitions, the company has brought many of the leading carpet brands into its corporate fold, including Armstrong, Philadelphia, Cabin Crafts, Kosset, Networx, Shawmark,

Trustmark, Crossley, Stratton, Salem, Sutton, Redbook, Minister, Invicta and Magee.

Founded in 1967 by brothers J.C. Shaw and Robert E. Shaw (who still serve as chairman and president, respectively), Shaw has been one of the nation's fastest-growing blue-chip companies. Over the past decade the company's revenues have grown 480 percent, and its earnings per share have grown 430 percent.

Shaw is vertically integrated, handling every step of the carpet-making process—spinning the fiber, dyeing it, weaving the rug and cutting it to size. Like 95 percent of the U.S. carpeting industry, Shaw makes tufted carpet from nylon yarn. In all, the company makes about 500 styles of carpet for residential and commercial customers. The company sells its carpeting through about 37,500 retail stores and 100 wholesale distributors throughout the United States. By integrating the operations of its acquired companies into one sales network, the company has been able to reduce overhead and marketing costs.

Shaw stock does tend to be more volatile than most of the stocks in the Best 100 because its sales are tied to the cyclical construction industry. But the company's long-term growth has been exceptional.

Shaw has 24,000 employees and 2,200 shareholders. Insiders (primarily the Shaw brothers) own 17 percent of the company stock.

EARNINGS-PER-SHARE GROWTH ★ ★

Past 5 years: 93 percent (14 percent per year)
Past 10 years: 424 percent (18 percent per year)

STOCK GROWTH ★ ★ ★ ★

Past 10 years: 800 percent (25 percent per year)
Dollar growth: $10,000 over 10 years (including reinvested dividends) would have grown to $109,000
Average annual compounded rate of return (including reinvested dividends): 27 percent

DIVIDEND YIELD

Average dividend yield in the past 3 years: 1.2 percent

DIVIDEND GROWTH ★ ★ ★ ★

Increased dividend: 11 consecutive years
Past 5-year increase: 144 percent (20 percent per year)

CONSISTENCY ★ ★

Increased earnings per share: 8 of past 10 years
Increased sales: 13 consecutive years

SHAREHOLDER PERKS

Shaw does not offer a dividend reinvestment plan, nor does it offer any other perks for its shareholders.

SHAW INDUSTRIES AT A GLANCE

Fiscal year ended: Dec. 31
Revenue and net income in $ millions

	1989	1990	1991	1992	1993	1994	5-year Growth Avg. Annual (%)	5-year Growth Total (%)
Revenue ($)	1,266	1,659	1,619	2,036	2,476	2,789	17	120
Net income ($)	56	60	36	79	118	127	18	127
Earnings/share ($)	.46	.50	.32	.59	.81	.89	14	93
Div. per share ($)	.10	.13	.13	.15	.18	.22	20	144
Dividend yield (%)	2.9	1.6	2.1	1.5	1.1	1.0	—	—
Avg. PE ratio	8.2	13.0	20.5	21.6	20.8	23.1	—	—

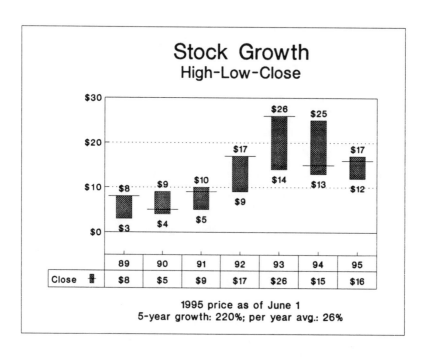

Stock Growth
High-Low-Close

	89	90	91	92	93	94	95
Close	$8	$5	$9	$17	$26	$15	$16

1995 price as of June 1
5-year growth: 220%; per year avg.: 26%

55

The Walt Disney Company

The **Walt Disney Company**©

500 South Buena Vista Street
Burbank, CA 91521
818-560-1000

Chairman and CEO: Michael D. Eisner

Earnings Growth	★	Dividend Growth	★ ★ ★
Stock Growth	★ ★ ★ ★	Consistency	★ ★ ★
Dividend Yield	★	Shareholder Perks	★
NYSE—DIS		**Total**	**13 points**

The Magic Kingdom has been rocked recently, but not ravaged. Walt Disney president Frank G. Wells was killed in an Easter Sunday helicopter crash in 1994 and chairman Michael Eisner underwent emergency quadruple heart bypass surgery. On top of that, board member Sam Williams died, and the Burbank-based operation was battered by the Los Angeles earthquake.

"A hectic year," said Eisner in his annual letter to shareholders, "but during all these events, all these devastations, all these uncertainties, the strength of our products and projects prevailed . . . and these strengths created the biggest year in our history."

It was a year when Disney had the number-one movie in the country (*The Lion King*), the number-one show on network TV ("Home Improvement"), two records that hit the top of the charts, a number-one show on Broadway (*Beauty and the Beast*), and the six best-attended theme parks in the world. In 1995, the company acquired Capital Cities/ABC in a blockbuster billion-dollar buy-out.

Aside from its new acquisition, Disney breaks its operations into three primary segments:

- **Filmed entertainment.** This is the company's largest segment, accounting for 48 percent of Disney's $10.1 billion in annual revenue. The company is well-diversified within this segment, with movies from Walt Disney Pictures, Touchstone Pictures, Hollywood Pictures, Miramax Films and Caravan Pictures. Among the company's leading movies recently have been *The Lion King, The Santa Clause, The Jungle Book, Pulp Fiction* and *Pocahontas.*

  The segment also includes the company's home video division, which claims about 600 titles, and its network and cable television offerings. Among its top shows are "Home Improvement," "Empty Nest," "Blossom," "Boy Meets World" and "Ellen."

- **Theme and parks resorts** (34 percent of revenue). The company operates a number of resorts. Its largest is Walt Disney World in Orlando, Florida, with three theme parks, The Magic Kingdom, Epcot Center and the Disney-MGM Studios Theme Park. Other parks include Disneyland in Anaheim, California, and Tokyo Disneyland. The company is a 39 percent shareholder of Disneyland Paris in France.

- **Consumer products** (18 percent). The division, which is responsible for the sale of Disney apparel, dolls, software games, books and assorted merchandise, is the fastest-growing of the three segments. The company has 350 Disney Stores—more than four times its store count of just four years earlier.

Disney has 65,000 employees and 460,000 shareholders.

EARNINGS-PER-SHARE GROWTH ★

Past 5 years: 61 percent (10 percent per year)
Past 10 years: 974 percent (27 percent per year)

STOCK GROWTH ★ ★ ★ ★

Past 10 years: 864 percent (25 percent per year)
Dollar growth: $10,000 over 10 years (including reinvested dividends) would have grown to $100,000

Average annual compounded rate of return (including reinvested dividends): 26 percent

DIVIDEND YIELD

Average dividend yield in the past 3 years: 0.7 percent

DIVIDEND GROWTH ★ ★ ★

Increased dividend: 7 consecutive years
Past 5-year increase: 142 percent (19 percent per year)

CONSISTENCY ★ ★ ★

Increased earnings per share: 9 of past 10 years
Increased sales: 12 consecutive years

SHAREHOLDER PERKS ★

The company does not offer a dividend reinvestment plan, but it does offer a couple of other shareholder perks. The company offers a direct deposit program allowing shareholders to have dividends deposited directly into their bank account.

For a limited time, shareholders also qualify for a $15 discount on the Magic Kingdom Club Gold Card (special price: $50). Gold Card membership provides a wide range of benefits including savings on admission at the theme parks and select resort hotel accommodations, and discounts on travel arrangements with Delta Airlines, National Car Rental and Premier Cruise Lines. Gold Card members also receive a personalized embossed membership card, an informative newsletter, a two-year subscription to Disney News magazine, a Disney vacation planning video, and a toll-free number for the Magic Kingdom Club Travel Centers. Further information is available by calling 714-490-3939.

DISNEY AT A GLANCE

Fiscal year ended: Sept. 30
Revenue and net income in $ millions

	1989	1990	1991	1992	1993	1994	5-year Growth Avg. Annual (%)	Total (%)
Revenue ($)	4,594	5,757	6,112	7,504	8,529	10,055	17	119
Net income ($)	703.3	824.0	636.6	816.7	671.3	1,110.4	10	58
Earnings/share ($)	1.27	1.50	1.20	1.52	1.63	2.04	10	61
Div. per share ($)	.12	.14	.17	.20	.24	.29	19	142
Dividend yield (%)	0.4	0.6	0.6	0.6	0.6	0.8	—	—
Avg. PE ratio	23.8	15.1	23.8	23.8	23.2	19.1	—	—

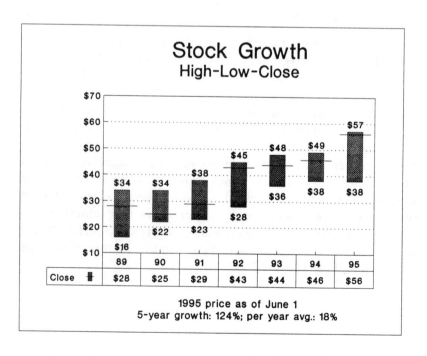

Stock Growth
High-Low-Close

	89	90	91	92	93	94	95
Close	$28	$25	$29	$43	$44	$46	$56

1995 price as of June 1
5-year growth: 124%; per year avg.: 18%

56

First Financial Management Corp.

3 Corporate Square
Suite 700
Atlanta, GA 30329
404-321-0120

Chairman, President and CEO: Patrick H. Thomas

Earnings Growth	★ ★ ★ ★	Dividend Growth	★
Stock Growth	★ ★ ★ ★	Consistency	★ ★ ★ ★
Dividend Yield		Shareholder Perks	
NYSE—FFM		**Total**	**13 points**

Now that the U.S. Postal Service has finally decided to join the 20th century, First Financial Management Corp. (FFMC) is there to help. The Postal Service has announced it intends to begin accepting credit cards, and FFMC will process all of those credit card transactions.

FFMC is the nation's leading vendor of merchant credit card services and offers a wide range of other information processing services for banks, financial institutions and other organizations. FFMC provides service to more than 300,000 commercial customers and 55 million consumers.

The Atlanta-based operation has been one of the nation's fastest-growing companies over the past decade, thanks in large part to a series of acquisitions. In all, the company has acquired more than 70 companies.

FFMC pulled off its biggest acquisition ever in 1994 when it bought out Western Union. Western Union, which is the world's largest nonbank immediate money transfer business, has added a new dimension to FFMC's operations. The company breaks its operations into three segments:

- **Merchant services.** The company's NaBANCO subsidiary is the largest merchant credit card processor in the United States. TeleCheck is a leader in check guarantee and verification services.

- **Health care services.** FFMC's First Health subsidiary provides health care claims processing and management services.
- **Data imaging services.** First Image Management Company offers computer data capture, data imaging, micro graphics, electronic database management and output printing and distribution.

FFMC has about 15,000 employees and 1,500 shareholders.

EARNINGS-PER-SHARE GROWTH   ★ ★ ★ ★

Past 5 years: 153 percent (21 percent per year)
Past 10 years: 924 percent (26 percent per year)

STOCK GROWTH   ★ ★ ★ ★

Past 10 years: 862 percent (25 percent per year)
Dollar growth: $10,000 over 10 years (including reinvested dividends) would have grown to $100,000
Average annual compounded rate of return (including reinvested dividends): 26 percent

DIVIDEND YIELD

Average dividend yield in the past 3 years: 0.2 percent

DIVIDEND GROWTH   ★

Increased dividend: 0 consecutive years
Past 5-year increase: 43 percent (7 percent per year)

CONSISTENCY   ★ ★ ★ ★

Increased earnings per share: 10 consecutive years
Increased sales: 10 consecutive years

SHAREHOLDER PERKS

The company offers no dividend reinvestment and stock purchase plan, nor does it provide any other shareholder perks.

FIRST FINANCIAL AT A GLANCE

Fiscal year ended: Dec. 31
Revenue and net income in $ millions

	1989	1990	1991	1992	1993	1994	5-year Growth Avg. Annual (%)	Total (%)
Revenue ($)	606.7	816.3	1,057.5	1,508.4	1,759.6	2,207.5	29	260
Net income ($)	39.4	47.7	62.7	86.2	131.8	160.2	33	310
Earnings/share ($)	1.01	1.10	1.23	1.43	2.12	2.56	21	153
Div. per share ($)	.07	.07	.07	.10	.10	.10	7	43
Dividend yield (%)	0.3	0.5	0.3	0.2	0.2	0.2	—	—
Avg. PE ratio	14.2	8.7	13.8	23.1	21.8	22.5	—	—

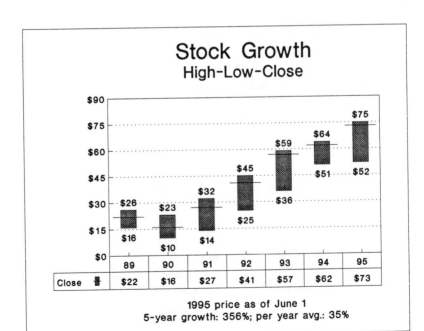

Stock Growth
High-Low-Close

	89	90	91	92	93	94	95
Close	$22	$16	$27	$41	$57	$62	$73

1995 price as of June 1
5-year growth: 356%; per year avg.: 35%

57

Cardinal Health, Inc.

655 Metro Place South, Suite 925
Dublin, OH 43017
614-761-8700

Chairman and CEO: Robet D. Walter
President: John C. Kane

Earnings Growth	★ ★ ★ ★	Dividend Growth	★ ★ ★
Stock Growth	★ ★ ★ ★	Consistency	★ ★
Dividend Yield		Shareholder Perks	
NYSE—CAH		**Total**	**13 points**

With the 1994 acquisition of drug wholesaler Whitmire Distribution Corp., Cardinal Health, Inc. has spread its wings across the country and become the nation's third-largest health care products distributor.

Upon adding the California-based wholesaler and its $3.1 billion in sales to its fold, Cardinal Distribution rechristened itself Cardinal Health. Cardinal and Whitmire appear to be an ideal match. Cardinal's distribution centers are in the eastern third of the country, while Whitmire generated most of its sales in the western two-thirds of the nation. Cardinal now has 38 distribution centers throughout the country.

The Dublin, Ohio, operation's extended breadth helps to accommodate the increasingly popular managed health care organizations, which themselves are broadening their geographic reach.

Cardinal supplies pharmaceuticals, surgical and hospital supplies, health and beauty care products and other products to hospitals, managed care facilities, independent and chain drug stores and the pharmacy departments of supermarkets and mass merchandisers.

About half the company's $5.8 billion in sales were to hospitals and managed care facilities, 23 percent were to chain drug stores and supermarket pharmacies, 21 percent to independent drug stores and 6 percent to specialty wholesalers.

Founded in 1971 as a food wholesaler, Cardinal entered the drug distribution business in 1979. It has rapidly expanded its business through a series of mergers and acquisitions. The company has about 3,500 employees.

EARNINGS-PER-SHARE GROWTH   ★ ★ ★ ★

Past 5 years: 158 percent (21 percent per year)
Past 10 years: 416 percent (18 percent per year)

STOCK GROWTH   ★ ★ ★ ★

Past 10 years: 849 percent (25 percent per year)
Dollar growth: $10,000 over 10 years (including reinvested dividends) would have grown to $98,000
Average annual compounded rate of return (including reinvested dividends): 25.5 percent

DIVIDEND YIELD

Average dividend yield in the past 3 years: 0.2 percent

DIVIDEND GROWTH   ★ ★ ★

Increased dividend: 11 consecutive years
Past 5-year increase: 233 percent (27 percent per year)

CONSISTENCY   ★ ★

Increased earnings per share: 8 of past 10 years
Increased sales: 9 of past 10 years

SHAREHOLDER PERKS

Cardinal offers no dividend reinvestment plan, nor does it offer any other perks for its shareholders.

CARDINAL HEALTH AT A GLANCE

Fiscal year ended: June 30
Revenue and net income in $ millions

	1989	1990	1991	1992	1993	1994	Avg. Annual (%)	Total (%)
							5-year Growth	
Revenue ($)	700.4	873.8	1,184.3	3,680.7	4,633.4	5,790.4	52	727
Net income ($)	8.5	12	17	28	40	35	33	312
Earnings/share ($)	.62	.66	.84	.74	1.10	1.60	21	158
Div. per share ($)	.03	.04	.05	.06	.07	.10	27	233
Dividend yield (%)	–	0.2	0.2	0.2	0.2	0.2	–	–
Avg. PE ratio	16.4	19.4	25.0	18.4	19.5	21.4	–	–

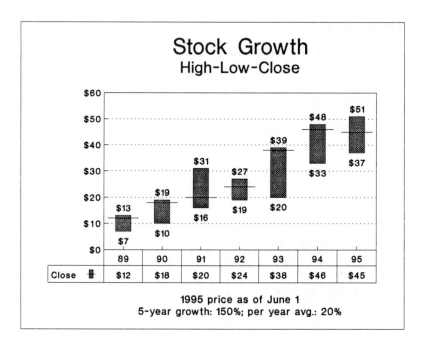

Stock Growth
High-Low-Close

	89	90	91	92	93	94	95
Close	$12	$18	$20	$24	$38	$46	$45

1995 price as of June 1
5-year growth: 150%; per year avg.: 20%

Great Lakes Chemical Corp.

One Great Lakes Blvd.
West Lafayette, IN 47906-0200
317-497-6100

President and CEO: Robert B. McDonald

Earnings Growth	★ ★ ★	Dividend Growth	★ ★ ★ ★
Stock Growth	★ ★ ★	Consistency	★ ★
Dividend Yield	★	Shareholder Perks	
NYSE—GLK		**Total**	**13 points**

Engines run smoother and knock less thanks to fuel tank additives produced by Great Lakes Chemical. The company is one of the world's leading producers of high-performance transport fuel additives such as antiknock boosters, combustion and cold fuel improvers for diesel fuel, corrosion inhibitors and gasoline and diesel detergents.

The West Lafayette, Indiana, operation serves more than 200 refineries in more than 65 countries. Petroleum additives account for 30 percent of the company's $2.1 billion in annual sales.

In addition to its fuel additives, the company is the world's leading producer of bromine, an element found deep under the earth's crust. Great Lakes has uncovered a wide range of commercial uses for bromine—from fire control to water treatment—and now markets it around the globe.

Bromine is used extensively for fire control applications, such as flame retardants in carpeting, electronics cabinetry and other products. Bromine-based fire extinguishing agents are used to fight fires and suppress explosions in oil pipelines, plant control rooms, aircraft and other locations. Flame retardants account for 13 percent of the company's total revenue.

The company's other segments include:

- **Intermediate and fine chemicals** (13 percent of revenue). The company produces chemicals for foundry resins, lube oil refining, pharmaceuticals, agrochemicals, photographic papers and films.
- **Polymer stabilizers** (8 percent). The company produces polymer stabilizer compounds used to enhance heat resistance and color consistency in manufactured products.
- **Water treatment** (18 percent). Great Lakes produces chemicals used in wastewater treatment and cooling water systems as well as water processing for manufacturing and recreational swimming pools and spas. The firm also manufactures pumps, filters and other pool operating equipment.
- **Specialized services and manufacturing** (18 percent). Specialized services include fluorine chemistry, environmental and oil field services, toxicological testing and engineered surface treatments.

Great Lakes Chemical has operations throughout North America and Europe. Foreign operations account for about 62 percent of total revenue. The company has about 7,000 employees and 4,000 shareholders.

EARNINGS-PER-SHARE GROWTH   ★ ★ ★

Past 5 years: 127 percent (18 percent per year)
Past 10 years: 590 percent (21 percent per year)

STOCK GROWTH   ★ ★ ★

Past 10 years: 512 percent (20 percent per year)
Dollar growth: $10,000 over 10 years (including reinvested dividends) would have grown to $67,000
Average annual compounded rate of return (including reinvested dividends): 21 percent

DIVIDEND YIELD   ★

Average dividend yield in the past 3 years: 0.5 percent

DIVIDEND GROWTH   ★ ★ ★ ★

Increased dividend: 22 consecutive years
Past 5-year increase: 100 percent (15 percent per year)

CONSISTENCY   ★ ★

Increased earnings per share: 8 consecutive years
Increased sales: 9 consecutive years

SHAREHOLDER PERKS

The company offers no dividend reinvestment plan, nor does it provide any
other special perks for shareholders.

GREAT LAKES CHEMICAL AT A GLANCE

Fiscal year ended: Dec. 31
Revenue and net income in $ millions

	1989	1990	1991	1992	1993	1994	5-year Growth Avg. Annual (%)	Total (%)
Revenue ($)	847.7	1,113.5	1,347.9	1,538.2	1,827.8	2,110.7	20	149
Net income ($)	123.0	141.0	157.5	232.7	272.8	278.7	18	127
Earnings/share ($)	1.76	2.01	2.23	2.37	3.82	4.00	18	127
Div. per share ($)	.19	.22	.26	.30	.34	.38	15	100
Dividend yield (%)	1.0	.8	.6	.5	.5	.5	—	—
Avg. PE ratio	10.7	13.6	19.0	19.3	19.0	15.6	—	—

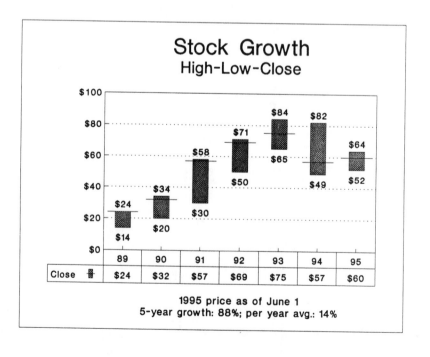

Stock Growth
High-Low-Close

	89	90	91	92	93	94	95
Close	$24	$32	$57	$69	$75	$57	$60

1995 price as of June 1
5-year growth: 88%; per year avg.: 14%

59

Hillenbrand Industries, Inc.

700 State Route 46 East
Batesville, IN 47006-8835
812-934-7000

Chairman: Daniel A. Hillenbrand
President and CEO: W. August Hillenbrand

Earnings Growth	★ ★	Dividend Growth	★ ★ ★ ★
Stock Growth	★ ★ ★	Consistency	★ ★ ★
Dividend Yield	★	Shareholder Perks	
NYSE—HB		**Total**	**13 points**

Hillenbrand is well poised to take advantage of the aging of America. The company is one of the nation's leading casket makers and a manufacturer of a variety of health care products. The company's Batesville Casket Company subsidiary, founded in 1884, is the nation's leading manufacturer of protective metal and hardwood burial caskets. Its Batesville Monoseal steel caskets are the only ones in the industry that use a magnesium alloy bar to protect the caskets from the ravages of time and decay. The Indiana operation also sells copper, bronze, walnut, mahogany, cherry, maple, pine, oak and poplar caskets, and it manufactures a line of urns used in cremations.

Hillenbrand also operates the Forecorp Insurance Group, which provides life insurance policies that allow customers to specify their own funeral benefits, including choice of funeral home, type of service, casket and related merchandise. Founded in 1985, Forecorp has been one of Hillenbrand's fastest-growing segments.

Hillenbrand's funeral-related division accounts for about 41 percent of its $1.58 billion in annual revenue. The company's other main segment is its health care division, which accounts for 59 percent of revenue. The health care segment has three key divisions, including Hill-Rom Company, a leading manufacturer of patient care equipment for hospitals; Block Medical, a leading manufacturer of portable, disposable and ambulatory electronic infusion pumps for home care patients; and Medeco Security Locks Company.

Based in Batesville, Indiana, Hillenbrand Industries has 10,000 employees and 11,000 shareholders.

EARNINGS-PER-SHARE GROWTH   ★ ★

Past 5 years: 108 percent (16 percent per year)
Past 10 years: 326 percent (16 percent per year)

STOCK GROWTH   ★ ★ ★

Past 10 years: 400 percent (17.5 percent per year)
Dollar growth: $10,000 over 10 years (including reinvested dividends) would have grown to $57,000
Average annual compounded rate of return (including reinvested dividends): 19 percent

DIVIDEND YIELD   ★

Average dividend yield in the past 3 years: 1.2 percent

DIVIDEND GROWTH   ★ ★ ★ ★

Increased dividend: 23 consecutive years
Past 5-year increase: 128 percent (18 percent per year)

CONSISTENCY   ★ ★ ★

Increased earnings per share: 9 consecutive years
Increased sales: 9 of past 10 years

SHAREHOLDER PERKS

The company offers no dividend reinvestment plan, nor does it provide any other special perks for its shareholders.

HILLENBRAND INDUSTRIES AT A GLANCE

Fiscal year ended: Dec. 31
Revenue and net income in $ millions

	1989	1990	1991	1992	1993	1994	5-year Growth Avg. Annual (%)	Total (%)
Revenue ($)	872.0	981.9	1,084.5	1,303.1	1,447.9	1,577.0	13	81
Net income ($)	70	76	90	115	133	142	15	103
Earnings/share ($)	.96	1.02	1.22	1.62	1.86	2.00	16	108
Div. per share ($)	.25	.28	.29	.35	.45	.57	18	128
Dividend yield (%)	1.5	1.3	1.3	0.9	1.1	1.6	—	—
Avg. PE ratio	16.5	20.3	19.0	23.5	22.6	17.7	—	—

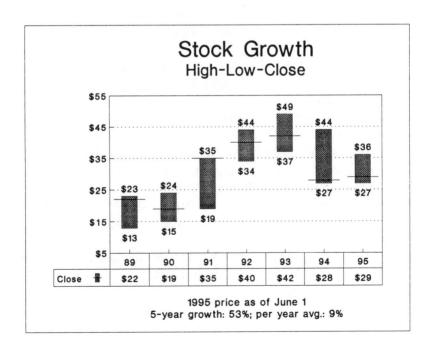

Stock Growth
High-Low-Close

	89	90	91	92	93	94	95
Close	$22	$19	$35	$40	$42	$28	$29

1995 price as of June 1
5-year growth: 53%; per year avg.: 9%

McDonald's Corp.

McDonald's Plaza
Oak Brook, IL 60521-2278
708-575-3000

Chairman and CEO: Michael R. Quinlan

Earnings Growth	★	Dividend Growth	★ ★ ★
Stock Growth	★ ★	Consistency	★ ★ ★ ★
Dividend Yield	★	Shareholder Perks	★ ★
NYSE—MCD		**Total**	**13 points**

Marketing dilemma: Your company name is synonymous with "all-beef patties" (on a sesame-seed bun), yet you want to enter an enormous new market where the cow is sacred. How do you do it?

If you're McDonald's, you drop your patented "Big Mac," and feature chicken and fish sandwiches along with some special veggie nuggets and a veggie burger. That's what McDonald's has done with its new restaurants in India, in Bombay and New Delhi. The company offers no beef products in those markets.

The international market has become increasingly important to the Oak Brook, Illinois, fast food franchiser, which has been edging ever closer to the saturation point in the United States. The company has sprouted golden arches in about 80 countries around the world.

In fact, about half of McDonald's operating income is now generated by its foreign operations, while about 40 percent of its $8.3 billion in annual revenue comes from overseas. The company has 9,800 restaurants in the United States and 5,500 abroad.

The rapid foreign growth of McDonald's has helped propel the company to 29 consecutive years of record earnings, dating back to the year the company went public.

In recent years, the company has been opening about twice as many restaurants in foreign markets as in the United States. The fast-food chain is now well-entrenched in the former Eastern Bloc and has also opened restaurants in Russia and China.

The company, which has been adding new restaurants at a rate of nearly 1,000 a year, has announced plans to begin opening as many as 1,200 to 1,500 restaurants per year. About two-thirds will be outside the United States.

McDonald's biggest foreign markets are Japan (about 1,100 outlets), Canada (700), England (480), Germany (500), and Australia (400). McDonald's is the most advertised brand name in the world.

In addition to its foreign expansion, McDonald's has also tried to keep its earnings growing by introducing a continuing line of new selections, such as ice cream, pizza, submarine sandwiches, salads, breakfast products and other specialties. McDonald's also maintains its marketing edge by keeping prices as low as any restaurant in the fast food business.

Most McDonald's restaurants are owned by independent businesspeople who operate them through a franchise agreement. Typically, the company tries to recruit investors who will be active, on-premises owners rather than outside investors. The conventional franchise arrangement is for a term of 20 years, and requires an investment of about $600,000, 60 percent of which may be financed. Each outlet is also subject to franchise fees based on a percentage of sales. With few exceptions, McDonald's does not supply food, paper or equipment to any restaurants, but approves suppliers from which those items can be purchased.

Restaurant managers receive training at the company's Hamburger University at the McDonald's corporate headquarters in Oak Brook, Illinois. About 2,000 managers a year go through the training program. In all, about 50,000 people have graduated from Hamburger U.

Since Ray Kroc founded McDonald's in 1955, the company has served about 80 billion burgers under the golden arches. The system serves about 26 million diners a day. McDonald's has 170,000 employees and 380,000 shareholders.

EARNINGS-PER-SHARE GROWTH   ★

Past 5 years: 71 percent (11.5 percent per year)
Past 10 years: 243 percent (13 percent per year)

STOCK GROWTH ★ ★

Past 10 years: 373 percent (17 percent per year)
Dollar growth: $10,000 over 10 years (including reinvested dividends) would have grown to $52,000
Average annual compounded rate of return (including reinvested dividends): 18 percent

DIVIDEND YIELD ★

Average dividend yield in the past 3 years: 0.8 percent

DIVIDEND GROWTH ★ ★ ★

Increased dividend: 29 consecutive years
Past 5-year increase: 87 percent (13.5 percent per year)

CONSISTENCY ★ ★ ★ ★

Increased earnings per share: 29 consecutive years
Increased sales: 29 consecutive years

SHAREHOLDER PERKS ★ ★

Outstanding dividend reinvestment and stock purchase plan: voluntary stock purchase plan allows contributions of $50 to $75,000 per year.

A wealth of literature on McDonald's and its locations and product ingredients is available to shareholders (or anyone else requesting it). The company also provides an investor hotline (not toll-free) that gives company news.

MCDONALD'S AT A GLANCE

Fiscal year ended: Dec. 31
Revenue and net income in $ millions

	1989	1990	1991	1992	1993	1994	5-year Growth Avg. Annual (%)	Total (%)
Revenue ($)	6,066	6,640	6,695	7,133	7,408	8,320	6.5	37
Net income ($)	727	802	860	959	1,083	1,224	11	68
Earnings/share ($)	.98	1.10	1.18	1.30	1.45	1.68	11.5	71
Div. per share ($)	.15	.17	.18	.20	.21	.28	13.5	87
Dividend yield (%)	1.0	1.1	1.1	0.9	0.8	0.8	—	—
Avg. PE ratio	15	14	14	17	18	17	—	—

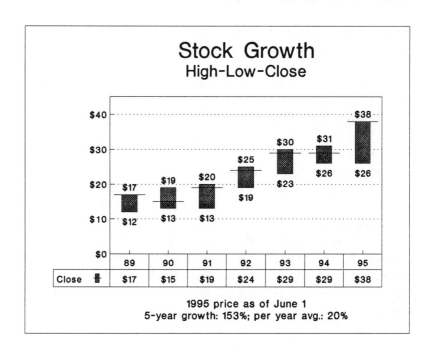

Stock Growth
High-Low-Close

	89	90	91	92	93	94	95
Close	$17	$15	$19	$24	$29	$29	$38

1995 price as of June 1
5-year growth: 153%; per year avg.: 20%

61

American Home Products Corp.

Five Giralda Farms
Madison, NJ 07940
201-660-5000

Chairman, President and CEO:
John R. Stafford

Earnings Growth		Dividend Growth	★ ★
Stock Growth	★	Consistency	★ ★ ★ ★
Dividend Yield	★ ★ ★ ★	Shareholder Perks	★ ★
NYSE—AHP		**Total**	**13 points**

American Home Products' merger in late 1994 with American Cyanamid Co. created a $13 billion global pharmaceutical and health care products powerhouse.

Operating in 145 companies, American Home can now boast that it ranks first in the sale of nonprescription drugs; first in vitamins and vaccines in the United States; and second in the world in nonprescription drugs. The "new" American Home, as the company bills itself, is also a leading player in generic pharmaceuticals, biotechnology, animal health care, agricultural chemicals and convenience food.

Overlapping products were jettisoned once the dust settled on the merger with American Cyanamid, a leading supplier of vaccines, vitamins and surgical products.

American Home has always had an impressive lineup of both prescription and over-the-counter drugs. Although pharmaceuticals have traditionally generated nearly 60 percent of American Home's revenues, its smaller stable of consumer health care products have household brand status and dominate certain markets.

For example, Anbesol is the leading topical analgesic for both babies and adults; Preparation H is the top-selling product in the hemorrhoidal relief category; and Primatene is the largest-selling nonprescription brand in the United States for asthma relief. All three products are made by American Home's Whitehall Laboratories and A.H. Robins units, which generate about 20 percent of the company's sales.

Other major over-the-counter brands include Advil, Anacin, Robitussin and Dimetapp. American Home believes it is well-positioned to capture a larger share of the growing self-medication market worldwide.

On the pharmaceutical side, which operates under the name Wyeth-Ayerst Research, the company produces Premarin, the most widely prescribed drug in the United States. Premarin, the company's flagship drug, is used to prevent and treat osteoporosis and is also used to treat short-term symptoms of menopause.

In 1994, Wyeth-Ayerst successfully launched Effexor, an antidepressant.

American Home has two other key operating units:

- The food products division produces an array of ready-to-eat convenience foods such as Chef Boyardee pasta, Dennison's chili and a recently introduced line of Sesame Street nutritional pasta for children.
- The medical supplies and instrumentation division manufactures such products as disposable syringes and needles, tubes, catheters, monitoring systems and endoscopic instruments.

The company has 74,000 employees and 71,600 shareholders.

EARNINGS-PER-SHARE GROWTH

Past 5 years: 40 percent (7 percent per year)
Past 10 years: 133 percent (9 percent per year)

STOCK GROWTH   ★

Past 10 years: 194 percent (11 percent per year)
Dollar growth: $10,000 over 10 years (including reinvested dividends) would have grown to $41,000
Average annual compounded rate of return (including reinvested dividends): 15 percent

DIVIDEND YIELD

Average dividend yield in the past 3 years: 4.3 percent

DIVIDEND GROWTH

Increased dividend: 42 consecutive years
Past 5-year increase: 51 percent (9 percent per year)

CONSISTENCY ★ ★ ★ ★

Increased earnings per share: 43 consecutive years
Increased sales: 43 consecutive years

SHAREHOLDER PERKS ★ ★

Good dividend reinvestment and stock purchase plan: voluntary stock purchase plan allows contributions of $50 to $10,000 per month.

Occasionally, the company sends coupons for some of its foods and health care products along with the dividend check.

AMERICAN HOME PRODUCTS AT A GLANCE

Fiscal year ended: Dec. 31
Revenue and net income in $ millions

	1989	1990	1991	1992	1993	1994	5-year Growth Avg. Annual (%)	5-year Growth Total (%)
Revenue ($)	6,747	6,775	7,079	7,874	8,305	8,966	6	33
Net income ($)	1,102	1,231	1,375	1,461	1,469	1,528	7	39
Earnings/share ($)	3.54	3.92	4.36	4.65	4.73	4.97	7	40
Div. per share ($)	1.95	2.15	2.38	2.66	2.86	2.94	9	51
Dividend yield (%)	3.6	4.1	2.8	3.9	4.4	4.7	—	—
Avg. PE ratio	13.5	13.6	14.6	16.9	13.5	12.1	—	—

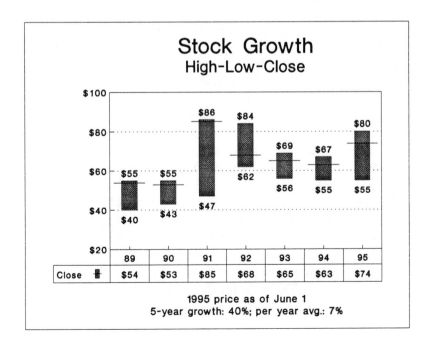

Stock Growth
High-Low-Close

Close	89	90	91	92	93	94	95
	$54	$53	$85	$68	$65	$63	$74

1995 price as of June 1
5-year growth: 40%; per year avg.: 7%

Banc One Corp.

100 E. Broad St.
Columbus, OH 43271
614-248-5944

Chairman and CEO: John B. McCoy

Earnings Growth		Dividend Growth	★ ★ ★
Stock Growth	★	Consistency	★ ★ ★
Dividend Yield	★ ★ ★ ★	Shareholder Perks	★ ★
NYSE—ONE		**Total**	**13 points**

Banc One, a company that has had a voracious appetite for acquisitions through the years, bit off a new chunk of territory in 1994 with the acquisition of Liberty National Bancorp in Louisville. The buyout helped make Banc One the largest banking organization in Kentucky.

Thanks to a series of past acquisitions, Banc One is also the largest bank in Arizona, second-largest in Indiana, Ohio and West Virginia, and third-largest in Colorado, Texas and Wisconsin. It also has operations in Illinois, Oklahoma and Utah.

But while it was buying one bank, Banc One was selling off others. The Columbus, Ohio, institution sold its affiliate bank in California and announced plans to sell its four banks in Michigan. Banc One chairman John B. McCoy said he didn't feel the company had "an opportunity to establish a meaningful presence" in those markets.

Banc One operates 68 banks with about 1,400 offices in its remaining 11 states. Like many other banks around the country, Banc One suffered through a lean year in 1994 thanks to a record six increases in the federal prime interest rate. In fact, 1994 marked the first time in Banc One's 26-year history that it did not post record earnings. (Earnings fell from $2.93 per share to $2.42. The company did, however, raise its dividend for the 24th consecutive year.) In spite of the sub-par year, Banc One remains first among the nation's largest 25 banks in terms of average return on assets over the past 10 years and second in terms of return on equity.

Banc One's loan portfolio breaks down this way: commercial loans, 28 percent; real estate, 27 percent; consumer loans, 30 percent; other, 15 percent. The company has 49,000 employees and 83,000 shareholders.

EARNINGS-PER-SHARE GROWTH

Past 5 years: 46 percent (8 percent per year)
Past 10 years: 155 percent (10 percent per year)

STOCK GROWTH ★

Past 10 years: 155 percent (10 percent per year)
Dollar growth: $10,000 over 10 years (including reinvested dividends) would have grown to $40,000
Average annual compounded rate of return (including reinvested dividends): 15 percent

DIVIDEND YIELD

Average dividend yield in the past 3 years: 3.0 percent
(The company has also paid out five special 10 percent dividends in the past 10 years.)

DIVIDEND GROWTH

Increased dividend: 24 consecutive years
Past 5-year increase: 97 percent (15 percent per year)

CONSISTENCY

Increased earnings per share: After 25 consecutive years of record earnings, the company saw its earnings drop in 1994.

SHAREHOLDER PERKS

Good dividend reinvestment and stock purchase plan: voluntary stock purchase plan allows contributions of $10 to $5,000 per quarter.

BANC ONE AT A GLANCE

Fiscal year ended: Dec. 31
Revenue and net income in $ millions

	1989	1990	1991	1992	1993	1994	5-year Growth Avg. Annual (%)	Total (%)
Assets ($)	26,552	30,336	46,293	61,417	79,919	88,923	27	234
Net income ($)	362.9	423.4	529.5	781.3	1,140.0	1,005.1	23	177
Earnings/share ($)	1.66	1.83	2.12	2.38	2.98	2.42	8	46
Div. per share ($)	.63	.69	.76	.89	1.07	1.24	15	97
Dividend yield (%)	2.4	3.1	1.8	2.1	2.7	3.7	—	—
Avg. PE ratio	10.7	9.9	12.5	14.0	13.0	13.1	—	—

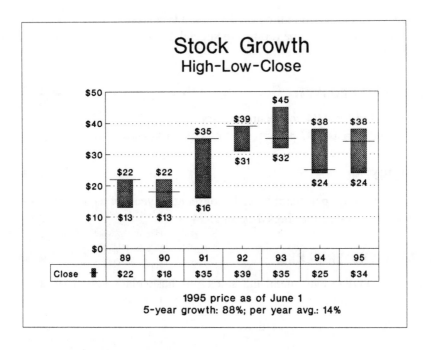

Stock Growth
High-Low-Close

	89	90	91	92	93	94	95
Close	$22	$18	$35	$39	$35	$25	$34

1995 price as of June 1
5-year growth: 88%; per year avg.: 14%

The May Department Stores Company

611 Olive Street
St. Louis, MO 63101-1799
314-342-6300

Chairman and CEO: David C. Farrell
President and COO: Jerome T. Loeb

Earnings Growth	★	Dividend Growth	★ ★
Stock Growth	★	Consistency	★ ★ ★ ★
Dividend Yield	★ ★ ★	Shareholder Perks	★ ★
NYSE—MA		**Total**	**13 points**

About one in every six Americans is walking around in shoes from May Department Stores subsidiary Payless ShoeSource. With more than 4,000 stores across the country, Payless sells nearly 200 million pairs of shoes each year. It is the nation's largest chain of self-service shoe stores, a distinction that should continue. Payless has been expanding at the rate of about 250 to 500 new stores a year.

Payless has also been expanding into the children's specialty arena with a growing chain of Payless Kids stores. The company has announced plans to open about 1,000 new Payless Kids stores and 1,200 new Payless ShoeSource stores over the next five years. Payless sales account for about 18 percent of May's $11.9 billion in annual revenue.

The balance of the company's revenue comes from its chain of department stores. May is the largest department store retailer in the country. The company operates about 315 stores in 29 states and the District of Columbia. Its five-year plan calls for an additional 110 new stores. The company breaks its department store operations into eight divisions, including: Lord & Taylor, New York, 49 stores (12 percent of total revenue); Hecht's, Washington, D.C., 45 stores (12 percent); Foley's, Houston, 48 stores (14 percent); Robinsons-May, Los Angeles, 48 stores (12 percent); Famous-Barr, St. Louis, 30 stores (8 percent); Kaufmann's, Pittsburgh, 40 stores (11 percent); Filene's, Boston, 33 stores (10 percent); and Meier & Frank, Portland, 8 stores (3 percent).

The St. Louis–based operation was founded by David May, who opened his first store in Leadville, Colorado, in 1877. The company has grown to about 120,000 employees and 46,000 shareholders.

EARNINGS-PER-SHARE GROWTH   ★

Past 5 years: 60 percent (10 percent per year)
Past 10 years: 135 percent (9 percent per year)

STOCK GROWTH   ★

Past 10 years: 175 percent (11 percent per year)
Dollar growth: $10,000 over 10 years (including reinvested dividends) would have grown to $37,000
Average annual compounded rate of return (including reinvested dividends): 14 percent

DIVIDEND YIELD   ★ ★ ★

Average dividend yield in the past 3 years: 2.5 percent

DIVIDEND GROWTH   ★ ★

Increased dividend: 20 consecutive years
Past 5-year increase: 51 percent (9 percent per year)

CONSISTENCY   ★ ★ ★ ★

Increased earnings per share: 15 consecutive years
Increased sales: 15 consecutive years

SHAREHOLDER PERKS   ★ ★

Good dividend reinvestment and stock purchase plan: voluntary stock purchase plan allows contributions of $25 and up (with no upper limit) per month.

MAY DEPARTMENT STORES AT A GLANCE

Fiscal year ended: Jan. 30
Revenue and net income in $ millions

	1989	1990	1991	1992	1993	1994	5-year Growth Avg. Annual (%)	Total (%)
Revenue ($)	9,602	10,066	10,615	11,150	11,529	11,877	5	24
Net income ($)	515	500	515	603	711	782	9	52
Earnings/share ($)	1.82	1.87	1.93	2.26	2.65	2.92	10	60
Div. per share ($)	.69	.77	.81	.83	.90	1.04	9	51
Dividend yield (%)	2.9	3.6	3.1	2.6	2.3	2.6	—	—
Avg. PE ratio	12	12	13	13	14	13	—	—

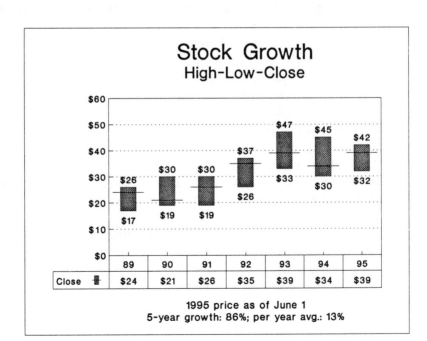

Stock Growth
High-Low-Close

	89	90	91	92	93	94	95
Close	$24	$21	$26	$35	$39	$34	$39

1995 price as of June 1
5-year growth: 86%; per year avg.: 13%

Microsoft Corp.

Microsoft ®

One Microsoft Way
Redmond, WA 98052-6399
206-882-8080

Chairman and CEO: William Gates

Earnings Growth	★ ★ ★ ★	Dividend Growth	
Stock Growth	★ ★ ★ ★	Consistency	★ ★ ★ ★
Dividend Yield		Shareholder Perks	
NASDAQ—MSFT		**Total**	**12 points**

Windows and MS-DOS. If you have a personal computer, there's a better than average chance your computer uses both. In fact, most new IBM-compatible personal computers are loaded with both sets of operating software before they leave the factory floor.

Windows is installed in more than 60 million computers worldwide. It is available in more than 25 languages. The recently introduced Windows 95 upgrade is expected to attain similar results in years to come.

At Microsoft, cofounder and chairman Bill Gates has built a multibillion-dollar empire on Windows, DOS and a variety of other software and computer products. The company produces software for both personal and business computers.

Over the past nine years, the Redmond, Washington, manufacturer has been the nation's fastest-growing publicly traded company. The company's success has made the 39-year-old Gates America's richest person, with a net worth in excess of $12 billion.

The company helps maintain its edge on the market by spending generously on product development. In 1994 alone, Microsoft spent more than $600 million on research and development.

While Microsoft's products are known worldwide, the North American market is by far the largest for Microsoft, accounting for 66 percent of total revenue in 1994. European operations generated 27 percent of revenue, while operations elsewhere around the world accounted for the remaining 7 percent.

Microsoft divides its operations into several key segments:

- **Personal operating systems.** Includes MS-DOS, Windows and Windows 95.
- **Business systems.** Includes Windows NT for business workstations, LAN Manager, Microsoft Mail, Schedule +, SQL Server and Microsoft At Work.
- **Desktop applications software.** The company produces Microsoft Word for word processing, Microsoft Excel spreadsheet software, and Microsoft Powerpoint presentation software.
- **Developer products.** Microsoft provides software development tools, database products and technical information to Windows software developers worldwide.
- **Consumer products.** The firm markets home office, entertainment, personal finance and other consumer-oriented software.
- **Books.** Founded in 1983, Microsoft Press publishes books about software products from Microsoft and other software developers.

The company, founded in 1975, has 16,000 employees and 27,000 shareholders.

EARNINGS-PER-SHARE GROWTH ★ ★ ★ ★

Past 5 years: 482 percent (42 percent per year)
Past 10 years: 4,850 percent (48 percent per year)

STOCK GROWTH ★ ★ ★ ★

Past 10 years: 3,900 percent (44 percent per year)
Dollar growth: $10,000 over 10 years (including reinvested dividends) would have grown to $400,000

Average annual compounded rate of return (including reinvested dividends): 44 percent

DIVIDEND YIELD

Pays no dividend

DIVIDEND GROWTH

Pays no dividend

CONSISTENCY   ★ ★ ★ ★

Increased earnings per share: 12 consecutive years
Increased sales: 12 consecutive years

SHAREHOLDER PERKS

The company offers no dividend reinvestment and stock purchase plan, nor does it provide any other shareholder perks.

MICROSOFT AT A GLANCE

Fiscal year ended: June 30
Revenue and net income in $ millions

	1989	1990	1991	1992	1993	1994	5-year Growth Avg. Annual (%)	5-year Growth Total (%)
Revenue ($)	803.5	1,183.4	1,843.5	2,758.7	3,753.0	4,649.0	42	480
Net income ($)	170.5	279.2	462.7	708.1	953.0	1,210.0	48	610
Earnings/share ($)	.34	.52	.82	1.21	1.58	1.98	42	482
Div. per share ($)	–	–	–	–	–	–	—	—
Dividend yield (%)	–	–	–	–	–	–	—	—
Avg. PE ratio	17.8	19.9	22.6	28.5	26.8	21.4	—	—

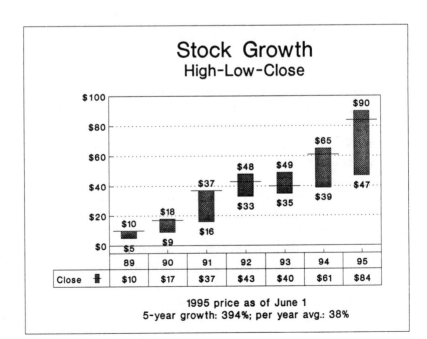

Stock Growth
High-Low-Close

	89	90	91	92	93	94	95
Close	$10	$17	$37	$43	$40	$61	$84

1995 price as of June 1
5-year growth: 394%; per year avg.: 38%

65

Harley-Davidson, Inc.

3700 West Juneau Ave.
P. O. Box 653
Milwaukee, WI 53201

Chairman: Vaughn L. Beals, Jr.
President and CEO: Richard F. Teerlink

Earnings Growth	★ ★ ★ ★	Dividend Growth	
Stock Growth	★ ★ ★ ★	Consistency	★ ★
Dividend Yield		Shareholder Perks	★ ★
NYSE—HDI		**Total**	**12 points**

There once was a time when you could tell a Harley rider by two traits—the bugs in his teeth and the oil on his boots.

That's only half true today. The sleek, finely honed riding machines of the 1990s have made believers of a growing throng of Harley riders—who may still proudly bare the bugs, but not the oil stains.

Harleys are now revered almost as works of art on wheels—and command $5,000 to $17,500 (plus extras) for riders lucky enough to get their hands on one. The wait for a new Harley can be as long as a couple of years. With its stringent emphasis on detail and quality, the company simply cannot turn out new machines fast enough to meet demand. Tough problem.

Harley-Davidson, in its present incarnation, was incorporated in 1981 by a private investment group which purchased Harley-Davidson Motorcycle from AMF, Inc., and took it public in 1986. The reputation of the bikes—and the profits of the company—has been rising ever since. From a net profit of $4.5 million in 1986, the company's profits have soared to $104 million in 1994.

The Milwaukee-based operation dominates the U.S. heavyweight motorcycle market (above 750 cubic centimeters engine displacement), holding a 56 percent share. That figure would be higher if Harley had the manufacturing capacity to turn out more bikes. In fact, the company is adding to its capacity and should be able to hike bike production from 65,000 units (in 1994) to 115,000 units by 1997.

Overseas sales are also on the rise. Harley has been aggressively attacking the European market, although production capacity is a problem there as well. The company sold 14,000 motorcycles in Europe in 1994, which represents a mere 11 percent of that market. As the company's production capacity increases, its foreign sales will rise as well. International sales currently account for about 29 percent of Harley's $1.54 billion in annual revenue.

In all, Harley manufactures 20 models of touring and custom heavyweight motorcycles. Its touring bikes are equipped for long-distance travel, with fairings, windshields, saddlebags and Harley Tour Paks. The custom bikes have distinctive styling, with customized trim and accessories. The company manufactures all of its chassis and engines itself. The bikes are based on four chassis variations and are powered by one of three air-cooled, twin-cylinder engines of V configurations with engine displacements of 883cc, 1200cc and 1340cc.

Motorcycles and related products account for 75 percent of the company's annual revenue. The other 25 percent of revenue comes from the company's Holiday Rambler division. Holiday Rambler builds three models of recreational vehicles, including the Navigator bus-style motor home (suggested price: $224,000 to $282,000), the Imperial motor home ($166,000 to $187,000) and the standard travel trailer ($47,000 to $72,500). Harley-Davidson has 6,000 employees and 19,000 shareholders.

EARNINGS-PER-SHARE GROWTH ★ ★ ★ ★

Past 5 years: 191 percent (24 percent per year)
Past 10 years: 1,370 percent (30 percent per year)

STOCK GROWTH ★ ★ ★ ★

Past 9 years: 2,500 percent (40 percent per year)
Dollar growth: $10,000 over 9 years (including reinvested dividends) would have grown to $260,000

Average annual compounded rate of return (including reinvested dividends): 40 percent

DIVIDEND YIELD

Average dividend yield in the past 3 years: 0.3 percent

DIVIDEND GROWTH

Increased dividend: 1 year

CONSISTENCY

Increased earnings per share: 7 of past 8 years
Increased sales: 8 consecutive years

SHAREHOLDER PERKS ★ ★

Good dividend reinvestment and stock purchase plan: voluntary stock purchase plan allows contributions of $30 to $5,000 per quarter.

HARLEY-DAVIDSON AT A GLANCE

Fiscal year ended: Dec. 31
Revenue and net income in $ millions

	1989	1990	1991	1992	1993	1994	5-year Growth Avg. Annual (%)	5-year Growth Total (%)
Revenue ($)	791	865	940	1,105	1,217	1,542	14	95
Net income ($)	32.6	37.8	37.0	53.8	77.6	104.3	26	220
Earnings/share ($)	.47	.54	.52	.76	.98	1.37	24	191
Div. per share ($)	–	–	–	–	.06	.14	–	–
Dividend yield (%)	–	–	–	–	0.3	0.5	–	–
Avg. PE ratio	8	9	18	19	20	18	–	–

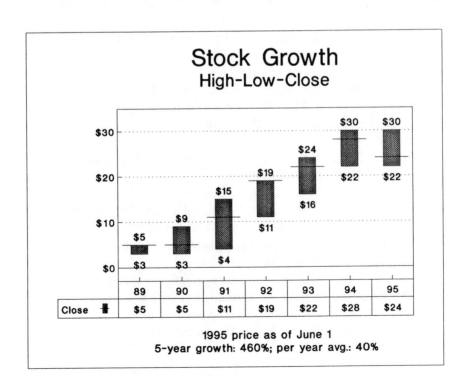

Stock Growth
High-Low-Close

	89	90	91	92	93	94	95
Close	$5	$5	$11	$19	$22	$28	$24

1995 price as of June 1
5-year growth: 460%; per year avg.: 40%

United HealthCare Corp.

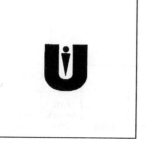

300 Opus Center
9900 Bren Road East
Minnetonka, MN 55343
612-936-1300

Chairman, President and CEO:
William W. McGuire, M.D.

Earnings Growth	★ ★ ★ ★	Dividend Growth	★ ★
Stock Growth	★ ★ ★ ★	Consistency	★ ★
Dividend Yield		Shareholder Perks	
NYSE—UNH		**Total**	**12 points**

Preventive medicine. Managed care. Cost containment. Accountability. All were key elements of the Great Health Care Reform Debate of 1994. And all are longstanding policies of United HealthCare.

Although the Clinton administration's Health Security Act failed to survive Congress, United HealthCare continues to draw from its formula of best practices to fuel one of the nation's fastest-growing health care management companies.

More than 2.5 million people are enrolled in the 21 health maintenance organizations (HMOs) the Minneapolis operation owns or manages in Minnesota, Illinois, Florida, Georgia, Tennessee and Iowa. Another 35 million in all 50 states are served by United HealthCare through such specialty services as prescription drug benefit programs and the National Transplant Network, which offers participants access to a network of health care facilities for transplant-related services.

Founded in 1974, the company has aggressively added HMOs to its stable. It is equally aggressive at controlling its own costs. Its medical-loss ratio, which measures medical costs as a percent of premium revenues, is one of the lowest in the business. To improve efficiency and reduce paperwork, United HealthCare has invested more than $130 million in recent years to develop the industry's most advanced information management systems.

United's management believes that regional, organized health care systems that were held up as a model during the health care debate can deliver quality, affordable health care to everyone and help reduce the billions of dollars in waste that continues to plague the nation's health system.

Utilization management is a cornerstone of United HealthCare's operations. The practice takes many forms—including programs to steer patients to the most appropriate care settings and away from expensive emergency room treatment when it's not needed. The company operates an around-the-clock "NurseLine" telephone information service which uses nurses to direct callers to proper medical attention. Company research showed that two-thirds of those who care for themselves with information provided by the service would otherwise have sought expensive emergency room care.

Hospitalization rates at United's health plans average only 67 admissions per 1,000 health plan commercial members, compared to 77 for the overall managed care industry. Average length of stay for a United member is 4.1 days versus the industry average of 4.8 days.

United HealthCare has taken a leading role in creating programs to treat mental illness and substance abuse and to assist its members in dealing with personal and workplace difficulties before they become serious health problems. Employers using United's mental health and substance abuse management services have reduced spending on this area from as much as 20 percent to as little as 5 percent of their overall health care costs. The company has 6,500 employees and 3,800 shareholders.

EARNINGS-PER-SHARE GROWTH ★ ★ ★ ★

Past 5 years: 617 percent (49 percent per year)
Past 10 years: 3,300 percent (41 percent per year)

STOCK GROWTH ★ ★ ★ ★

Past 10 years: 1,800 percent (34 percent per year)

Dollar growth: $10,000 over 10 years (including reinvested dividends) would have grown to $190,000
Average annual compounded rate of return (including reinvested dividends): 34 percent

DIVIDEND YIELD

Average dividend yield in the past 3 years: 0.07 percent

DIVIDEND GROWTH   ★ ★

Increased dividend: 2 consecutive years
Past 5-year increase: 200 percent (25 percent per year)

CONSISTENCY   ★ ★

Increased earnings per share: 7 consecutive years
Increased sales: 5 consecutive years

SHAREHOLDER PERKS

The company offers no dividend reinvestment and stock purchase plan, nor does it provide any other shareholder perks.

UNITED HEALTHCARE AT A GLANCE

Fiscal year ended: Dec. 31
Revenue and net income in $ millions

	1989	1990	1991	1992	1993	1994	5-year Growth Avg. Annual (%)	5-year Growth Total (%)
Revenue ($)	551	1,056	1,416	2,201	3,115	3,769	42	584
Net income ($)	20.9	39.5	83.3	132.2	214.0	290.1	70	1,390
Earnings/share ($)	.23	.35	.61	.79	1.24	1.65	49	617
Div. per share ($)	–	.01	.01	.02	.02	.03	25	200
Dividend yield (%)	–	.3	.1	.03	0.04	.1	—	—
Avg. PE ratio	15.0	12.5	19.5	27.4	24.7	26.2	—	—

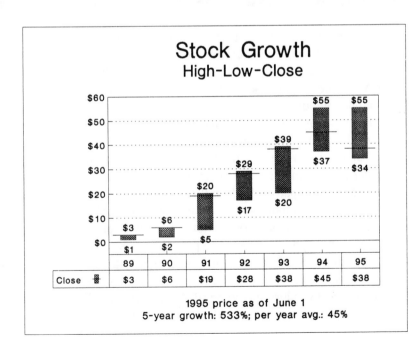

Stock Growth
High-Low-Close

	89	90	91	92	93	94	95
Close	$3	$6	$19	$28	$38	$45	$38

1995 price as of June 1
5-year growth: 533%; per year avg.: 45%

Computer Associates International, Inc.

One Computer Associates Plaza
Islandia, NY 11788-7000
516-342-5224

Chairman and CEO: Charles B. Wang
President and COO: Sanjay Kumar

Earnings Growth	★ ★ ★	Dividend Growth	★
Stock Growth	★ ★ ★ ★	Consistency	★ ★ ★
Dividend Yield	★	Shareholder Perks	
NYSE—CA		**Total**	**12 points**

When Computer Associates first opened for business in 1976, its entire mission was to develop operating software for large IBM mainframe computers. But as American industry shifted to smaller computers, Computer Associates began expanding its product base to include applications for smaller computers as well.

The company now puts out more than 300 software applications for large, medium and small computers and networks. While Computer Associates has been working to add new products for the smaller end of the computer market, mainframe software sales still account for about three-quarters of the company's $2.15 billion in annual revenue.

Most of the company's software is designed to enhance data processing functions by providing tools to measure and improve computer hardware and software performance and programmer productivity.

The company also makes database management, business applications and graphics software for mainframes, midrange and desktop computers from a variety of vendors, including IBM, DEC, Hewlett-Packard, Amdahl, Data General, Sun, Sequent, Tandem, Compaq and Apple.

The company's hottest software product is the CA-Unicenter software, originally designed to enhance the computer "client/server environment" for Hewlett-Packard hardware.

The Islandia, New York, operation has offices in 30 countries. Foreign sales (outside North America) account for about 46 percent of total revenue. The company has 7,000 employees and 10,000 shareholders.

EARNINGS-PER-SHARE GROWTH

Past 5 years: 129 percent (18 percent per year)
Past 10 years: 1,460 percent (32 percent per year)

STOCK GROWTH

Past 10 years: 1,635 percent (33 percent per year)
Dollar growth: $10,000 over 10 years (including reinvested dividends) would have grown to $180,000
Average annual compounded rate of return (including reinvested dividends): 33 percent

DIVIDEND YIELD ★

Average dividend yield in the past 3 years: 0.7 percent

DIVIDEND GROWTH ★

Increased dividend: 1 year
Past 5-year increase: 40 percent (7 percent per year)

CONSISTENCY ★★★

Increased earnings per share: 9 of past 10 years
Increased sales: 13 consecutive years

SHAREHOLDER PERKS

The company offers no dividend reinvestment plan, nor does it provide any other shareholder perks.

COMPUTER ASSOCIATES AT A GLANCE

Fiscal year ended: March 31
Revenue and net income in $ millions

	1989	1990	1991	1992	1993	1994	5-year Growth Avg. Annual (%)	5-year Growth Total (%)
Revenue ($)	925.6	1,244.4	1,300.6	1,508.8	1,841.0	2,149.0	18	132
Net income ($)	164	158	159	163	246	401	20	144
Earnings/share ($)	1.02	.85	.86	.92	1.44	2.34	18	129
Div. per share ($)	–	–	.10	.10	.10	.14	7	40
Dividend yield (%)	–	–	1.0	1.0	.6	.4	—	—
Avg. PE ratio	14.7	18.4	11.4	11.4	12.1	14.3	—	—

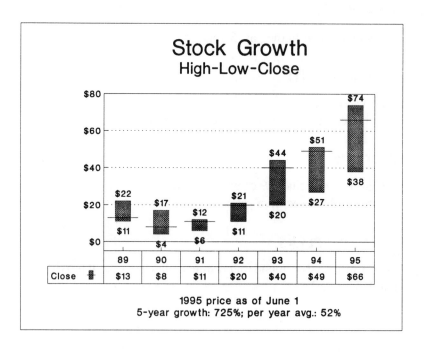

Stock Growth
High-Low-Close

	89	90	91	92	93	94	95
Close	$13	$8	$11	$20	$40	$49	$66

1995 price as of June 1
5-year growth: 725%; per year avg.: 52%

A. Schulman,

3550 W. Market St.
Akron, OH 44333
216-666-3751

Chairman: Robert A. Stefanko
President and CEO: Terry L. Haines

Earnings Growth		Dividend Growth	★ ★ ★ ★
Stock Growth	★ ★ ★ ★	Consistency	★ ★ ★
Dividend Yield	★	Shareholder Perks	
NASDAQ—SHLM		**Total**	**12 points**

Plastic has come a long way from its brittle beginnings. It's now used for car parts, baseball helmets, computer casings, lawn furniture and thousands of other applications that require durability, flexibility and economy. This golden age of plastics has been a remarkable era of opportunity for plastics maker A. Schulman.

The Akron-based manufacturer has posted increased earnings 12 of the past 13 years. Its foreign operations continue to expand and now account for nearly 70 percent of the company's $749 million in annual sales.

Schulman provides the plastic resins for a vast range of products and, in many cases, also provides the chemical concentrate that give the plastics their color. Among those products are:

- Automotive parts such as window seals, bumper guards, air ducts, steering wheels, fan shrouds, valance panels and other automotive components.
- Consumer products such as toys, pens, outdoor furniture, disposable diapers, shelving, videocassettes, batteries and toys;

- Electrical and electronic products such as telephone parts, wire insulation, transformers, outdoor lighting and wire and cable insulation;
- Packaging for foods, soap, flowers and household items;
- Office equipment such as computer cases and stack trays; and
- Agricultural products such as greenhouse coverings.

Schulman also manufactures flame retardants used in such applications as telephone system terminal blocks, color television tube covers, appliance housings and electrical components. The company, founded in 1928, has about 1,800 employees and 1,450 shareholders.

EARNINGS-PER-SHARE GROWTH

Past 5 years: 45 percent (8 percent per year)
Past 10 years: 297 percent (15 percent per year)

STOCK GROWTH ★ ★ ★ ★

Past 10 years: 841 percent (25 percent per year)
Dollar growth: $10,000 over 10 years (including reinvested dividends) would have grown to $102,000
Average annual compounded rate of return (including reinvested dividends): 26 percent

DIVIDEND YIELD ★

Average dividend yield in the past 3 years: 1.1 percent

DIVIDEND GROWTH ★ ★ ★ ★

Increased dividend: 12 consecutive years
Past 5-year increase: 107 percent (16 percent per year)

CONSISTENCY ★ ★ ★

Increased earnings per share: 9 of past 10 years
Increased sales: 8 of past 10 years

SHAREHOLDER PERKS

The company has no dividend reinvestment plan, nor does it offer any other shareholder perks.

A. SCHULMAN AT A GLANCE

Fiscal year ended: Aug. 31
Revenue and net income in $ millions

	1989	1990	1991	1992	1993	1994	5-year Growth Avg. Annual (%)	Total (%)
Revenue ($)	624.4	678.6	736.0	732.2	685.1	748.8	4	20
Net income ($)	31	36	42	44	37	45	8	45
Earnings/share ($)	.82	.96	1.14	1.18	1.04	1.19	8	45
Div. per share ($)	.14	.15	.19	.22	.25	.29	16	107
Dividend yield (%)	1.3	1.2	1.1	0.9	1.1	1.2	—	—
Avg. PE ratio	12.6	13.5	16.5	20.1	22.4	21.0	—	—

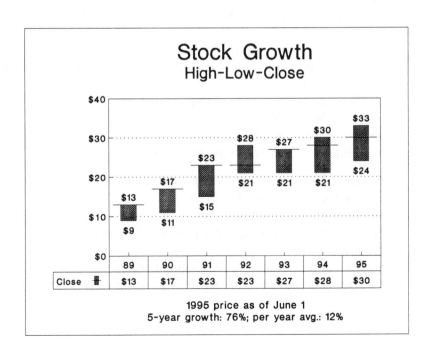

Stock Growth
High-Low-Close

Close	89	90	91	92	93	94	95
	$13	$17	$23	$23	$27	$28	$30

1995 price as of June 1
5-year growth: 76%; per year avg.: 12%

69

Nordson Corp.

28601 Clemens Road
Westlake, OH 44145
216-892-1580

Chairman: Eric T. Nord
President and CEO: William P. Madar

Earnings Growth		Dividend Growth	★ ★ ★
Stock Growth	★ ★ ★ ★	Consistency	★ ★
Dividend Yield	★	Shareholder Perks	★ ★
NASDAQ—NDSN		**Total**	**12 points**

It's a sticky business, but Nordson has prospered over the years by producing a growing line of industrial dispensing systems for adhesives, sealants and coatings.

The Ohio-based operation makes products for a broad range of industrial customers, from bookbinders and packagers to automotive and appliance manufacturers.

The company has international divisions in Europe, Japan and Australia, and sales offices in 30 other countries. Foreign sales account for nearly 60 percent of Nordson's $506 million in annual revenue.

The company breaks its operations into these 10 segments:

- **Packaging**. The firm makes automated hot-melt adhesive dispensing systems for sealing cartons and cases.
- **Product assembly**. Nordson manufactures adhesive and sealant dispensing systems for bonding plastic, metal and wood products in a wide range of industries.
- **Nonwovens**. The company makes equipment for applying adhesives and liquids in the assembly of diapers and feminine hygiene products.

- **Converting**. The firm makes coating and laminating systems used to manufacture continuous-roll goods such as back-coated textiles, medical disposables and automotive body cloth.
- **Advanced gasketing**. Nordson produces custom-engineered systems to dispense foamed adhesives and sealants in gaskets for automotive components, appliances and electrical enclosures.
- **Powder coating**. The company makes electrostatic spray systems for applying powder paints and coatings to appliances, automotive components and other applications.
- **Liquid finishing**. The firm makes electrostatic spray systems for applying paints and coatings to plastic, metal and wood products.
- **Automotive**. Nordson creates liquid and powder finishing systems for spray-coating automotive parts. It also makes adhesive dispensing systems for bonding glass and sealing interior seams.
- **Container coating**. It makes equipment for adding coatings to food and beverage metal containers.
- **Electronics**. Nordson manufactures equipment for applying protective coatings and solder flux to printed circuit boards and electronic assemblies.

Founded in 1954, Nordson has 3,200 employees and 2,900 shareholders.

EARNINGS-PER-SHARE GROWTH

Past 5 years: 39 percent (7 percent per year)
Past 10 years: 345 percent (16 percent per year)

STOCK GROWTH   ★ ★ ★ ★

Past 10 years: 602 percent (21.5 percent per year)
Dollar growth: $10,000 over 10 years (including reinvested dividends) would have grown to $80,000
Average annual compounded rate of return (including reinvested dividends): 23 percent

DIVIDEND YIELD   ★

Average dividend yield in the past 3 years: 1 percent

DIVIDEND GROWTH   ★ ★ ★

Increased dividend: 13 consecutive years
Past 5-year increase: 75 percent (12 percent per year)

CONSISTENCY   ★ ★

Increased earnings per share: 8 of past 10 years
Increased sales: 9 consecutive years

SHAREHOLDER PERKS   ★ ★

Good dividend reinvestment and stock purchase plan: voluntary stock
purchase plan allows contributions of $10 to $4,000 per quarter.

NORDSON AT A GLANCE

Fiscal year ended: Oct. 31
Revenue and net income in $ millions

	1989	1990	1991	1992	1993	1994	5-year Growth Avg. Annual (%)	Total (%)
Revenue ($)	282,098	344,904	387,962	425,618	461,557	506,692	13	80
Net income ($)	34,187	29,346	33,787	39,537	35,991	46,654	7	36
Earnings/share ($)	1.76	1.52	1.77	2.03	2.13	2.45	7	39
Div. per share ($)	.32	.36	.40	.44	.48	.56	12	75
Dividend yield (%)	1.3	1.6	1.5	.9	1.1	1.0	—	—
Avg. PE ratio	14	15	15	23	21	23	—	—

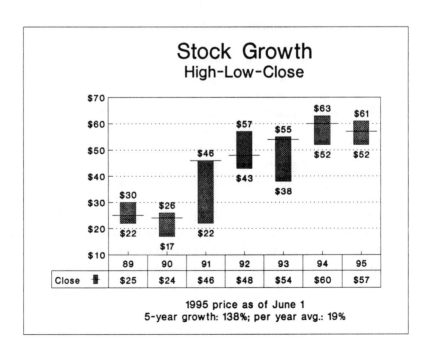

Stock Growth
High-Low-Close

	89	90	91	92	93	94	95
Close	$25	$24	$46	$48	$54	$60	$57

1995 price as of June 1
5-year growth: 138%; per year avg.: 19%

International Flavors & Fragrances, Inc.

521 W. 57th St.
New York, NY 10019-2960
212-765-5500

Chairman and President: Eugene P. Grisanti

Earnings Growth	★	Dividend Growth	★ ★ ★
Stock Growth	★ ★	Consistency	★ ★ ★
Dividend Yield	★ ★ ★	Shareholder Perks	★ ★ ★
NYSE—IFF		**Total**	**12 points**

As a growing legion of health-conscious consumers scans the grocery shelves for healthier alternatives, food companies have been turning increasingly to International Flavors & Fragrances (IFF) to spice up their otherwise bland low-fat, low-calorie offerings.

IFF specializes in developing tastes and scents for foods, beverages, soaps, perfumes and other products. It has established a growing business helping food companies turn their diet yogurt, snacks, desserts, meat alternatives and other low-calorie concoctions into tempting treats.

The New York–based manufacturer sells its flavor products primarily to the food, beverage and tobacco industries.

The company also produces extracts, concentrated juices and concentrates derived from various fruits, vegetables, nuts, herbs and spices. Flavors account for 41 percent of IFF's $1.3 billion in annual revenue.

The other part of IFF's business is its fragrances, which account for 59 percent of total revenue. It sells its scents primarily to manufacturers of consumer products such as soaps, detergents, cosmetic creams, lotions and powders, lipsticks, after-shave lotions, deodorants, hair preparations, air fresheners, perfumes and colognes.

IFF has 27 fragrance and flavor laboratories in 21 countries. The company has operations in more than 50 countries, drawing about 68 percent of its sales come from outside North America.

The company makes its products from both synthetic and natural compounds such as flowers, fruits and other botanical and animal products. Founded in 1909, IFF has 4,400 employees and 4,600 shareholders.

EARNINGS-PER-SHARE GROWTH ★

Past 5 years: 66 percent (11 percent per year)
Past 10 years: 222 percent (12 percent per year)

STOCK GROWTH ★ ★

Past 10 years: 364 percent (17 percent per year)
Dollar growth: $10,000 over 10 years (including reinvested dividends) would have grown to $63,000
Average annual compounded rate of return (including reinvested dividends): 20 percent

DIVIDEND YIELD ★ ★ ★

Average dividend yield in the past 3 years: 2.7 percent

DIVIDEND GROWTH ★ ★ ★

Increased dividend: 34 consecutive years
Past 5-year increase: 64 percent (10 percent per year)

CONSISTENCY ★ ★ ★

Increased earnings per share: 9 consecutive years
Increased sales: 12 consecutive years

SHAREHOLDER PERKS

The company offers no dividend reinvestment plan, nor does it provide any other special perks for its shareholders.

INTERNATIONAL FLAVORS & FRAGRANCES AT A GLANCE

Fiscal year ended: Dec. 31
Revenue and net income in $ millions

	1989	1990	1991	1992	1993	1994	5-year Growth Avg. Annual (%)	Total (%)
Revenue ($)	869.5	962.8	1,016.9	1,126.4	1,188.6	1,315.2	9	51
Net income ($)	138.5	157	169	171	202.5	226	10	63
Earnings/share ($)	1.22	1.37	1.47	1.48	1.78	2.03	11	66
Div. per share ($)	.66	.74	.83	.93	1.02	1.08	10	64
Dividend yield (%)	3.4	3.4	3.0	2.6	2.7	2.8	—	—
Avg. PE ratio	15.8	16.0	18.8	21.5	20.8	19.9	—	—

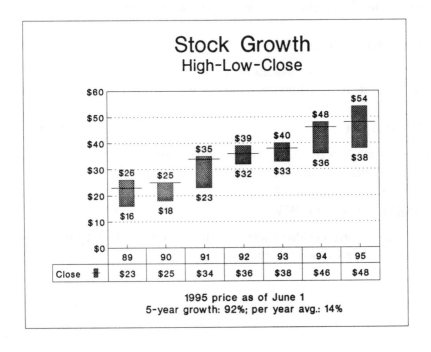

Stock Growth
High-Low-Close

	89	90	91	92	93	94	95
Close	$23	$25	$34	$36	$38	$46	$48

1995 price as of June 1
5-year growth: 92%; per year avg.: 14%

Sensormatic Electronics Corp.

Sensormatic

500 N.W. 12th Ave.
Deerfield Beach, FL 33442-1795
305-420-2000

Chairman, President and CEO: Ronald G. Assaf

Earnings Growth	★ ★ ★ ★	Dividend Growth	★ ★
Stock Growth	★ ★ ★	Consistency	★ ★
Dividend Yield	★	Shareholder Perks	
NYSE—SRM		**Total**	**12 points**

Shoplifting may be the bane of the retail business, but it's been a boon to Sensormatic Electronics. Sensormatic specializes in manufacturing electronic surveillance equipment and security tags for retailers, offices and manufacturing facilities. The Deerfield Beach, Florida, operation makes electronic article surveillance and electronic asset protection systems (including the reusable tags and disposable labels used with those systems), closed-circuit television systems and access control systems.

Sensormatic's equipment is used not only to deter shoplifting, but also to discourage internal or other theft in a wide variety of clothing and hard goods retail stores and in commercial and industrial facilities.

The company has enjoyed exceptional growth, with 28 consecutive quarters of revenue growth of 20 percent or more. The company markets its products throughout North America, Europe and South America. It also has sales operations in Japan, Taiwan, Indonesia and South Africa. Foreign sales account for 46 percent of the firm's $656 million in annual revenue.

Its systems typically consist of electronic detection units housed in pedestals or overhead units or concealed in the walls, ceilings or floors.

The units are also placed at exits of stores, departments within stores or at checkout aisles. These devices are used in conjunction with specially designed tabs and labels that are affixed to the merchandise.

Some of the company's newer applications are also used by non-retail businesses to protect equipment such as personal computers, fax and copy machines. Its systems also protect newborns in hospitals.

Sensormatic even offers specialized systems for the protection of newborn infants in hospitals and patients in long-term care facilities.

The company's closed-circuit monitoring systems are used for retail and non-retail businesses. Sensormatic has 5,500 employees and 4,700 shareholders.

EARNINGS-PER-SHARE GROWTH   ★ ★ ★ ★

Past 5 years: 183 percent (23 percent per year)
Past 10 years: 170 percent (10.5 percent per year)

STOCK GROWTH   ★ ★ ★

Past 10 years: 447 percent (18.5 percent per year)
Dollar growth: $10,000 over 10 years (including reinvested dividends) would have grown to $60,000
Average annual compounded rate of return (including reinvested dividends): 19.5 percent

DIVIDEND YIELD   ★

Average dividend yield in the past 3 years: 0.9 percent

DIVIDEND GROWTH   ★ ★

Increased dividend: 1 year
Past 5-year increase: 600 percent (47 percent per year)

CONSISTENCY   ★ ★

Increased earnings per share: 8 consecutive years
Increased sales: 8 consecutive years

SHAREHOLDER PERKS

The company offers no dividend reinvestment and stock purchase plan, nor does it provide any other shareholder perks.

SENSORMATIC ELECTRONICS AT A GLANCE

Fiscal year ended: June 30
Revenue and net income in $ millions

	1989	1990	1991	1992	1993	1994	5-year Growth Avg. Annual (%)	5-year Growth Total (%)
Revenue ($)	150.9	191.3	239.2	309.9	487.3	656.0	34	330
Net income ($)	16.7	20.0	24.7	31.5	54.1	72.1	34	330
Earnings/share ($)	.40	.48	.60	.73	.93	1.13	23	183
Div. per share ($)	.03	.12	.20	.20	.20	.21	47	600
Dividend yield (%)	.5	1.5	1.8	1.2	0.7	0.7	—	—
Avg. PE ratio	17.0	17.5	18.8	23.5	24.2	27.8	—	—

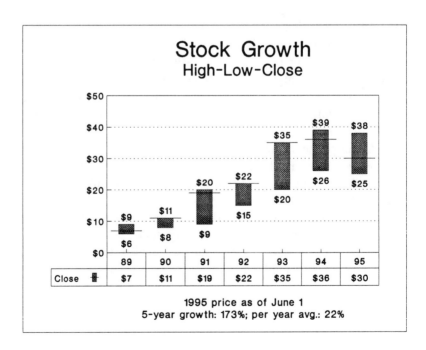

Stock Growth
High-Low-Close

Close	$7	$11	$19	$22	$35	$36	$30
	89	90	91	92	93	94	95

1995 price as of June 1
5-year growth: 173%; per year avg.: 22%

Cincinnati Financial Corp.

6200 S. Gilmore Road
Fairfield, OH 45014
513-870-2000

Chairman: J. J. Schiff, Jr.
President and CEO: Robert B. Morgan

Earnings Growth	★	Dividend Growth	★ ★ ★
Stock Growth	★ ★	Consistency	★ ★
Dividend Yield	★ ★	Shareholder Perks	★ ★
NASDAQ—CINF		**Total**	**12 points**

True to its Midwestern roots, Cincinnati Financial Corp. is a solid, conservative holding company whose units write several lines of insurance throughout America's heartland, where the ground never quakes and a hurricane's devastating winds never blow.

Cincinnati's three property and casualty subsidiaries are considered to be among the best regional operations in the insurance business. Because the subsidiaries don't write policies in natural-disaster–prone coastal states, Cincinnati Financial rarely has to absorb the costs associated with major disasters.

Although the Midwest is vulnerable to flooding, Cincinnati Financial has never paid a claim because it does not market flood insurance. What it does sell is tightly underwritten property and casualty, life and health, workers' compensation and other policies.

Its strict underwriting standards are understandable considering employees own a large stake of the company stock. Cost controls have helped keep Cincinnati Financial's productivity level in the upper ranks of the insurance industry and have allowed the firm to increase its dividend 34 years in a row.

Cincinnati Financial's three property and casualty companies are Cincinnati Insurance, Cincinnati Casualty and Cincinnati Indemnity. Life and health policies are written through the Cincinnati Life Insurance Co.

Cincinnati Financial invests heavily in the training of the approximately 1,000 independent agents who sell its products. Training focuses on the theme of providing extraordinary customer service. Staff development ranges from computer training to claims and underwriting classes as well as self-study courses from the leading insurance institutes.

The company management believes that making it easier for local agents to do business through training and support pays off in the long run through the stronger customer and community relationships the agents can strike. Independent consumer surveys continue to rate Cincinnati Financial's claim service higher than any other agent-represented company.

A fifth subsidiary, CFC Investment Co., writes leases and loans on office and medical equipment, computers, vehicles and other types of equipment. It also manages corporately owned real estate, including the unit's headquarters building and three office buildings held for investment purposes.

About 31 percent of Cincinnati Financial's premiums are for automobile insurance, 22 percent for multi-peril, and 18 percent for workers' compensation. The remaining 29 percent consist of other commercial policies. The company has 2,000 employees and 7,300 shareholders.

EARNINGS-PER-SHARE GROWTH ★

Past 5 years: 68 percent (11 percent per year)
Past 10 years: 447 percent (16 percent per year)

STOCK GROWTH ★ ★

Past 10 years: 268 percent (14 percent per year)
Dollar growth: $10,000 over 10 years (including reinvested dividends) would have grown to $47,000
Average annual compounded rate of return (including reinvested dividends): 17 percent

DIVIDEND YIELD   ★ ★

Average dividend yield in the past 3 years: 2.2 percent

DIVIDEND GROWTH   ★ ★ ★

Increased dividend: 34 consecutive years
Past 5-year increase: 78 percent (12 percent per year)

CONSISTENCY   ★ ★

Increased earnings per share: 8 of past 10 years
Increased premiums earned: 10 straight years

SHAREHOLDER PERKS   ★ ★

Good dividend reinvestment and stock purchase plan: voluntary stock
purchase plan allows contributions of $25 to $1,000 per month. Participants
are assessed a nominal fee of $1 to $3 per transaction.

CINCINNATI FINANCIAL AT A GLANCE

Fiscal year ended: Dec. 31
Revenue and net income in $ millions

	1989	1990	1991	1992	1993	1994	5-year Growth Avg. Annual (%)	5-year Growth Total (%)
Revenue ($)	974	1,049	1,161	1,304	1,442	1,513	9	55
Net income ($)	114	129	146	171	216	201	12	76
Earnings/share ($)	2.33	2.61	2.94	3.39	4.20	3.91	11	68
Div. per share ($)	.72	.81	.91	1.03	1.12	1.28	12	78
Dividend yield (%)	3.1	3.1	2.5	2.2	1.9	2.4	—	—
Avg. PE ratio	10.1	10.0	12.1	14.0	14.9	13.5	—	—

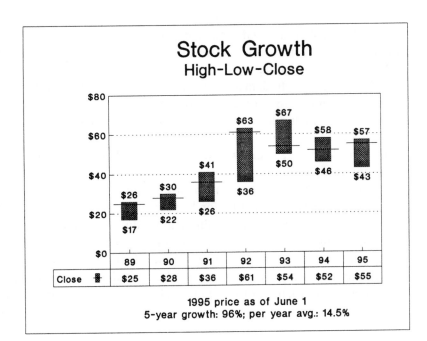

Stock Growth
High-Low-Close

Close	89	90	91	92	93	94	95
	$25	$28	$36	$61	$54	$52	$55

1995 price as of June 1
5-year growth: 96%; per year avg.: 14.5%

H. J. Heinz Company

600 Grant St.
P. O. Box 57
Pittsburgh, PA 15320-0057
412-456-5700

Chairman, President and CEO:
Anthony J. F. O'Reilly

Earnings Growth		Dividend Growth	★ ★ ★
Stock Growth	★	Consistency	★ ★ ★
Dividend Yield	★ ★ ★	Shareholder Perks	★ ★
NYSE—HNZ		**Total**	**12 points**

Pet food, diet food, baby food and tuna—Heinz is a lot more than ketchup. In fact, the Pittsburgh-based foods company is also the nation's leading producer of frozen potatoes. Its Ore-Ida brand holds a 48 percent of the U.S. frozen spuds market.

The company's trademark ketchup accounts for 50 percent of all ketchup sold in the United States. Several other Heinz segments are also market leaders, including Star-Kist Tuna, which holds a 40 percent share of the U.S. tuna market; 9 Lives cat food, which holds a 26 percent market share; and Weight Watchers, which accounts for 51 percent of the weight management market.

Heinz ketchup and other condiments remain the largest part of the company's business, accounting for 19 percent of the firm's $7.8 billion in sales. The company has marketing and production operations world-wide, generating about 50 percent of its total revenue abroad.

One of its fastest growing areas is baby food, which accounts for 9 percent of the company's revenue. In the United States, the company offers about 130 varieties of Heinz brand baby food. The company has also made some acquisitions abroad to bolster its international baby food sales. Among its largest areas of growth are China, India and the Pacific Rim.

The company's other leading segment is its Star-Kist Tuna and other sea foods, which account for about 10 percent of total revenue.

The Heinz pet food division continues to expand. The firm recently announced intentions of acquiring the Quaker Oats North American pet foods division. That would add Kibbles 'n Bits and Cycle to the company's other list of pet foods, including 9 Lives, Vets, Recipe and Skippy Premium.

The balance of the company's sales comes from its Weight Watchers programs and diet foods and from its broad variety of other foods. Heinz is a leading producer of canned soup, desserts, beans, sauces, pasta, candy, pickles, chilled salads, rice cakes, frozen meats, vinegar, flavored rice products and other processed foods. The company has 34,000 employees and 49,000 shareholders.

EARNINGS-PER-SHARE GROWTH

Past 5 years: 41 percent (7 percent per year)
Past 10 years: 142 percent (9 percent per year)

STOCK GROWTH ★

Past 10 years: 201 percent (12 percent per year)
Dollar growth: $10,000 over 10 years (including reinvested dividends) would have grown to $40,000
Average annual compounded rate of return (including reinvested dividends): 15 percent

DIVIDEND YIELD ★ ★ ★

Average dividend yield in the past 3 years: 3.0 percent

DIVIDEND GROWTH ★ ★ ★

Increased dividend: Every year since 1967
Past 5-year increase: 84 percent (13 percent per year)

CONSISTENCY   ★ ★ ★

Increased earnings per share: 9 of past 10 years
Increased sales: 9 of past 10 years

SHAREHOLDER PERKS

Good dividend reinvestment and stock purchase plan: voluntary stock purchase plan allows contributions of $25 to $5,000 per month.

Shareholders who attend the annual meeting receive a gift package of some of the company's newer products.

The company puts out one of corporate America's best quarterly reports. The reports, which generally run about 30 pages, are packed with new product information and company developments. They also occasionally carry special offers or product discounts for Heinz shareholders.

H. J. HEINZ AT A GLANCE

Fiscal year ended: April 30
Revenue and net income in $ millions

	1989	1990	1991	1992	1993	1994	5-year Growth Avg. Annual (%)	Total (%)
Revenue ($)	5,800.8	6,085.7	6,647.1	6,581.9	7,103.4	7,046.7	4	20
Net income ($)	440	504	568	638	530	603	6.5	37
Earnings/share ($)	1.67	1.90	2.13	2.40	2.04	2.35	7	41
Div. per share ($)	.70	.81	.93	1.05	1.17	1.29	13	84
Dividend yield (%)	3.0	2.3	2.7	2.7	2.7	3.6	—	—
Avg. PE ratio	16.0	16	16	21	16	17	—	—

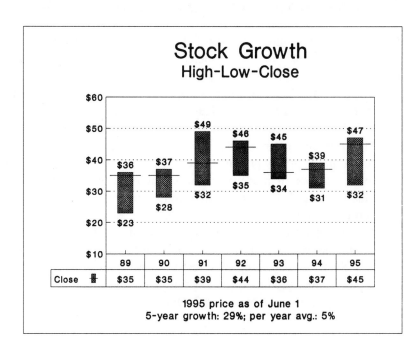

Stock Growth
High-Low-Close

Close	89	90	91	92	93	94	95
	$35	$35	$39	$44	$36	$37	$45

1995 price as of June 1
5-year growth: 29%; per year avg.: 5%

Pitney Bowes, Inc.

⊞ Pitney Bowes

Walter H. Wheeler Drive
Stamford, CT 06926
203-356-5000

Chairman, President and CEO: George B. Harvey

Earnings Growth		Dividend Growth	★ ★ ★ ★
Stock Growth	★	Consistency	★ ★ ★
Dividend Yield	★ ★	Shareholder Perks	★ ★
NYSE—PBI		**Total**	**12 points**

Pitney Bowes does more than just help businesses get the mail out. The world's largest maker of postage meters and mailing equipment also helps its customers with office systems, logistics and facilities management.

The company has long outgrown the days when it churned out manually operated postage meters. Nearly all of its equipment is software controlled and can be connected to a customer's internal computer network.

Pitney, which has invested more than half a billion dollars in research and development of new products in recent years, has made a special study of the key trends in modern business. Called The Study Group, the organization helps Pitney get a better understanding of its customers and position itself for the future.

The 75-year-old company refined its focus in the fall of 1994 by announcing its was divesting its Dictaphone Corporation and Monarch Marking Systems. The company's restructuring process also calls for the phase-out of older product lines and continued investment in technology products such as its state-of-the art Paragon Mailing Processor System.

The unit, which can sort and fold material as well as address, weigh and stamp envelopes, has become a mainstay in many corporate mailrooms where cost control are the watchwords. The Paragon was recently introduced in Germany and France—markets that Pitney believes hold enormous potential for the product.

About 71 percent of Pitney's $3.27 billion in annual revenues comes from its business equipment segment, which includes mailing systems, shipping and weighing systems, fax machines and copiers.

Pitney is the only facsimile systems supplier in the United States that markets exclusively through its own direct sales force. The company concentrates its copier sales on larger corporations with multiunit installations. It endears itself to the large companies with preventive maintenance program covering all elements of copier performance.

Pitney's Management Services unit has been helping a growing number of companies in the retail industry integrate their software systems. The acquisition of Ameriscribe has significantly increased the unit's size and scope and better positioned Pitney in the market for on-site management of business support services.

Pitney offers management services for a variety of business support functions such as mail centers, copy centers, fax services and electronic printing. Targeted customers are large industrial companies, banking and financial institutions, and services organizations such as law firms and accounting firms. Management services and business supplies contribute about 12 percent of annual sales.

The company's financial services unit provides lease financing programs for customers who use products marketed by Pitney Bowes companies. Financial services generate about 17 percent of total revenue. Pitney has 32,500 employees and 31,500 shareholders.

EARNINGS-PER-SHARE GROWTH

Past 5 years: 39 percent (7 percent per year)
Past 10 years: 151 percent (10 percent per year)

STOCK GROWTH

Past 10 years: 213 percent (12 percent per year)

Dollar growth: $10,000 over 10 years (including reinvested dividends) would have grown to $39,000
Average annual compounded rate of return (including reinvested dividends): 14.5 percent

DIVIDEND YIELD   ★ ★

Average dividend yield in the past 3 years: 2.4 percent

DIVIDEND GROWTH   ★ ★ ★ ★

Increased dividend: 12 consecutive years
Past 5-year increase: 100 percent (15 percent per year)

CONSISTENCY   ★ ★ ★

Increased earnings per share: 9 of past 10 years
Increased sales: 9 of past 10 years

SHAREHOLDER PERKS   ★ ★

Good dividend reinvestment and stock purchase plan: voluntary stock purchase plan allows contributions of $100 to $3,000 per quarter.

PITNEY BOWES AT A GLANCE

Fiscal year ended: Dec. 31
Revenue and net income in $ millions

	1989	1990	1991	1992	1993	1994	5-year Growth Avg. Annual (%)	Total (%)
Revenue ($)	2,876	3,196	3,333	3,434	3,543	3,271	2.5	14
Net income ($)	253	259	288	312	353	348	7	38
Earnings/share ($)	1.59	1.62	1.80	1.96	2.22	2.21	7	39
Div. per share ($)	.52	.60	.68	.78	.90	1.04	15	100
Dividend yield (%)	2.2	2.8	2.5	2.3	2.2	2.7	—	—
Avg. PE ratio	16	13	15.5	17	18	17.5	—	—

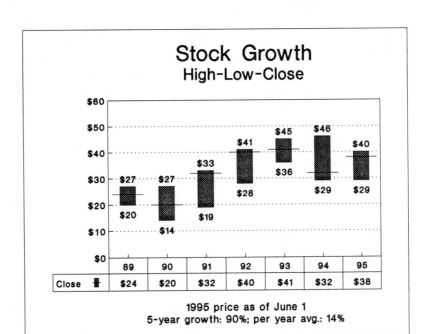

Stock Growth
High-Low-Close

Close	$24	$20	$32	$40	$41	$32	$38

1995 price as of June 1
5-year growth: 90%; per year avg.: 14%

Emerson Electric Co.

8000 West Florissant Ave.
P. O. Box 4100
St. Louis, MO 63136-8506
314-553-2000

Chairman and CEO: Charles F. Knight

Earnings Growth		Dividend Growth	★ ★
Stock Growth	★	Consistency	★ ★ ★ ★
Dividend Yield	★ ★ ★	Shareholder Perks	★ ★
NYSE—EMR		**Total**	**12 points**

After 37 consecutive years of record profits, Emerson Electric is not about to rest on its laurels. In 1994 alone, the St. Louis–based manufacturer introduced 345 new products. About 100 of those items were expected to generate at least $8 million in the first five years after their introduction.

Emerson relies on new product sales (products introduced within the past five years) for 24 percent of its $8.6 billion in annual sales.

The company produces a wide range of electrical equipment, including motors for industrial and heavy commercial applications, industrial automation equipment, gear drives, power distribution equipment and temperature and environmental control systems.

Emerson divides its operations into two key segments:

- **Commercial and industrial components and systems** (57.5 percent of revenue). The company manufactures process control instruments and systems, industrial motors and drives, industrial machinery and computer support products.
- **Appliance and construction-related components** (42.5 percent of revenue). Emerson manufactures a wide range of small motors; appliance components; heating, ventilating and air-conditioning components; refrigeration and comfort control components; timers; switches; humidifiers; exhaust fans; wrenches; pipe cutters and related equipment. Among its consumer products are portable and stationary power tools,

hobby tools, hand tools, garbage disposers, hot water dispensers, dishwasher, ladders and shop vacuums.

Emerson sells its products worldwide. Foreign sales account for 38 percent of the company's total revenue.

Emerson Electric was founded by John Wesley Emerson in 1890—shortly after Thomas A. Edison installed his first electrical generators. In his small St. Louis shop, Emerson manufactured room fans, ceiling fans and electrical motors. Today, Emerson Electric has about 72,000 employees and 33,000 shareholders.

EARNINGS-PER-SHARE GROWTH

Past 5 years: 34 percent (6 percent per year)
Past 10 years: 107 percent (7.5 percent per year)

STOCK GROWTH ★

Past 10 years: 160 percent (10 percent per year)
Dollar growth: $10,000 over 10 years (including reinvested dividends) would have grown to $34,000
Average annual compounded rate of return (including reinvested dividends): 13 percent

DIVIDEND YIELD ★ ★ ★

Average dividend yield in the past 3 years: 2.6 percent

DIVIDEND GROWTH ★ ★

Increased dividend: 38 consecutive years
Past 5-year increase: 39 percent (7 percent per year)

CONSISTENCY ★ ★ ★ ★

Increased earnings per share: 37 consecutive years
Increased sales: 9 of past 10 years

SHAREHOLDER PERKS ★ ★

Good dividend reinvestment and stock purchase plan: voluntary stock purchase plan allows contributions of $25 to $2,500 per quarter.

EMERSON ELECTRIC AT A GLANCE

Fiscal year ended: Sept. 31
Revenue and net income in $ millions

	1989	1990	1991	1992	1993	1994	5-year Growth Avg. Annual (%)	5-year Growth Total (%)
Revenue ($)	7,071.3	7,573.4	7,427.0	7,706.0	8,173.8	8,607.2	4	22
Net income ($)	588.0	613.2	631.9	662.9	708.1	788.5	6	34
Earnings/share ($)	2.63	2.75	2.83	2.96	3.15	3.52	6	34
Div. per share ($)	1.12	1.26	1.32	1.38	1.44	1.56	7	39
Dividend yield (%)	3.4	3.4	3.2	2.7	2.6	2.8	—	—
Avg. PE ratio	12.4	13.9	15.1	17.2	18.1	17.0	—	—

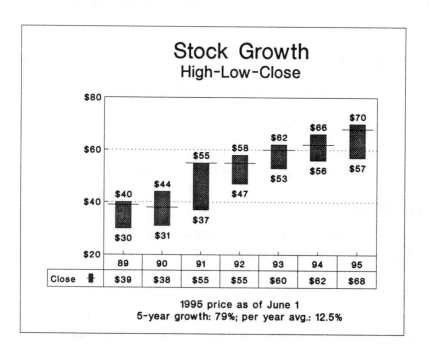

Stock Growth
High-Low-Close

	89	90	91	92	93	94	95
Close	$39	$38	$55	$55	$60	$62	$68

1995 price as of June 1
5-year growth: 79%; per year avg.: 12.5%

Genuine Parts Company

2999 Circle 75 Parkway
Atlanta, GA 30339
404-953-1700

Chairman and CEO: Larry L. Prince
President: Thomas C. Gallagher

Earnings Growth		Dividend Growth	★ ★
Stock Growth	★	Consistency	★ ★ ★ ★
Dividend Yield	★ ★ ★	Shareholder Perks	★ ★
NYSE—GPC		**Total**	**12 points**

Through the nearly 6,000 NAPA auto parts stores it supplies, Genuine Parts Company helps keep America's used cars and trucks purring. It supplies more than 150,000 different replacement parts and accessory items.

Genuine Parts is the market leader in the auto parts industry, with annual revenue of $4.86 billion. The firm's auto parts division accounts for 55 percent of its total revenue. The company owns about 725 automotive parts stores in 37 states. It also serves more than 5,000 independently owned stores (primarily NAPA Auto Parts) throughout the United States. Each center carries about 100,000 different parts for domestic and foreign automobiles. The company also handles parts for trucks, buses, motorcycles, watercraft, recreational vehicles, farm equipment, small engines and heavy-duty equipment.

In Canada, Genuine owns a 49 percent interest in UAP/NAPA, which operates 9 automotive parts distribution centers and 125 auto parts stores.

Genuine does no manufacturing itself, but serves strictly as a wholesale distributor. It buys parts from about 150 suppliers.

Genuine also operates in two other segments:

- **Industrial parts** (27 percent of revenue). Through its Motion Industries and Berry Bearing subsidiaries, the company is a distributor of industrial replacement parts. In all, the company serves about 150,000 customers in the United States and Canada.

- **Office products** (18 percent of revenue). Genuine's S.P. Richards Company subsidiary distributes a broad line of computer supplies, office furniture, office machines and general office supplies.

Founded in 1928, Genuine has enjoyed 45 consecutive years of record sales and 34 consecutive years of increased net income. It has raised its dividend for 38 straight years. The Atlanta-based operation has 21,300 employees and about 6,700 shareholders.

EARNINGS-PER-SHARE GROWTH

Past 5 years: 36 percent (6 percent per year)
Past 10 years: 138 percent (9 percent per year)

STOCK GROWTH   ★

Past 10 years: 156 percent (10 percent per year)
Dollar growth: $10,000 over 10 years (including reinvested dividends) would have grown to $35,000
Average annual compounded rate of return (including reinvested dividends): 13 percent

DIVIDEND YIELD   ★ ★ ★

Average dividend yield in the past 3 years: 3.1 percent

DIVIDEND GROWTH   ★ ★

Increased dividend: 38 consecutive years
Past 5-year increase: 44 percent (8 percent per year)

CONSISTENCY   ★ ★ ★ ★

Increased earnings per share: 34 consecutive years
Increased sales: 45 consecutive years

SHAREHOLDER PERKS   ★ ★

Good dividend reinvestment and stock purchase plan: voluntary stock purchase plan allows contributions of $10 to $3,000 per quarter.

GENUINE PARTS AT A GLANCE

Fiscal year ended: Dec. 31
Revenue and net income in $ millions

	1989	1990	1991	1992	1993	1994	5-year Growth Avg. Annual (%)	Total (%)
Revenue ($)	3,485.3	3,660.4	3,763.7	4,016.8	4,384.3	4,858.4	7	40
Net income ($)	215.3	223.7	224.0	237.0	257.8	288.5	5	30
Earnings/share ($)	1.71	1.79	1.81	1.91	2.08	2.33	6	36
Div. per share ($)	.80	.92	.97	1.00	1.06	1.15	8	44
Dividend yield (%)	3.1	3.5	3.5	3.2	2.9	3.2	—	—
Avg. PE ratio	15.1	14.2	15.3	16.4	17.3	15.4	—	—

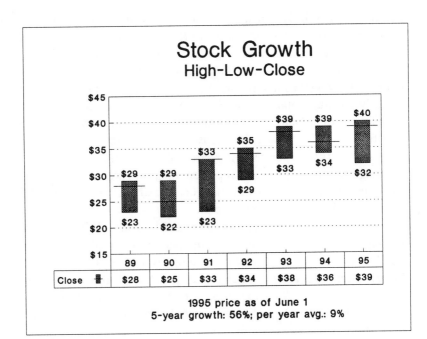

Stock Growth
High-Low-Close

	89	90	91	92	93	94	95
Close	$28	$25	$33	$34	$38	$36	$39

1995 price as of June 1
5-year growth: 56%; per year avg.: 9%

PacifiCare Health Systems, Inc.

5995 Plaza Drive
Cypress, CA 90630
714-952-1121

Chairman: Terry Hartshorn
President and CEO: Alan Hoops

Earnings Growth	★ ★ ★ ★	Dividend Growth	
Stock Growth	★ ★ ★ ★	Consistency	★ ★ ★
Dividend Yield		Shareholder Perks	
NASDAQ—PHSY "A"		**Total**	**11 points**

PacifiCare Health Systems, a growing health maintenance organization, has managed to maintain one of the healthiest balance sheets in the industry, with more than 50 consecutive quarters of profitability.

The Cypress, California, HMO continues to build enrollment in its home state as well as in Oregon, Washington, Oklahoma, Texas and most recently Florida. Total membership is more than 1.4 million.

Since 1985, PacifiCare has provided health care services to Medicare beneficiaries. The Secure Horizons program serves more than 400,000 members and is the largest Medicare risk program in the United States. Although Medicare members represent only 30 percent of the company's customer base, the senior citizens generate about 56 per cent of PacifiCare's $2.9 billion in annual revenue.

PacifiCare, which operates group and network HMOs, also recently launched a medical services program available to millions of Medicaid-eligible residents of California. The company also offers pharmacy benefit management, military health care management, coordination of managed care products for multiregion employers, health and life insurance, behavioral health, workers' compensation, dental and vision services and health promotion.

PacifiCare tries to make its services attractive to employers and employees through the development of innovative health care services and products. For example, in California, PacifiCare has developed a program called "The Art of Caring," a workshop designed to serve as a customer service primer for physicians and their office staff.

About 68 percent of PacifiCare's members are in California; 9 percent in Oklahoma; 7 percent in Texas; 7 percent in Oregon; 5 percent in Florida; and 4 percent in Washington. PacifiCare has about 4,000 employees and 1,000 shareholders.

EARNINGS-PER-SHARE GROWTH ★ ★ ★ ★

Past 5 years: 571 percent (46 percent per year)
Past 10 years: 1,093 percent (27 percent per year)

STOCK GROWTH ★ ★ ★ ★

Past 10 years: 1,442 percent (70 percent per year)
Dollar growth: $10,000 over 10 years (including reinvested dividends) would have grown to $154,000
Average annual compounded rate of return (including reinvested dividends): 70 percent

DIVIDEND YIELD

Pays no dividend

DIVIDEND GROWTH

Pays no dividend

CONSISTENCY ★ ★ ★

Increased earnings per share: 8 consecutive years
Increased sales: 9 consecutive years

SHAREHOLDER PERKS

The company offers no stock purchase plan, nor does it provide any other shareholder perks.

PACIFICARE HEALTH SYSTEMS AT A GLANCE

Fiscal year ended: Sept. 30
Revenue and net income in $ millions

	1989	1990	1991	1992	1993	1994	5-year Growth Avg. Annual (%)	Total (%)
Revenue ($)	650.2	975.8	1,242.4	1,686.3	2,221.1	2,893.3	28	345
Net income ($)	10.6	17.6	25.7	43.6	62.7	90.3	53	752
Earnings/share ($)	.48	.74	1.10	1.78	2.25	3.22	46	571
Div. per share ($)	–	–	–	–	–	–	—	—
Dividend yield (%)	–	–	–	–	–	–	—	—
Avg. PE ratio	12.7	15.7	11.4	14.4	18.2	16.8	—	—

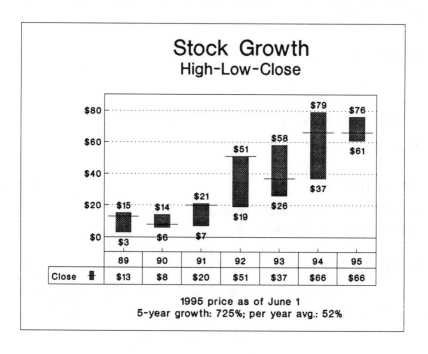

Stock Growth
High-Low-Close

	89	90	91	92	93	94	95
Close	$13	$8	$20	$51	$37	$66	$66

1995 price as of June 1
5-year growth: 725%; per year avg.: 52%

Office Depot, Inc.

2200 Old Germantown Road
Delray Beach, FL 33445
407-278-4800

Chairman and CEO: David I. Fuente
President: Mark D. Begelman

Earnings Growth	★ ★ ★ ★	Dividend Growth	
Stock Growth	★ ★ ★ ★	Consistency	★ ★ ★
Dividend Yield		Shareholder Perks	
NYSE—ODP		**Total**	**11 points**

For anyone who's ever had to pay full retail prices for pens, pencils, notebooks, folders and other office supplies, the new wave of giant, warehouse-style office supply discounters has been a welcome relief. Entrepreneurs and small business owners have embraced these new no-frills superstores, where they can buy office products in bulk at less than half the standard retail price.

Office Depot is the largest and most successful of the office discount chains. The company has grown at a staggering pace since going public in 1988. Its sales have grown more than thirtyfold from $132 million in 1988 to $4.3 billion in 1994, and its earnings have grown nearly ninetyfold from $1.2 million to $104 million.

The company has about 440 stores in 35 states and Canada. Office Depot has also opened stores in Colombia, Israel and Poland, and has announced plans to open stores in Mexico.

The company's growth has come both from new store openings and from acquisitions. Office Depot has made a concerted effort to push into the larger commercial market by expanding its catalog and delivery business and by acquiring a number of "contract stationers" who deal directly with larger business customers.

Each of the company's stores offers a broad range of more than 5,000 office products, including a variety of paper products, computer hardware and software, calculators, copiers, telephones, fax machines, office furniture, envelopes, pens, pencils, notebooks and related products.

General office supplies account for about 46 percent of the company's total revenue, while business machines make up 41 percent and office furniture accounts for the other 13 percent. The Delray Beach, Florida, retailer has about 22,000 employees.

EARNINGS-PER-SHARE GROWTH   ★ ★ ★ ★

Past 5 years: 667 percent (51 percent per year)
Past 10 years: Company had its first profit in 1988

STOCK GROWTH   ★ ★ ★ ★

Past 7 years (stock began trading in 1988): 900 percent (39 percent per year)
Dollar growth: $10,000 over 7 years (including reinvested dividends) would have grown to $100,000
Average annual compounded rate of return (including reinvested dividends): 39 percent

DIVIDEND YIELD

Pays no dividend

DIVIDEND GROWTH

Pays no dividend

CONSISTENCY   ★ ★ ★

Increased earnings per share: 7 straight years
Increased sales: 8 straight years

SHAREHOLDER PERKS

The company offers no dividend reinvestment and stock purchase plan (since it pays no dividend) and offers no other shareholder perks.

OFFICE DEPOT AT A GLANCE

Fiscal year ended: Dec. 31
Revenue and net income in $ millions

	1989	1990	1991	1992	1993	1994	5-year Growth Avg. Annual (%)	5-year Growth Total (%)
Revenue ($)	621.2	1,987.5	1,497.9	1,963.0	2,836.8	4,266.2	45	587
Net income ($)	7.7	16.4	18.8	45.3	70.8	105.0	70	1,264
Earnings/share ($)	.09	.14	.15	.32	.48	.69	51	667
Div. per share ($)	–	–	–	–	–	–	—	—
Dividend yield (%)	–	–	–	–	–	–	—	—
Avg. PE ratio	47	26.5	37	43.5	40	34	—	—

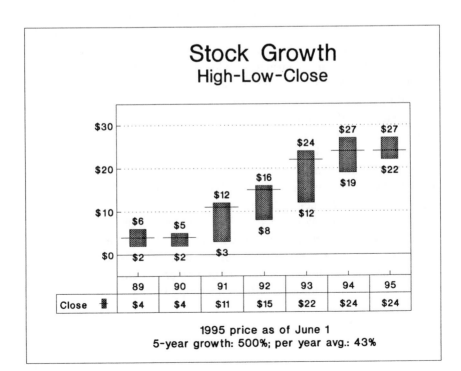

Stock Growth
High-Low-Close

	89	90	91	92	93	94	95
Close	$4	$4	$11	$15	$22	$24	$24

1995 price as of June 1
5-year growth: 500%; per year avg.: 43%

Novell, Inc.

122 East 1700 South
Provo, UT 84606
801-429-7000

Chairman, President and CEO:
Robert J. Frankenberg

Earnings Growth	★ ★ ★ ★	Dividend Growth	
Stock Growth	★ ★ ★ ★	Consistency	★ ★ ★
Dividend Yield		Shareholder Perks	
NASDAQ–NOVL		**Total**	**11 points**

Already the world's leading manufacturer of computer networking products, Novell is attacking other areas of the computer industry as well.

The Provo, Utah, manufacturer acquired WordPerfect and QuatroPro in July 1994 and quickly hit the market with its own updated and newly bundled versions of those products under the Novell banner. WordPerfect is among the world's top-selling brands of word processing software, and QuatroPro is among the top sellers of all brands of spreadsheet software.

Founded in 1983, Novell underwent a key management transition in 1994. Gone is 70-year-old Raymond J. Noorda, one of the original founders and the guiding hand of the company since 1986. He was replaced as chairman, president and CEO by Robert Frankenberg, a 25-year veteran of Hewlett-Packard. Frankenberg, 47, had been the vice president and general manager of Hewlett-Packard's personal information products group.

Novell is best known for its NetWare networking products, which are used worldwide. Its products can link thousands of computers together. In fact, a key advantage of Novell's systems is that they enable varying types of host computers to link up with other computers whether they use DOS, Windows, OS/2, MacIntosh or UNIX operating systems.

The company also manufactures a wide range of other networking products, including network routers, network monitoring systems and store-in-forward products used to transmit messages between computer users and remote access software. Novell also owns a major stake in UNIX Systems Laboratories, a subsidiary of AT&T that develops and licenses the UNIX operating system and other software to vendors worldwide.

About 43 percent of the company's $2 billion in annual revenue comes from its foreign operations. The company has 31 foreign field offices and 113 foreign distributors. Its largest foreign markets are Canada, Japan, France, Australia, Germany, Hong Kong, Belgium and the United Kingdom. Novell has about 4,400 employees and 10,000 shareholders.

EARNINGS-PER-SHARE GROWTH

Past 5 years: 376 percent (37 percent per year)
Past 10 years: 2,600 percent (39 percent per year)

STOCK GROWTH ★ ★ ★ ★

Past 10 years: 2,400 percent (37 percent per year)
Dollar growth: $10,000 over 10 years (including reinvested dividends) would have grown to $250,000
Average annual compounded rate of return (including reinvested dividends): 37 percent

DIVIDEND YIELD

Pays no dividend

DIVIDEND GROWTH

Pays no dividend

CONSISTENCY

Increased earnings per share: 8 of past 9 years
Increased sales: 9 consecutive years

SHAREHOLDER PERKS

The company offers no dividend reinvestment and stock purchase plan, nor does it provide any other shareholder perks.

NOVELL AT A GLANCE

Fiscal year ended: Oct. 31
Revenue and net income in $ millions

	1989	1990	1991	1992	1993	1994	5-year Growth Avg. Annual (%)	Total (%)
Revenue ($)	421.9	497.5	640.1	933.4	1,122.9	1,999	36.5	370
Net income ($)	48.5	94.3	162.5	322	283.3	206.7	34	330
Earnings/share ($)	.17	.34	.55	.81	.90	.81	37	376
Div. per share ($)	–	–	–	–	–	–	—	—
Dividend yield (%)	–	–	–	–	–	–	—	—
Avg. PE ratio	22.5	15.2	24.1	34.2	30.0	23.3	—	—

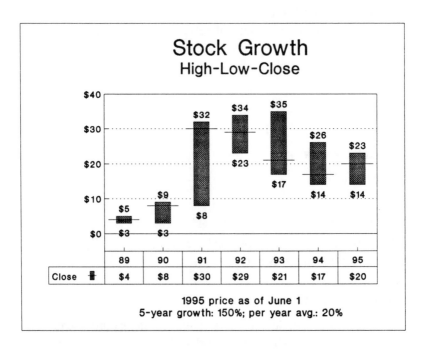

Stock Growth
High-Low-Close

	89	90	91	92	93	94	95
Close	$4	$8	$30	$29	$21	$17	$20

1995 price as of June 1
5-year growth: 150%; per year avg.: 20%

Tyson Foods, Inc.

2210 West Oaklawn Dr.
Springdale, AR 72762-6999
501-756-4000

Chairman: Don Tyson
President and CEO: Leland E. Tollett

Earnings Growth	★	Dividend Growth	★ ★
Stock Growth	★ ★ ★ ★	Consistency	★ ★ ★ ★
Dividend Yield		Shareholder Perks	
NASDAQ—TYSN "A"		**Total**	**11 points**

Tyson Foods has taken to heart the Depression-era expression, "a chicken in every pot." Except that Tyson, which is by far the dominant chicken producer in the United States, would like to put a chicken in every pot around the world.

The Springdale, Arkansas, producer is expanding rapidly overseas, with sales in 43 countries. Foreign sales now account for about 10 percent of Tyson's $5.1 billion in annual revenue. Russia and Mexico are two of its faster-growing foreign markets, but Tyson management has high expectations for China as well, where the company recently signed letters of intent to begin marketing chicken to the 1.2 billion Chinese consumers.

Tyson is rapidly expanding its production facilities to accommodate its growing market. By the end of 1997, the company expects to have increased its poultry production capacity from 30 million head per week to about 37 million per week.

Poultry sales account for about 75 percent of the company's total revenue, while beef and pork make up 11 percent, seafood accounts for 5 percent, Mexican foods comprise 3 percent and other products make up the other 6 percent.

Tyson's stock-in-trade has been its ability to make strategic acquisitions of companies that can be easily integrated into its overall operation. But Tyson's growth can be traced to more than just its aggressive acquisition strategy. The nation's appetite for poultry has grown dramatically over the past decade, as health-conscious consumers looked for alternatives to red meat. Poultry consumption is expected to continue to grow at a rate of 10 to 15 percent per year through the rest of this decade.

Tyson markets its fowl to grocery stores, restaurant chains and institutional food services. About 50 percent of the company's revenue comes from the retail trade, while restaurants and food services account for the other 50 percent. The company does business with about 80 percent of the nation's restaurant chains.

Tyson runs a fully integrated operation, processing its poultry through every phase of the production process. It operates a nationwide network of hatcheries, feed mills and processing plants.

The company packages its fowl in many forms—fresh, frozen, mixed and marinated, plus more than 50 sizes, shapes and styles of boneless breasts and breaded patties. These "value-enhanced" products make up about 85 percent of the poultry Tyson sells. "It significantly reduces our exposure to fresh or iced chicken, which is the least profitable, most volatile side of the poultry business," says Tyson Foods founder and chairman Don Tyson. "By moving into value-enhanced products, we have more stable profits."

In all, the company offers more than 500 different meat products to the food services market. Tyson, which was founded in 1935 and first incorporated in 1947, has 50,000 employees and 32,000 shareholders. Insiders (primarily the Tyson family) control about 60 percent of the company stock.

EARNINGS-PER-SHARE GROWTH ★

Past 5 years: 76 percent (12 percent per year)
Past 10 years: 756 percent (24 percent per year)

STOCK GROWTH ★ ★ ★ ★

Past 10 years: 797 percent (24.5 percent per year)
Dollar growth: $10,000 over 10 years (including reinvested dividends) would have grown to $92,000

Average annual compounded rate of return (including reinvested dividends): 25 percent

DIVIDEND YIELD

Average dividend yield in the past 3 years: 0.2 percent

DIVIDEND GROWTH

Increased dividend: 2 consecutive years
Past 5-year increase: 600 percent (49 percent per year)

CONSISTENCY ★ ★ ★ ★

Increased earnings per share: 14 consecutive years
Increased sales: 14 consecutive years

SHAREHOLDER PERKS

The company does not offer a dividend reinvestment and stock purchase plan, nor does it offer any other perks.

TYSON FOODS AT A GLANCE

Fiscal year ended: Dec. 31
Revenue and net income in $ millions

	1989	1990	1991	1992	1993	1994	5-year Growth Avg. Annual (%)	Total (%)
Revenue ($)	2,538	3,825	3,922	4,169	4,707	5,110	15	101
Net income ($)	101	120	145	160	180	203	15	101
Earnings/share ($)	.78	.90	1.05	1.16	1.22	1.37	12	76
Div. per share ($)	.01	.01	.03	.04	.04	.07	49	600
Dividend yield (%)	.1	.1	.2	.2	.2	.03	—	—
Avg. PE ratio	12	15	17	16	18	16.5	—	—

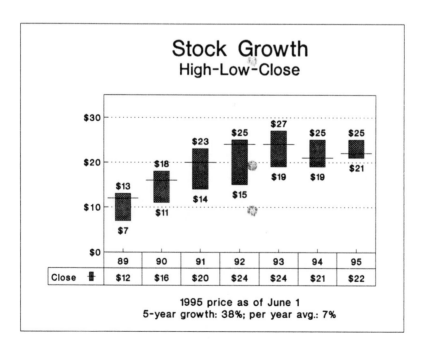

Stock Growth
High-Low-Close

	89	90	91	92	93	94	95
Close	$12	$16	$20	$24	$24	$21	$22

1995 price as of June 1
5-year growth: 38%; per year avg.: 7%

8.

Vishay Intertechnology, Inc.

63 Lincoln Highway
Malvern, PA 19355-2120
610-644-1300

Chairman, President and CEO: Dr. Felix Zandman

Earnings Growth	★ ★ ★	Dividend Growth	
Stock Growth	★ ★ ★ ★	Consistency	★ ★ ★ ★
Dividend Yield		Shareholder Perks	
NYSE—VSH		**Total**	**11 points**

You'll find its components in computers, cars, phones, appliances, TVs, radios, jets, weapons, medical equipment and a wide range of other high-tech equipment. Vishay Intertechnology is the largest manufacturer of passive electronic components in the United States and Europe.

The company's leading products are resistors, capacitors and inductors. Resistors are the most common component in electronic circuits and are used to adjust and regulate levels of control, timing and filtering functions in electrical equipment.

Founded in 1962 by Dr. Felix Zandman (who continues to serve as chairman, president and CEO), Vishay has grown quickly through new product introductions and global acquisitions. It now has 56 manufacturing plants. Only about 39 percent of the company's $988 million in annual sales are generated by U.S. customers. European sales account for most of the remaining 61 percent.

The company's sales and earnings have grown rapidly over the past decade. Sales have grown twentyfold during that period, while earnings per share have increased about sixfold. The growth has come primarily as a result of Vishay's four-pronged business strategy, including:

1. Acquisitions of components manufacturers with established positions in major markets;
2. Streamlining of sales and general administration functions;
3. Production cost savings through transfer and expansion of manufacturing operations to countries with lower labor cost;
4. Maintaining production facilities in the company's major markets to enhance customer service.

Vishay, based in Malvern, Pennsylvania, has about 17,000 employees and 1,500 shareholders.

EARNINGS-PER-SHARE GROWTH   ★ ★ ★

Past 5 years: 114 percent (16.5 percent per year)
Past 10 years: 471 percent (19 percent per year)

STOCK GROWTH   ★ ★ ★ ★

Past 10 years: 684 percent (23 percent per year)
Dollar growth: $10,000 over 10 years (including reinvested dividends) would have grown to $78,400
Average annual compounded rate of return: 23 percent

DIVIDEND YIELD

Pays no dividend

DIVIDEND GROWTH

Pays no dividend

CONSISTENCY   ★ ★ ★ ★

Increased earnings per share: 13 consecutive years
Increased sales: 9 of past 10 years

SHAREHOLDER PERKS

The company offers no dividend reinvestment plan, nor does it offer any other perks.

VISHAY INTERTECHNOLOGY AT A GLANCE

Fiscal year ended: Dec. 31
Revenue and net income in $ millions

	1989	1990	1991	1992	1993	1994	5-year Growth Avg. Annual (%)	Total (%)
Revenue ($)	415.6	445.6	442.3	664.2	856.3	987.8	19	140
Net income ($)	17.8	23.2	20.9	30.4	44.1	58.9	34	330
Earnings/share ($)	1.12	1.34	1.14	1.55	1.88	2.40	16.5	114
Div. per share ($)	–	–	–	–	–	–	—	—
Dividend yield (%)	–	–	–	–	–	–	—	—
Avg. PE ratio	12.0	9.2	11.2	13.8	16.2	16.4	—	—

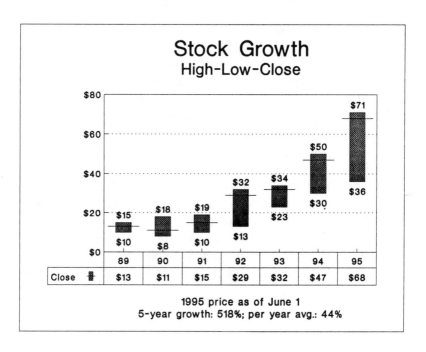

Stock Growth
High-Low-Close

	89	90	91	92	93	94	95
Close	$13	$11	$15	$29	$32	$47	$68

1995 price as of June 1
5-year growth: 518%; per year avg.: 44%

82

Thermo Instrument Systems, Inc.

504 Airport Road
P. O. Box 2108
Santa Fe, NM 87504-2108
617-622-1000

President and CEO: Arvin H. Smith

Earnings Growth	★ ★ ★ ★	Dividend Growth	
Stock Growth	★ ★ ★ ★	Consistency	★ ★ ★
Dividend Yield		Shareholder Perks	
AMEX—THI		**Total**	**11 points**

If it's in the air, Thermo Instrument Systems can probably detect it. The company's new pollution analyzer, for instance, can monitor ambient pollutants down to the part-per-billion level.

The Sante Fe operation makes a wide range of analytical, environmental monitoring instruments used to detect and measure air pollution, nuclear radioactivity, complex chemical compounds, toxic metals and other elements in a wide variety of materials.

The company also manufactures process monitoring and control instruments for the oil, gas and petrochemical industries.

Thermo Instrument, which did not become a publicly traded company until 1986, has grown quickly through acquisitions and internal development of new products and technologies.

The company is worldwide in scope, drawing about 30 percent of its $662 million in annual revenue from its foreign sales.

Thermo Instrument breaks its product line into these key product categories:

- **Analytical instruments.** The company makes atomic emission and atomic absorption spectrometers, which identify and measure trace quantities of metals and other elements in a variety of materials such as soil, water, wastes, foods, drugs, cosmetics and alloys.

* **Monitoring instruments.** Thermo Instrument makes nuclear radiation monitoring instruments used to detect and measure alpha, beta, gamma, neutron and X-ray radiation emitted by natural sources.

The company markets its products to manufacturers, government agencies, environmental labs, utilities and waste management and treatment facilities. Thermo Instrument has 4,000 employees and 2,100 shareholders.

EARNINGS-PER-SHARE GROWTH ★ ★ ★ ★

Past 5 years: 172 percent (22 percent per year)
Past 8 years: 508 percent (25 percent per year)

STOCK GROWTH ★ ★ ★ ★

Past 10 years: 715 percent (23 percent per year)
Dollar growth: $10,000 over 10 years (including reinvested dividends) would have grown to $81,500
Average annual compounded rate of return (including reinvested dividends): 23 percent

DIVIDEND YIELD

Pays no dividend

DIVIDEND GROWTH

Pays no dividend

CONSISTENCY ★ ★ ★

Increased earnings per share: 8 straight years
Increased sales: 10 straight years

SHAREHOLDER PERKS

The company offers no stock purchase plan, nor does it offer any other shareholder perks.

THERMO INSTRUMENT SYSTEMS AT A GLANCE

Fiscal year ended: Dec. 31
Revenue and net income in $ millions

	1989	1990	1991	1992	1993	1994	5-year Growth Avg. Annual (%)	Total (%)
Revenue ($)	184.7	285.3	338.7	423.2	584.2	662.2	29	258
Net income ($)	8	19	25	33	44	60	49	628
Earnings/share ($)	.29	.33	.41	.51	.66	.79	22	172
Div. per share ($)	–	–	–	–	–	–	—	—
Dividend yield (%)	–	–	–	–	–	–	—	—
Avg. PE ratio	18	20	24	23	30	26	—	—

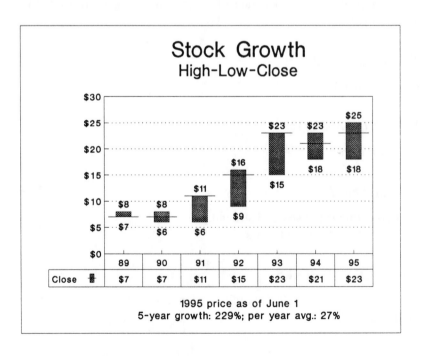

Stock Growth
High-Low-Close

	89	90	91	92	93	94	95
Close	$7	$7	$11	$15	$23	$21	$23

1995 price as of June 1
5-year growth: 229%; per year avg.: 27%

Loctite Corp.

10 Columbus Blvd.
Hartford, CT 06106
203-520-5000

Chairman: Kenneth W. Butterworth
President and CEO: David Freeman

Earnings Growth		Dividend Growth	★ ★
Stock Growth	★ ★ ★	Consistency	★ ★
Dividend Yield	★ ★	Shareholder Perks	★ ★
NYSE–LOC		**Total**	**11 points**

With a name that says it all, Loctite Corp. makes a line of products that stick and seal.

The company's most recognizable consumer products include Super Glue, Duro and Loctite glues. But it is Loctite's industrial products that provide the bulk of the company's earnings and revenue.

Loctite's industrial-strength sealants, adhesives and other chemical specialties are used by a variety of industries including electronics, plastics, health care and the automotive aftermarket. Loctite has customers all over the world. About 55 percent of the company's $703 million in annual sales is generated in foreign markets. Relying on international markets for the lion's share of its revenues can have a downside, however. When the European economy went flat in 1992 and 1993, Loctite felt the pinch. The relative strength of the dollar against major European currencies compounded the problem. But Loctite's European fortunes turned around when the dollar weakened and most European economies came roaring back.

To better position itself in Europe—where Loctite does more than 40 percent of its business—the company changed its structure to allow it to focus on the management of a European-wide marketplace rather than management of products within an individual company. The new structure will permit closer coordination of pan-European product launches and marketing programs.

To strike closer bonds with the fast-growing Asia/Pacific market, Loctite is gradually abandoning its practice of selling through national distributors in favor of establishing wholly owned subsidiaries or joint ventures. The operations are managed by Loctite employees who are well versed in the company's selling techniques.

In Latin America, Loctite has made strong investments in its manufacturing, technical, logistics and sales capabilities as it prepares for stronger growth in that region of the world.

Loctite also manufactures and markets metal-care products and cleaners for tile, porcelain, wood, metal and fiberglass surfaces, as well as hand cleaners. In 1985, it began making electroluminescent lights, a relatively new and versatile lighting device. Founded in 1953, Loctite has 3,700 employees and 2,300 shareholders.

EARNINGS-PER-SHARE GROWTH

Past 5 years: 44 percent (8 percent per year)
Past 10 years: 248 percent (13 percent per year)

STOCK GROWTH ★ ★ ★

Past 10 years: 525 percent (20 percent per year)
Dollar growth: $10,000 over 10 years (including reinvested dividends) would have grown to $73,000
Average annual compounded rate of return (including reinvested dividends): 22 percent

DIVIDEND YIELD

Average dividend yield in the past 3 years: 1.8 percent

DIVIDEND GROWTH   ★ ★

Increased dividend: 11 consecutive years
Past 5-year increase: 55 percent (9 percent per year)

CONSISTENCY   ★ ★

Increased earnings per share: 8 of past 10 years
Increased sales: 11 consecutive years

SHAREHOLDER PERKS   ★ ★

Good dividend reinvestment and stock purchase plan: voluntary stock purchase plan allows contributions of $25 to $1,000 per month.

The company sometimes hands out various product (such as tubes of Super Glue) to shareholders attending the annual meeting and recently offered free samples of two new products to all shareholders in the annual report mailing.

LOCTITE AT A GLANCE

Fiscal year ended: July 31
Revenue and net income in $ millions

	1989	1990	1991	1992	1993	1994	5-year Growth Avg. Annual (%)	Total (%)
Revenue ($)	473.9	555.2	561.2	608.0	612.6	703.6	8.5	49
Net income ($)	58.2	66.3	69.6	72.1	68.3	82.4	7	41
Earnings/share ($)	1.62	1.82	1.91	1.98	1.92	2.33	.8	44
Div. per share ($)	.53	.59	.68	.74	.79	.82	9	55
Dividend yield (%)	2.5	2.3	1.9	1.6	2.0	1.9	—	—
Avg. PE ratio	13	14	19	23	21	18	—	—

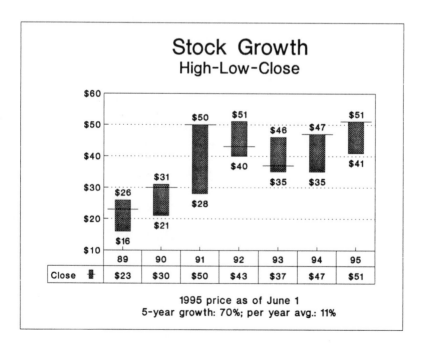

Stock Growth
High-Low-Close

Close	89	90	91	92	93	94	95
	$23	$30	$50	$43	$37	$47	$51

1995 price as of June 1
5-year growth: 70%; per year avg.: 11%

Thermo Electron Corp.

Æ Thermo Electron

81 Wyman Street
P. O. Box 9046
Waltham, MA 02254-9046
617-622-1000

Chairman, President and CEO: George N. Hatsopoulos

Earnings Growth	★ ★ ★ ★	Dividend Growth	
Stock Growth	★ ★ ★	Consistency	★ ★ ★
Dividend Yield		Shareholder Perks	
NYSE—TMO		**Total**	**11 points**

For decades, engineers and futurists have talked about the possibility of making vehicles that run on alternative energy. But Thermo Electron is the one company that has actually gone beyond the talk to deliver a working product, which is now on the streets logging long hours every day.

The company builds natural-gas–fueled TecoDrive engines that are used in several buses in California, 20 United Parcel Service vans in Washington D.C., several U.S. Postal Service trucks in four other U.S. cities and bus fleets in Belgium, Brazil and Canada.

Thermo Electron is a major manufacturer of alternative energy systems, environmental monitoring and analysis instruments, paper recycling equipment and biomedical products.

The Waltham, Massachusetts, operation recently received Food and Drug Administration approval for a left ventricular assist device that can serve as an alternative to certain heart transplant operations. Thermo Electron spent 28 years researching and developing the device.

The company has strong international sales, particularly in Europe. Foreign exports account for about 20 percent of the company's $1.6 billion in annual revenue.

Thermo Electron's key segments include:

- **Instruments.** The company makes a wide range of analytical and monitoring instruments used to detect and measure air pollution, nuclear radioactivity, toxic substances, chemical compounds and trace quantities of metals and other elements.

- **Alternative energy systems.** The firm builds and operates alternative energy power plants, such as waste-to-energy electric power plants and fossil fuel cogeneration plants, which generate electricity and thermal energy in the form of steam or hot or chilled water.

- **Process equipment.** Thermo Electron develops computer-controlled thermal processing systems used to treat, mold and strengthen metals and metal parts. The company also manufactures systems for the thermal treatment of toxic wastes, such as soil contaminated by petroleum products.

- **Biomedical products.** The company makes a variety of biomedical devices and special instruments, including instruments used to detect ultratrace concentrations of nitrogen-based compounds, ventricular assist devices and high-voltage power conversion systems, modulators and related equipment.

- **Services.** The company provides lab testing, engineering and environmental science services such as the monitoring of hazardous wastes and radioactive materials, the design and construction inspection of water supply and wastewater treatment facilities, and metallurgical heat-treating services for customers in aerospace and other industries.

Thermo Electron was founded in 1956 by George Hatsopoulos, who still serves as chairman, president and CEO. He started the company while still a graduate student at the Massachusetts Institute of Technology (MIT) so he could research commercial aspects of his doctoral thesis in energy conversion. The company now has 9,000 employees and 6,400 shareholders.

EARNINGS-PER-SHARE GROWTH   ★ ★ ★ ★

Past 5 years: 144 percent (19.5 percent per year)
Past 10 years: 600 percent (21.5 percent per year)

STOCK GROWTH ★ ★ ★

Past 10 years: 584 percent (19 percent per year)
Dollar growth: $10,000 over 10 years (including reinvested dividends)
would have grown to $58,400
Average annual compounded rate of return (including reinvested dividends): 19 percent

DIVIDEND YIELD

Pays no dividend

DIVIDEND GROWTH

Pays no dividend

CONSISTENCY ★ ★ ★ ★

Increased earnings per share: 11 consecutive years
Increased sales: 10 consecutive years

SHAREHOLDER PERKS

The company offers no stock purchase plan, nor does it provide any other
shareholder perks.

THERMO ELECTRON AT A GLANCE

Fiscal year ended: Dec. 31
Revenue and net income in $ millions

	1989	1990	1991	1992	1993	1994	5-year Growth Avg. Annual (%)	5-year Growth Total (%)
Revenue ($)	623.0	720.7	805.5	949.0	1,249.7	1,585.3	20.5	154
Net income ($)	26.6	35.0	47.1	59.2	76.6	103.4	31	282
Earnings/share ($)	.86	1.09	1.31	1.48	1.75	2.10	19.5	144
Div. per share ($)	–	–	–	–	–	–	—	—
Dividend yield (%)	–	–	–	–	–	–	—	—
Avg. PE ratio	18.3	19.7	20.0	25.3	23.5	20.2	—	—

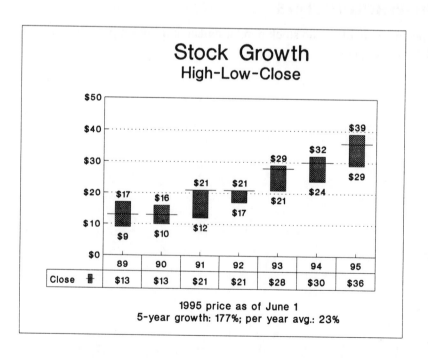

Stock Growth
High-Low-Close

	89	90	91	92	93	94	95
Close	$13	$13	$21	$21	$28	$30	$36

1995 price as of June 1
5-year growth: 177%; per year avg.: 23%

The Pro...
Gamble Company

One Procter & Gamble Plaza
Cincinnati, OH 45202
513-983-1100

Chairman and CEO: Edwin L. Artzt
President: John Pepper

Earnings Growth	★	Dividend Growth	★ ★ ★
Stock Growth	★	Consistency	★ ★ ★
Dividend Yield	★ ★	Shareholder Perks	★
NYSE—PG		**Total**	**11 points**

With its *Bounty* of well-known consumer products and its *Tide* of increasing profitability, Procter & Gamble has long been a *Joy* for shareholders. The company produces many of the nation's most-recognized brand names, from Pampers and Pringles to Crest and Cheer.

Founded in 1837 by William Procter and James Gamble, the Cincinnati operation is the world's leading producer of soaps and cosmetics. It also churns out a wide range of other consumer staples. In fact, the company puts more than 300 brands on the market in more than 140 countries around the world. Foreign sales account for about 50 percent of the company's $30.3 billion in annual revenue.

Procter & Gamble has managed to maintain its strong market position through a relentless advertising approach. For many years, the company has been TV's biggest advertiser.

The firm divides its product offerings into several key categories:

- **Laundry and cleaning products.** Leading brands include Tide, Cheer, Spic and Span, Comet, Lestoil, Mr. Clean, Bold, Dash, Dreft, Era, Gain, Ivory, Oxydol, Top Job, Cascade, Dawn, Bounce, Downy and Joy.

- **Personal care products.** The company makes a wide range of personal care products, including Clearasil, Noxzema, Camay, Coast, Lava, Oil of Olay, Safeguard, Zest, Cover Girl, Max Factor, Sure, Secret and Old Spice. Other products include Pampers, Always, Metamucil, Pepto-Bismol, Vidal Sassoon, Prell, Head & Shoulders, Pert, Crest, Gleem, Vicks, NyQuil, Scope, Puffs and Bounty.
- **Food and beverages.** Leading products include Crisco, Duncan Hines, Pringles, Fisher Nuts, Folgers Coffee, Hawaiian Punch, Jif, Pringles, and Sunny Delight Florida Citrus Punch.

Procter & Gamble also produces a number of prescription and over-the-counter medications and offers a line of commercial soaps and detergents for the cleaning industry. P&G has about 97,000 employees and 200,000 shareholders.

EARNINGS-PER-SHARE GROWTH ★

Past 5 years: 74 percent (12 percent per year)
Past 10 years: 140 percent (9 percent per year)

STOCK GROWTH ★

Past 10 years: 230 percent (13 percent per year)
Dollar growth: $10,000 over 10 years (including reinvested dividends) would have grown to $44,000
Average annual compounded rate of return (including reinvested dividends): 16 percent

DIVIDEND YIELD ★ ★

Average dividend yield in the past 3 years: 2.2 percent

DIVIDEND GROWTH ★ ★ ★

Increased dividend: 38 consecutive years
Past 5-year increase: 65 percent (11 percent per year)

CONSISTENCY

Increased earnings per share: 9 consecutive years
Increased sales: 9 of past 10 years

SHAREHOLDER PERKS ★

The company offers a dividend reinvestment plan, but it recently discontinued its voluntary stock purchase option.

PROCTER & GAMBLE AT A GLANCE

Fiscal year ended: June 30
Revenue and net income in $ millions

	1989	1990	1991	1992	1993	1994	5-year Growth Avg. Annual (%)	5-year Growth Total (%)
Revenue ($)	21,398	34,081	27,026	29,362	30,433	30,296	7	42
Net income ($)	1,206	1,602	1,773	1,872	2,078	2,211	13	83
Earnings/share ($)	1.78	2.25	2.46	2.62	2.91	3.09	12	74
Div. per share ($)	.75	.88	.98	1.03	1.10	1.24	11	65
Dividend yield (%)	3.4	2.6	2.4	2.3	2.2	2.3	—	—
Avg. PE ratio	12.2	16.2	16.7	17.4	17.8	17.5	—	—

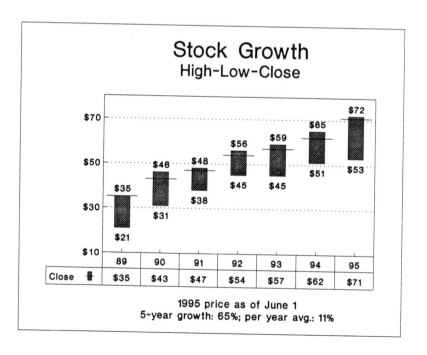

Stock Growth
High-Low-Close

Close	89	90	91	92	93	94	95
	$35	$43	$47	$54	$57	$62	$71

1995 price as of June 1
5-year growth: 65%; per year avg.: 11%

86

Hubbell, Inc.

584 Derby Milford Road
Orange, CT 06477-4024
203-799-4100

Chairman, President and CEO:
G. J. Ratcliffe

Earnings Growth		Dividend Growth	★ ★
Stock Growth	★	Consistency	★ ★ ★
Dividend Yield	★ ★ ★	Shareholder Perks	★ ★
NYSE—HUB "B"		**Total**	**11 points**

In 1888, when Hubbell put its first electrical products on the market, its entire line consisted of just a few electrical connectors and wiring devices for industrial applications. Now the company produces thousands of electric products, including outlets, adapters, lighting fixtures, measurement equipment and electrical transmission and distribution products.

Over the years, the Orange, Connecticut, manufacturer has been among the most consistent companies in America, posting 32 consecutive years of increased operating income through 1992. A restructuring charge to streamline the operation in 1993 broke that string, but in 1994, earnings snapped back again to a record level.

Hubbell's leading product line is low-voltage devices such as fuses, switches, wall plates, cables, plugs, surge suppressor units, connectors, adaptors and wall outlets. The company's lighting division sells lights for athletic fields, service stations and roadways.

Other low-voltage products include industrial controls such as motor speed controls, power and grounding resistors and overhead crane controls.

Hubbell's low-voltage segment accounts for 52 percent of its $1.01 billion in annual revenue. Hubbell's other segments include:

- **High-voltage products** (16 percent of sales). Hubbell makes insulated wire and cable, electrical transmission and distribution products, and high-voltage test and measurement equipment.

- **Other electronics products** (32 percent of sales). Hubbell manufactures steel and plastic boxes used at outlets, switch locations, junction points, fittings, tubing and enclosures through its Raco subsidiary.

Hubbell has subsidiaries in Canada, Mexico, England and Puerto Rico and has sales in several other countries. Foreign operations account for about 5 percent of total revenue. The company has 6,000 employees, 5,700 class B (nonvoting) shareholders and 1,400 class A (voting) shareholders. (Officers and directors control 43% of class A shares.)

EARNINGS-PER-SHARE GROWTH

Past 5 years: 33 percent (6 percent per year)
Past 10 years: 142 percent (9 percent per year)

STOCK GROWTH ★

Past 10 years: 212 percent (12 percent per year)
Dollar growth: $10,000 over 10 years (including reinvested dividends) would have grown to $40,000
Average annual compounded rate of return (including reinvested dividends): 15 percent

DIVIDEND YIELD ★ ★ ★

Average dividend yield in the past 3 years: 3 percent

DIVIDEND GROWTH ★ ★

Increased dividend: 34 consecutive years
Past 5-year increase: 51 percent (9 percent per year)

CONSISTENCY ★ ★ ★

Increased earnings per share: 9 of past 10 years
Increased sales: 12 consecutive years

SHAREHOLDER PERKS ★ ★

Modest dividend reinvestment and stock purchase plan: voluntary stock purchase plan allows contributions of $100 to $1,000 per quarter.

HUBBELL AT A GLANCE

Fiscal year ended: Dec. 31
Revenue and net income in $ millions

	1989	1990	1991	1992	1993	1994	5-year Growth Avg. Annual (%)	Total (%)
Revenue ($)	668.8	719.5	756.1	786.1	832.4	1,013.7	9	50
Net income ($)	79.4	86.0	90.6	94.1	66.3	106.5	6	30
Earnings/share ($)	2.40	2.61	2.73	2.83	2.00	3.20	6	33
Div. per share ($)	1.07	1.25	1.40	1.51	1.55	1.62	9.	51
Dividend yield (%)	3.4	3.4	3.0	3.0	3.0	3.0	—	—
Avg. PE ratio	13.2	13.9	16.9	17.8	26.0	16.9	—	—

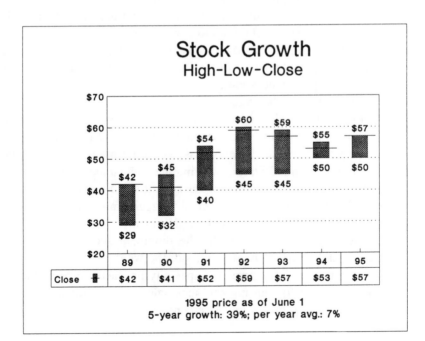

Stock Growth
High-Low-Close

	89	90	91	92	93	94	95
Close	$42	$41	$52	$59	$57	$53	$57

1995 price as of June 1
5-year growth: 39%; per year avg.: 7%

Reebok International, Ltd.

100 Technology Center Dr.
Stoughton, MA 02072
617-341-5000

Chairman, President and CEO:
Paul Fireman

Earnings Growth	★ ★	Dividend Growth	
Stock Growth	★ ★ ★ ★	Consistency	★ ★ ★
Dividend Yield	★	Shareholder Perks	
NYSE—RBK		**Total**	**10 points**

When the world's Olympians take the field in 1996, you'll see one national team decked out in Reebok-sponsored shoes and uniforms. Not the U.S. national team, however, although Reebok sponsors many individual U.S. athletes. But the Stoughton, Massachusetts, shoemaker is the official 1996 footwear and apparel sponsor of the Russian Olympic Committee and its 25 associated sports federations.

How times have changed.

For Reebok, it's all part of the marketing. The company sells its shoes in 140 countries. Foreign sales account for about 39 percent of its $3.3 billion in annual revenue. Reebok has also run a high-impact marketing campaign in the United States, enlisting the endorsements of some of the biggest names in sports, including basketball star Shaquille O'Neal, Superbowl MVP Emmitt Smith, baseball slugger Frank Thomas, Olympic skater Nancy Kerrigan and golfer Greg Norman.

Athletic shoes continue to be the dominant segment of Reebok's balance sheet. In the U.S. market, sales of footwear account for 72 percent of total revenue, while apparel and specialty products make up the other 28 percent. In the foreign market, shoe sales account for 86 percent of revenue and apparel makes up 14 percent.

Reebok's current claim to fame is The Pump, an athletic shoe with a special cushion that inflates around the foot to provide added support while keeping the shoe lightweight. With the air cushion technology and the newest generation of ultralight foams and plastics, Reebok has reduced the weight of its shoes by more than 50 percent over the past decade. Its high-performance running shoes today weigh just 5.5 ounces, compared with 12 ounces in 1985 and 16 ounces in 1975.

Along with The Pump, Reebok markets several other popular brands, including the Instapump shoe, Rockport shoes, Greg Norman golf shoes and apparel, Avia shoes and apparel, and Boks casual shoes. Founded in 1979, Reebok has 4,700 employees and 9,000 shareholders.

EARNINGS-PER-SHARE GROWTH

Past 5 years: 97 percent (15 percent per year)
Past 10 years: 3,675 percent (43 percent per year)

STOCK GROWTH ★ ★ ★ ★

Past 10 years: 800 percent (25 percent per year)
Dollar growth: $10,000 over 10 years (including reinvested dividends) would have grown to $100,000
Average annual compounded rate of return (including reinvested dividends): 26 percent

DIVIDEND YIELD ★

Average dividend yield in the past 3 years: 0.9 percent

DIVIDEND GROWTH

Increased dividend: 0 consecutive years
Past 5-year increase: 0 percent (0 percent per year)

CONSISTENCY

Increased earnings per share: 9 of past 10 years
Increased sales: 9 of past 10 years

SHAREHOLDER PERKS

The company offers no dividend reinvestment plan, nor does it offer any other perks.

REEBOK INTERNATIONAL AT A GLANCE

Fiscal year ended: Dec. 31
Revenue and net income in $ millions

	1989	1990	1991	1992	1993	1994	5-year Growth Avg. Annual (%)	5-year Growth Total (%)
Revenue ($)	1,822.1	2,159.2	2,734.4	3,022.6	2,893.9	3,280.4	13	80
Net income ($)	175	177	235	115	223	255	8	45
Earnings/share ($)	1.53	1.54	2.37	1.24	2.53	3.02	15	97
Div. per share ($)	.30	.30	.30	.30	.30	.30	—	—
Dividend yield (%)	2.1	2.0	1.2	1.0	1.0	.8	—	—
Avg. PE ratio	10	10	11	12	12	11	—	—

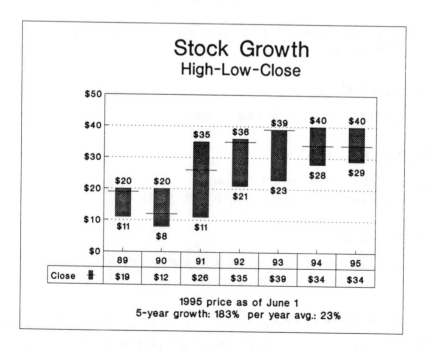

Stock Growth
High-Low-Close

	89	90	91	92	93	94	95
Close	$19	$12	$26	$35	$39	$34	$34

1995 price as of June 1
5-year growth: 183% per year avg.: 23%

FIserv, Inc.

25 FIserv Dr.
Brookfield, WI 53045
414-879-5000
800-425-FISV (investor relations)

Chairman and CEO: George D. Dalton
President and COO: Leslie M. Muma

Earnings Growth	★ ★ ★	Dividend Growth	
Stock Growth	★ ★ ★ ★	Consistency	★ ★ ★
Dividend Yield		Shareholder Perks	
NYSE—FISV		**Total**	**10 points**

As banks across the country add to their list of sophisticated services, such as automatic teller machines, credit cards, wire transfers, brokerage services and retirement accounts, the demand on their time and technological capabilities continues to mount. FIserv has carved its niche by helping these overburdened institutions keep up with the mountain of paperwork that comes with the additional services.

Founded in 1984 by George Dalton and Leslie Muma (who continue to serve as chairman and president, respectively), FIserv has quickly become the nation's leading independent data processing provider for banks, savings institutions and credit unions with assets over $25 million. It has also established the nation's largest check clearing customer base.

The suburban Milwaukee operation has grown quickly through a rapid-fire succession of acquisitions. The company has made more than 50 acquisitions over the past 10 years.

FIserv provides a wide range of data processing services. It also provides account processing services, administration and trusteeship of self-directed retirement plans, marketing communications and graphic design services, plastic card products and services and disaster recovery services.

Basically, FIserv is able to step in and take over the responsibilities of the financial institutions' data processing departments—and do it more effectively and inexpensively than the banks can do it themselves. That is why more than 1,500 banks and financial institutions have turned their data processing duties over to FIserv. FIserv has 6,200 employees and 10,000 shareholders.

EARNINGS-PER-SHARE GROWTH   ★ ★ ★

Past 5 years: 138 percent (19 percent per year)

STOCK GROWTH   ★ ★ ★ ★

Past 9 years: 525 percent (23 percent per year)
Dollar growth: $62,500 over 9 years (including reinvested dividends) would have grown to $100,000
Average annual compounded rate of return (including reinvested dividends): 23 percent

DIVIDEND YIELD

Pays no dividend

DIVIDEND GROWTH

Pays no dividend

CONSISTENCY   ★ ★ ★

Increased earnings per share: 9 consecutive years
Increased sales: 9 consecutive years

SHAREHOLDER PERKS

The company offers no dividend reinvestment and stock purchase plan, nor does it provide any other shareholder perks.

FISERV AT A GLANCE

Fiscal year ended: Dec. 31
Revenue and net income in $ millions

	1989	1990	1991	1992	1993	1994	5-year Growth Avg. Annual (%)	Total (%)
Revenue ($)	164.0	183.2	281.3	332.1	454.7	563.6	28	240
Net income ($)	11.4	13.8	18.3	23.0	30.7	37.7	27	230
Earnings/share ($)	.40	.47	.56	.67	.80	.95	19	138
Div. per share ($)	–	–	–	–	–	–	—	—
Dividend yield (%)	–	–	–	–	–	–	—	—
Avg. PE ratio	16.1	14.8	22.0	23.3	25.0	22.2	—	—

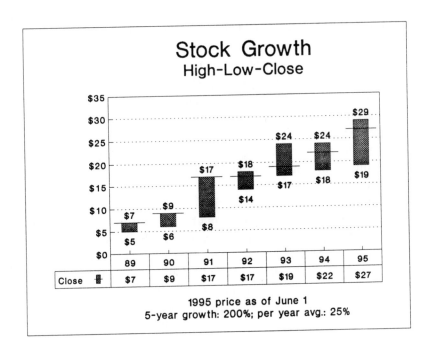

Stock Growth
High-Low-Close

Close	89	90	91	92	93	94	95
	$7	$9	$17	$17	$19	$22	$27

1995 price as of June 1
5-year growth: 200%; per year avg.: 25%

89

The Olsten Corp.

Olsten
Corporation™

175 Broad Hollow Road
Melville, NY 11747-8905
516-844-7800

Chairman and CEO: Frank N. Liguori
President: Stuart Olsten

Earnings Growth	★ ★ ★	Dividend Growth	★
Stock Growth	★ ★ ★	Consistency	★ ★
Dividend Yield	★	Shareholder Perks	
NYSE—OLS		**Total**	**10 points**

With its ready corps of stand-in office clerks and factory workers, Olsten Corp. has long been one of the nation's fastest-growing temp help services. Now the company has broadened its services to dominate a new arena. Through a series of acquisitions and agreements, Olsten has become the nation's leading provider of home health care services.

In 1994, Olsten reached an agreement with Columbia/HCA Healthcare Corp. (the nation's largest hospital system) to manage home health agencies in 22 of its hospitals. The company has reached agreements for similar services with a number of other managed care organizations.

Health care services now account for about 51 percent of Olsten's $2.26 billion in annual revenue. Staffing services make up the other 49 percent of revenue.

The company provides services for business, industry, health care organizations and government through a 1,200-office network that covers the United States, Canada, Mexico and Great Britain.

In all, the Melville, New York, operation serves more than 500,000 patient and client accounts and employs about 650,000 people.

Its health care services include skilled nursing and home health aides, as well as a variety of other related services.

Olsten's staffing services include general office and administrative services, office automation and records management, and other services for corporations.

The firm's temporary workers are typically used by client businesses to bolster their full-time staff during peak periods or to replace workers during vacations or illnesses. Olsten has more than 3,000 permanent employees and 1,200 shareholders.

EARNINGS-PER-SHARE GROWTH ★ ★ ★

Past 5 years: 110 percent (16 percent per year)
Past 10 years: 523 percent (43 percent per year)

STOCK GROWTH ★ ★ ★

Past 10 years: 567 percent (21 percent per year)
Dollar growth: $10,000 over 10 years (including reinvested dividends) would have grown to $75,000
Average annual compounded rate of return (including reinvested dividends): 22 percent

DIVIDEND YIELD ★

Average dividend yield in the past 3 years: 0.9 percent

DIVIDEND GROWTH ★

Increased dividend: 8 of past 10 years
Past 5-year increase: 73 percent (12 percent per year)

CONSISTENCY ★ ★

Increased earnings per share: 8 of past 10 years
Increased sales: 15 consecutive years

SHAREHOLDER PERKS

The company offers no dividend reinvestment plan, nor does it offer any other shareholder perks.

OLSTEN AT A GLANCE

Fiscal year ended: Dec. 31
Revenue and net income in $ millions

	1989	1990	1991	1992	1993	1994	5-year Growth Avg. Annual (%)	Total (%)
Revenue ($)	580.1	1,331.5	1,696.7	1,956.1	2,157.5	2,260.3	31	290
Net income ($)	18.1	14.7	14.6	21.1	45.8	68.0	29.5	278
Earnings/share ($)	.78	.63	.62	.87	1.16	1.62	16	110
Div. per share ($)	.15	.16	.16	.19	.24	.26	12	73
Dividend yield (%)	1.1	1.7	1.2	.9	.9	.8	—	—
Avg. PE ratio	17	14.5	21	23	23	20	—	—

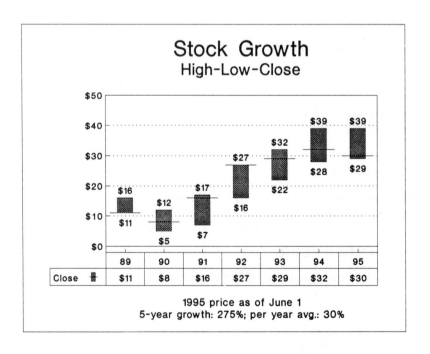

Stock Growth
High-Low-Close

	89	90	91	92	93	94	95
Close	$11	$8	$16	$27	$29	$32	$30

1995 price as of June 1
5-year growth: 275%; per year avg.: 30%

Bandag, Inc.

Bandag Center
2905 N. Hwy. 61
Muscatine, IA 52761-5886
319-262-1400

Chairman, President and CEO:
Martin G. Carver

Earnings Growth		Dividend Growth	★ ★
Stock Growth	★ ★	Consistency	★ ★ ★
Dividend Yield	★	Shareholder Perks	★ ★
NYSE—BDG		**Total**	**10 points**

Bandag's retreads roll daily across the highways and byways of the world. The Muscatine, Iowa, manufacturer markets its tire retreading process in more than 110 countries. Nearly two-thirds of its 1,325 franchisees are located outside the United States.

The world's largest producer of procured tread rubber and equipment, Bandag manufactures more than 500 separate tread designs and sizes. Its retreading process is used for tires on industrial equipment, off-road equipment and passenger cars. But truck and bus retreads comprise by far the largest share of the company's business, accounting for more than 90 percent of the firm's $651 million in annual revenue.

In the U.S. market, Bandag retreads make up 16 percent of the total light and heavy truck tire replacement market (including new tire sales).

Bandag's two-step cold-bonding retreading process was introduced in 1957 by the late Roy C. Carver, the company founder.

The process begins at the Bandag factory, where the rubber is molded under high pressure and high temperatures to make it denser, harder and more durable. Then the tread is shipped to the franchise shops, where it is bonded to tires using a lower temperature, lower pressure process.

The company claims that its two-step process, while more expensive than the alternative "hot-capped" retreating processes, produces tires that are more durable and ultimately cost less per mile. Bandag retreads also cost considerably less than new tires. In addition to its retreading process, Bandag custom-formulates rubber compounds to customer specifications for a variety of other uses. Retread materials and supplies account for 93 percent of Bandag's revenue, while its other products provide 7 percent of revenue. Bandag has 2,400 employees and 4,500 shareholders. The Carver family controls 73 percent of the voting stock.

EARNINGS-PER-SHARE GROWTH

Past 5 years: 34 percent (6 percent per year)
Past 10 years: 216 percent (12 percent per year)

STOCK GROWTH ★ ★

Past 10 years: 335 percent (16 percent per year)
Dollar growth: $10,000 over 10 years (including reinvested dividends) would have grown to $50,000
Average annual compounded rate of return (including reinvested dividends): 17.5 percent

DIVIDEND YIELD ★

Average dividend yield in the past 3 years: 1.2 percent

DIVIDEND GROWTH ★ ★

Increased dividend: 18 consecutive years
Past 5-year increase: 59 percent (10 percent per year)

CONSISTENCY ★ ★ ★

Increased earnings per share: 9 of past 10 years
Increased sales: 9 of past 10 years

SHAREHOLDER PERKS

Good dividend reinvestment and stock purchase plan: voluntary stock purchase plan allows contributions of $50 to $10,000 per quarter.

BANDAG AT A GLANCE

Fiscal year ended: Dec. 31
Revenue and net income in $ millions

	1989	1990	1991	1992	1993	1994	5-year Growth Avg. Annual (%)	Total (%)
Revenue ($)	525.3	586.2	582.9	591.4	590.2	650.6	5	24
Net income ($)	75.9	78.8	79.6	83.0	78.7	94.0	5	24
Earnings/share ($)	2.61	2.75	2.86	2.99	2.88	3.51	6	34
Div. per share ($)	.46	.51	.56	.61	.66	.73	10	59
Dividend yield (%)	1.2	1.3	1.1	.9	1.2	1.3	—	—
Avg. PE ratio	15	15	18	21.5	19	16	—	—

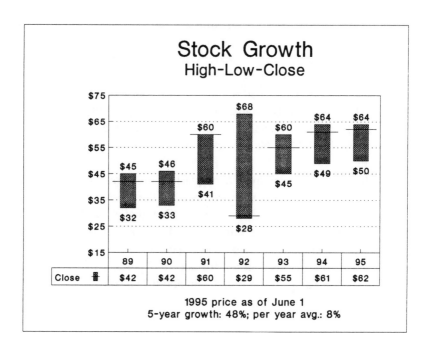

Stock Growth
High-Low-Close

	89	90	91	92	93	94	95
Close	$42	$42	$60	$29	$55	$61	$62

1995 price as of June 1
5-year growth: 48%; per year avg.: 8%

91

American International Group, Inc.

70 Pine St.
New York, NY 10270
212-770-7000

Chairman and CEO: Maurice R. Greenberg
President: Thomas R. Tizzio

Earnings Growth	★	Dividend Growth	★ ★
Stock Growth	★ ★	Consistency	★ ★ ★ ★
Dividend Yield	★	Shareholder Perks	
NYSE—UNH		**Total**	**10 points**

Founded in China in 1919 by an American entrepreneur, American International Group has grown to become one of the world's leading insurance organizations and the largest underwriter of commercial and industrial coverage in the United States.

When C.V. Starr opened a small insurance agency called American Asiatic Underwriters, Shanghai was the bustling commercial center of China and East Asia. Because of political unrest, however, Starr relocated his company in 1939 to New York, where the company later adopted its current name.

Although the company's headquarters was moved to New York, Starr's insurance company never abandoned the world stage. As a sign of the times, AIG reestablished a presence in Shanghai in 1992 as China began to reembrace capitalism. The same year, AIG opened an office in Moscow, the first American insurance company to do so.

Overseas operations account for about 47 percent of AIG's revenue. Its member companies write policies in about 130 countries.

AIG's mainstay is property and casualty insurance. It also offers individual and group life and health insurance, risk management and insurance agency services, and personal auto insurance.

AIG's largest business segment is its domestic general brokerage group (38 percent of income), which markets property-casualty insurance products to corporations and commercial customers.

The other segments include life insurance (29 percent of pretax income), foreign general (16 percent), financial services (15.5 percent); and other services about 1 percent. The company has 33,000 employees and 10,400 shareholders.

EARNINGS-PER-SHARE GROWTH   ★

Past 5 years: 55 percent (9 percent per year)
Past 10 years: 548 percent (21 percent per year)

STOCK GROWTH   ★ ★

Past 10 years: 368 percent (16.5 percent per year)
Dollar growth: $10,000 over 10 years (including reinvested dividends) would have grown to $48,000
Average annual compounded rate of return (including reinvested dividends): 17 percent

DIVIDEND YIELD   ★

Average dividend yield in the past 3 years: 0.5 percent

DIVIDEND GROWTH   ★ ★

Increased dividend: 8 consecutive years
Past 5-year increase: 74 percent (12 percent per year)

CONSISTENCY   ★ ★ ★ ★

Increased earnings per share: 10 consecutive years

SHAREHOLDER PERKS

The company does not offer a dividend reinvestment and stock purchase plan, nor does it provide any other shareholder perks.

AMERICAN INTERNATIONAL GROUP AT A GLANCE

Fiscal year ended: Dec. 31
Revenue and net income in $ millions

	1989	1990	1991	1992	1993	1994	5-year Growth Avg. Annual (%)	Total (%)
Revenue ($)	14,150	15,702	16,884	18,389	20,135	22,442	10	59
Net income ($)	1,367	1,442	1,553	1,657	1,939	2,176	10	59
Earnings/share ($)	4.42	4.61	4.86	5.20	6.11	6.87	9	55
Div. per share ($)	.23	.27	.31	.35	.39	.40	12	74
Dividend yield (%)	0.5	0.6	0.5	0.6	0.4	0.5	—	—
Avg. PE ratio	11.2	10.9	12.1	12.6	14.4	13.2	—	—

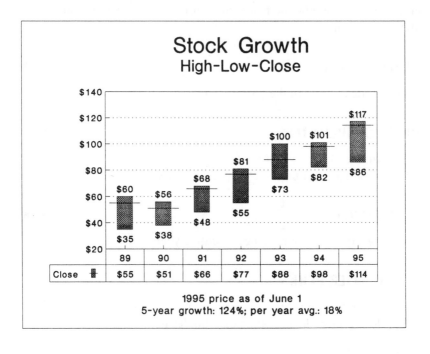

Stock Growth
High-Low-Close

	89	90	91	92	93	94	95
Close	$55	$51	$66	$77	$88	$98	$114

1995 price as of June 1
5-year growth: 124%; per year avg.: 18%

Sigma-Aldrich Co.

SIGMA-ALDRICH
CORPORATION

3050 Spruce St.
St. Louis, MO 63103
314-771-5765

Chairman, President and CEO:
Dr. Tom Cori

Earnings Growth	★	Dividend Growth	★ ★
Stock Growth	★ ★	Consistency	★ ★ ★ ★
Dividend Yield	★	Shareholder Perks	
NASDAQ—SIAL		**Total**	**10 points**

Sigma-Aldrich may not unlock the cures of modern medicine, but it does contribute to the chain of success. The company supplies more than 75,000 chemical compounds for research laboratories around the world.

The company produces organic and inorganic chemicals, radio labeled chemicals, diagnostic reagents and a wide variety of other compounds for use in research and development, in the diagnosis of disease, and as specialty chemicals for manufacturing. The St. Louis–based operation also handles 60,000 rare esoteric chemicals for special research projects.

Scientist use Sigma-Aldrich's chemicals in the fields of biochemistry, synthetic chemistry, quality control and testing, immunology, hematology, pharmacology, microbiology, neurology, endocrinology and agriculture. Sigma diagnostic products are used in the detection of heart, liver and kidney diseases and various metabolic disorders. In all, the company's chemical products division accounts for 81 percent of its $851 million in total annual revenue.

The other 19 percent of Sigma-Aldrich's revenue comes from its B-Line Systems unit, which manufactures metal components for strut, cable tray and pipe support systems in power plants, refineries and manufacturing facilities.

Sigma-Aldrich has clients in nearly every country in the world. Foreign sales account for about 51 percent of the company's revenue.

The company sells its chemicals to about 134,000 customers, including scientists and technicians in hospitals, universities, clinical laboratories and private and governmental research laboratories. The firm was formed in 1975 through the merger of Sigma and Aldrich. It has posted 20 consecutive years of record earnings since the merger. The company has 5,100 employees and 2,000 shareholders.

EARNINGS-PER-SHARE GROWTH ★

Past 5 years: 71 percent (11.5 percent per year)
Past 10 years: 370 percent (17 percent per year)

STOCK GROWTH ★ ★

Past 10 years: 294 percent (15 percent per year)
Dollar growth: $10,000 over 10 years (including reinvested dividends) would have grown to $42,000
Average annual compounded rate of return (including reinvested dividends): 15.5 percent

DIVIDEND YIELD ★

Average dividend yield in the past 3 years: 0.6 percent

DIVIDEND GROWTH ★ ★

Increased dividend: 20 consecutive years
Past 5-year increase: 79 percent (12.5 percent per year)

CONSISTENCY ★ ★ ★ ★

Increased earnings per share: 20 consecutive years
Increased sales: 20 consecutive years

SHAREHOLDER PERKS

Sigma-Aldrich offers no dividend reinvestment plan, nor does it offer any other shareholder perks.

SIGMA-ALDRICH AT A GLANCE

Fiscal year ended: Dec. 31
Revenue and net income in $ millions

	1989	1990	1991	1992	1993	1994	5-year Growth Avg. Annual (%)	5-year Growth Total (%)
Revenue ($)	441.1	529.1	589.4	654.4	739.4	851.2	14	93
Net income ($)	64	71	80	96	96	110	12	72
Earnings/share ($)	1.29	1.44	1.60	1.92	2.15	2.21	11.5	71
Div. per share ($)	.19	.21	.23	.26	.30	.34	12.5	79
Dividend yield (%)	0.7	0.7	0.6	0.5	0.6	0.8	—	—
Avg. PE ratio	19.5	21	25	26	23	18.5	—	—

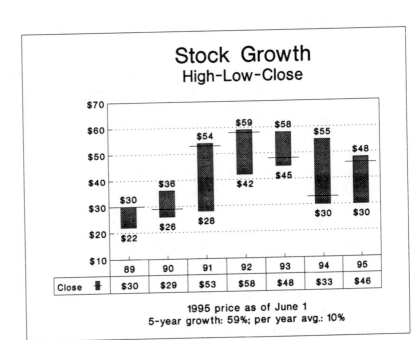

Stock Growth
High-Low-Close

	89	90	91	92	93	94	95
Close		$30	$29	$53	$58	$48	$33	$46

1995 price as of June 1
5-year growth: 59%; per year avg.: 10%

Torchmark Corp.

2001 Third Avenue South
Birmingham, AL 35233
205-325-4200

Chairman, President and CEO:
R. K. Richey

Earnings Growth		Dividend Growth	★
Stock Growth	★	Consistency	★ ★ ★ ★
Dividend Yield	★ ★	Shareholder Perks	★ ★
NYSE—TMK		**Total**	**10 points**

Insurance and financial services stalwart Torchmark Corp. continues building on its strength in the life insurance field with the 1994 acquisition of the $560 million American Income Holdings, which sells life insurance to credit unions and union members.

Through its life insurance subsidiaries, Torchmark generates about 59 percent of its $1.9 billion in annual income. The company has enjoyed a 43-year streak of increased earnings and dividends per share on the strength of its simple operating philosophy. It states that Torchmark will focus on managing well the things it can control so that it can respond to or take advantage of things it cannot control.

Among the things it could not control was President Clinton's 1993 proposed Health Security Act. Although Congress killed the proposal, the uncertainty weighed on Torchmark's stock price as well as that of other insurance and health care concerns.

Torchmark's principal life insurance subsidiary is Liberty National Life Insurance. The unit, which employs more than 3,000 full-time sales representatives throughout the southeastern United States, also sells health, interest-sensitive life and cancer coverage insurance.

About 40 percent of the company's income comes through premiums and fees paid for health insurance. Other principal subsidiaries include United American Insurance Company, which sells senior life and health care insurance through 57,000 independent agents; Global Life and Accident Insurance Company; and United Investors Life Insurance Company.

Another Torchmark subsidiary is Waddell & Reed, which sells individual life insurance and annuities through 2,800 sales representatives and independent agents nationwide. Agents also sell a broad range of mutual funds and provide financial planning services.

The Birmingham, Alabama, operation has 6,300 employees and 8,300 shareholders.

EARNINGS-PER-SHARE GROWTH

Past 5 years: 47 percent (8 percent per year)
Past 10 years: 263 percent (14 percent per year)

STOCK GROWTH ★

Past 10 years: 183 percent (11 percent per year)
Dollar growth: $10,000 over 10 years (including reinvested dividends) would have grown to $37,000
Average annual compounded rate of return (including reinvested dividends): 14 percent

DIVIDEND YIELD ★ ★

Average dividend yield in the past 3 years: 2.4 percent

DIVIDEND GROWTH ★

Increased dividend: 43 consecutive years
Past 5-year increase: 35 percent (6 percent per year)

CONSISTENCY ★ ★ ★ ★

Increased earnings per share: 43 consecutive years

SHAREHOLDER PERKS

Good dividend reinvestment and stock purchase plan: voluntary stock purchase plan allows contributions of $100 to $3,000 eight times per year.

TORCHMARK AT A GLANCE

Fiscal year ended: Dec. 31
Revenue and net income in $ millions

	1989	1990	1991	1992	1993	1994	5-year Growth Avg. Annual (%)	5-year Growth Total (%)
Revenue ($)	1,633.6	1,787.1	1,907.4	2,045.8	2,176.8	1,922.6	3	18
Net income ($)	218.9	238.2	255.3	277.0	288.3	262.6	3	20
Earnings/share ($)	2.59	2.85	3.13	3.58	3.76	3.81	8	47
Div. per share ($)	.83	.93	1.00	1.07	1.09	1.12	6	35
Dividend yield (%)	2.2	2.9	2.6	1.9	2.4	3.2	—	—
Avg. PE ratio	10.6	10.6	11.1	12.6	14.5	14.7	—	—

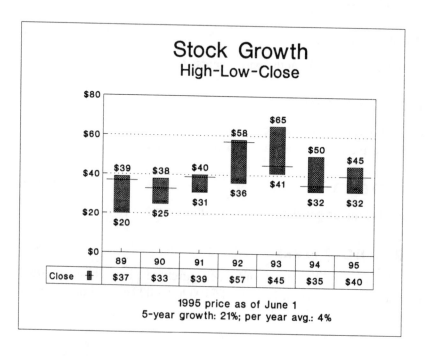

Stock Growth
High-Low-Close

	89	90	91	92	93	94	95
Close	$37	$33	$39	$57	$45	$35	$40

1995 price as of June 1
5-year growth: 21%; per year avg.: 4%

9

Crown Cork & Seal Company

9300 Ashton Road
Philadelphia, PA
215-698-5100

Chairman, President and CEO:
William J. Avery

Earnings Growth	★ ★	Dividend Growth	
Stock Growth	★ ★ ★	Consistency	★ ★ ★ ★
Dividend Yield		Shareholder Perks	
NYSE—CCK		**Total**	**9 points**

Crown Cork & Seal, the king of cans, containers and closures, is maintaining its claim to the industry throne though a series of reorganizations, plant closings and new operations around the world.

The restructurings and major capital expenditures to boost productivity at its 160 plants worldwide are designed to help Crown Cork better serve its core clients in the food, citrus, brewing, soft drink, oil, paint, toiletry, drug, antifreeze, chemical and pet food industries.

The Philadelphia-based manufacturer has enjoyed steady growth, with 12 consecutive years of increased earnings.

Crown Cork not only manufactures metal and plastic containers but also manufactures and markets packaging and handling machinery. The production of metal cans is Crown Cork's mainstay, generating about 66 percent of the company's $4.45 billion in annual revenue.

In 1994, Crown Cork opened a food can plant in Owatonna, Minnesota, that produces more than a billion cans a year for companies that pack fresh vegetables and processed food.

Crown Cork is the largest U.S. producer of plastic containers. The sale of plastic containers and closures accounts for about 22 percent of the company's revenue.

Metal crowns, closures and packaging machinery account for about 12 percent of annual sales. The company makes no glass containers.

Crown Cork, which draws about a third of its revenues from international operations, has plants in North America, South America, Europe, Africa and Asia. The firm recently established joint ventures for beverage container manufacturing in China, Brazil and Vietnam. The 103-year-old operation has about 23,000 employees and 6,000 shareholders.

EARNINGS-PER-SHARE GROWTH ★ ★

Past 5 years: 92 percent (14 percent per year)
Past 10 years: 332 percent (16 percent per year)

STOCK GROWTH ★ ★ ★

Past 10 years: 473 percent (19 percent per year)
Dollar growth: $10,000 over 10 years (including reinvested dividends) would have grown to $57,000
Average annual compounded rate of return (including reinvested dividends): 19 percent

DIVIDEND YIELD

Pays no dividend

DIVIDEND GROWTH

Pays no dividend

CONSISTENCY ★ ★ ★ ★

Increased earnings per share: 12 consecutive years
Increased sales: 9 of past 10 years

SHAREHOLDER PERKS

The company offers no dividend reinvestment plan (it pays no dividend), nor does it offer any other shareholder perks.

CROWN CORK & SEAL AT A GLANCE

Fiscal year ended: Dec. 31
Revenue and net income in $ millions

	1989	1990	1991	1992	1993	1994	5-year Growth Avg. Annual (%)	5-year Growth Total (%)
Revenue ($)	1,909.8	3,072.1	3,807.4	3,780.7	4,162.6	4,452.2	18.5	133
Net income ($)	94.2	107.1	128.1	155.4	180.9	204.0	17	117
Earnings/share ($)	1.19	1.24	1.48	1.79	2.08	2.29	14	92
Div. per share ($)	–	–	–	–	–	–	—	—
Dividend yield (%)	–	–	–	–	–	–	—	—
Avg. PE ratio	14	15	17	18.5	18	16	—	—

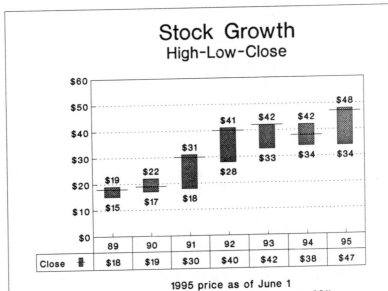

Stock Growth
High-Low-Close

	89	90	91	92	93	94	95
Close		$18	$19	$30	$40	$42	$38	$47

1995 price as of June 1
5-year growth: 147%; per year avg.: 20%

95

Michaels Stores, Inc.

5931 Campus Circle Dr.
Las Colinas Business Park
Irving, TX 75063
214-714-7000

Chairman and CEO: Sam Wyly
President: Jack E. Bush

Earnings Growth	★ ★ ★ ★	Dividend Growth	
Stock Growth	★ ★ ★	Consistency	★ ★
Dividend Yield		Shareholder Perks	
NASDAQ—MIKE		**Total**	**9 points**

It's an imagination destination. Michaels Stores, Inc., is the nation's largest chain of arts and crafts stores, with more than 385 stores in 41 states and Canada. The stores are expansive crafts centers that average 15,000 square feet of sales space. Each store offers about 30,000 different items, including general crafts, art, silk and dried flowers, picture framing material, art and hobby supplies and party merchandise. But Michaels Stores offer more than just merchandise. The stores also provide classes and demonstrations to give hands-on experience for customers.

The company has also added a growing list of young customers through Michaels Kids Club, which boasts more than 250,000 members.

The Irving, Texas, retailer sells merchandise in these departments: general craft materials, including those for stenciling, doll making, jewelry making, woodworking, wall decor and specialty painting; wearable art, including garments, fabric paints, embellishments, jewels and sequins, transfers and appliques; silk flowers, artificial plants and floral arrangements; picture framing materials and services; fine art materials, including paints, brushes, easels and canvas; hobby items, including dollhouses, plastic models and paint-by-number kits; party supplies, greeting cards, invitations and candy; needlecraft items, yarns and needles; and ribbon, including satins, laces, florals and other styles.

In addition to its standard stores, the company has opened a few Michaels Craft and Floral Warehouse outlets that cover 40,000 square feet—more than twice the size of their regular stores. The warehouse stores offer a greater selection of merchandise at discounted prices. Michaels Stores has about 12,000 employees.

EARNINGS-PER-SHARE GROWTH ★ ★ ★ ★

Past 5 years: 656 percent (50 percent per year)
Past 10 years: 9,300 percent (57 percent per year)

STOCK GROWTH ★ ★ ★

Past 10 years: 466 percent (19 percent per year)
Dollar growth: $10,000 over 10 years (including reinvested dividends) would have grown to $57,000
Average annual compounded rate of return (including reinvested dividends): 19 percent

DIVIDEND YIELD

Pays no dividend

DIVIDEND GROWTH

Pays no dividend

CONSISTENCY ★ ★

Increased earnings per share: 8 of past 10 years
Increased sales: 10 consecutive years

SHAREHOLDER PERKS

The company offers no dividend reinvestment and stock purchase plan, nor does it provide any other shareholder perks.

MICHAELS STORES AT A GLANCE

Fiscal year ended: Dec. 31
Revenue and net income in $ millions

	1989	1990	1991	1992	1993	1994	5-year Growth Avg. Annual (%)	Total (%)
Revenue ($)	289.8	362.0	410.9	493.2	619.7	994.5	28	243
Net income ($)	15	21	26	34	41	39	21	160
Earnings/share ($)	.25	.57	.87	1.21	1.52	1.89	50	656
Div. per share ($)	–	–	–	–	–	–	—	—
Dividend yield (%)	–	–	–	–	–	–	—	—
Avg. PE ratio	28	8	13	20	21	25.5	—	—

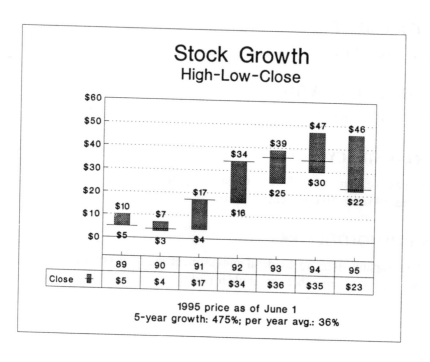

Stock Growth
High-Low-Close

	89	90	91	92	93	94	95
Close	$5	$4	$17	$34	$36	$35	$23

1995 price as of June 1
5-year growth: 475%; per year avg.: 36%

96

W. W. Grainger, Inc.

W.W. GRAINGER, INC.

5500 W. Howard St.
Skokie, IL 60077-2699
708-982-9000

Chairman: David W. Grainger
President and CEO: Richard L. Keyser

Earnings Growth	★	Dividend Growth	★ ★
Stock Growth	★ ★	Consistency	★ ★ ★
Dividend Yield	★	Shareholder Perks	
NYSE—GWW		**Total**	**9 points**

This is a business that's floating on air. W. W. Grainger specializes in air compressors, air tools and paint sprayers, blowers, fans and air conditioning and refrigeration equipment. The Skokie, Illinois, manufacturer also makes other industrial equipment, such as electric motors, gas-engine-driven power plants, heating equipment and controls, hydraulic equipment, janitorial supplies, and lighting fixtures and components.

It also manufactures pumps, material handling and storage equipment, motor controls, office equipment, outdoor equipment, plant and office maintenance equipment, power and hand tools, power transmission components, safety products and shop tools.

In addition to its core business, Grainger also operates Lab Safety Supply, Inc., which it acquired in 1992. Lab Safety sells respiratory systems, protective clothing and other equipment used in the workplace and in environmental cleanup operations. The firm, based in Janesville, Wisconsin, boasts some 350,000 customers.

In all, W. W. Grainger markets about 500,000 products (not all of which are produced by Grainger). The products are marketed through the firm's 338 branches in all 50 states and Puerto Rico.

Grainger sells primarily to contractors, service shops, industrial and commercial maintenance departments, manufacturers, hotels, and health care and educational facilities.

The company offers an innovative "electronic catalog" for customers. The catalog uses PC-based software and CD-ROM technology. With the software or CDs, customers can call up Grainger products on their own PCs. The listings come complete with specifications, prices and pictures. More than 26,000 copies of the electronic catalog are currently in use. Founded in 1927, Grainger has 11,300 employees and 2,100 shareholders.

EARNINGS-PER-SHARE GROWTH ★

Past 5 years: 56 percent (9 percent per year)
Past 10 years: 189 percent (11 percent per year)

STOCK GROWTH ★ ★

Past 10 years: 255 percent (13 percent per year)
Dollar growth: $10,000 over 10 years (including reinvested dividends) would have grown to $40,000
Average annual compounded rate of return (including reinvested dividends): 15 percent

DIVIDEND YIELD ★

Average dividend yield in the past 3 years: 1.2 percent

DIVIDEND GROWTH ★ ★

Increased dividend: 23 consecutive years
Past 5-year increase: 56 percent (9 percent per year)

CONSISTENCY ★ ★ ★

Increased earnings per share: 9 consecutive years
Increased sales: 11 consecutive years

SHAREHOLDER PERKS

The company offers no dividend reinvestment or stock purchase plan, nor does it offer any other shareholder perks.

W. W. GRAINGER AT A GLANCE

Fiscal year ended: Dec. 31
Revenue and net income in $ millions

	1989	1990	1991	1992	1993	1994	5-year Growth Avg. Annual (%)	5-year Growth Total (%)
Revenue ($)	1,727.5	1,935.2	2,077.2	2,364.4	2,628.4	3,023.1	12	75
Net income ($)	119.6	126.8	127.8	137.2	148.4	178	8	48
Earnings/share ($)	2.20	2.31	2.37	2.58	2.88	3.44	9	56
Div. per share ($)	.50	.57	.61	.65	.71	.78	9	56
Dividend yield (%)	1.7	1.7	1.4	1.2	1.2	1.4	—	—
Avg. PE ratio	14	14	18	20	20	18	—	—

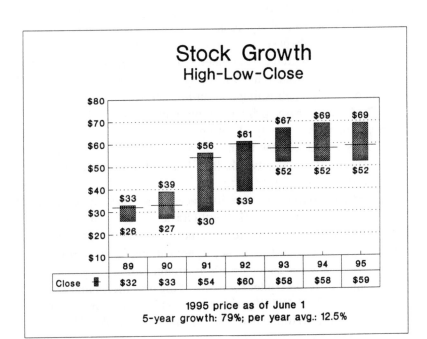

Stock Growth
High-Low-Close

	89	90	91	92	93	94	95
Close	$32	$33	$54	$60	$58	$58	$59

1995 price as of June 1
5-year growth: 79%; per year avg.: 12.5%

97

R. R. Donnelley & Sons Co.

77 West Wacker Drive
Chicago, IL 60601
312-326-8000

Chairman and CEO: John R. Walter

Earnings Growth		Dividend Growth	★
Stock Growth	★	Consistency	★ ★ ★
Dividend Yield	★ ★	Shareholder Perks	★ ★
NYSE—DNY		**Total**	**9 points**

Is there room on the information superhighway for a 132-year-old printing company? R. R. Donnelley thinks so.

The world's largest commercial printer has been repositioning itself to prosper in the digital age. Donnelley has spent more than $2.5 billion in recent years upgrading plant and equipment and investing in CD-ROM or computer diskette publishing and on-line services.

The Chicago-based printer is committed to taking editorial content and reproducing it in a variety of different media. In late 1994, for example, Donnelley announced the formation of its new Digital Division, a world-wide print-on-demand network. It will allow Donnelley to focus on short-run jobs of 5,000 or fewer pieces.

Print will continue to have its place in the world of communications. The myth of the paperless office notwithstanding, Donnelley believes that every new digital medium creates a need for more printed products. For example, *CompuServe* Magazine, a publications for subscribers to the on-line service, now has about 1 million circulation.

Donnelley is the printer for many of the new media magazines such as *CompuServe, CD-ROM World* and *Internet World*. Donnelley remains the printer of more traditional top-selling magazines like *TV Guide, Time,*

Reader's Digest, the National Enquirer, Sports Illustrated and *Modern Maturity.* Donnelley prints nine of the nation's 10 largest-circulated magazines. Magazines constitute about 18 percent of Donnelley's business.

Its largest segment is publishing for catalogers and retailers. Donnelley generates about a third of its revenue by providing digital prepress services and specialty printing for merchants around the world. Although Sears has scrapped its "Big Book" catalog, Donnelley's commercial printing work has continued to grow.

About 14 percent of the company's revenue comes from the printing of telephone directories throughout the world. Donnelley has contracts with most of the largest directory publishers in the United States and the United Kingdom.

Donnelley began doing business in the United Kingdom in 1978 and has since expanded into other countries. About 10 percent of its revenue comes from international ventures. In the coming years, Donnelley will target high-growth markets in Asia, Latin America and Central Europe. New operations in Europe, Asia and Latin America during the third quarter of 1994 helped increase total international sales by nearly 40 percent.

Other sources of income for Donnelley include:

- **Book publishing** (14 percent of revenue). Donnelley prints everything from Michael Crichton's latest bestseller to the all-time best seller—the Bible.
- **Documentation services** (12 percent). This segment provides computer hardware and software documentation and disk replication for companies such as Microsoft and Novell.
- **Financial services publishing, graphic design and database management** (11 percent).

Donnelley has 34,000 employees and 10,500 shareholders.

EARNINGS-PER-SHARE GROWTH

Past 5 years: 22 percent (4 percent per year)
Past 10 years: 99 percent (7 percent per year)

STOCK GROWTH

Past 10 years: 146 percent (9 percent per year)

Dollar growth: $10,000 over 10 years (including reinvested dividends) would have grown to $30,000
Average annual compounded rate of return (including reinvested dividends): 11 percent

DIVIDEND YIELD   ★ ★

Average dividend yield in the past 3 years: 1.8 percent

DIVIDEND GROWTH   ★

Increased dividend: More than 19 consecutive years
Past 5-year increase: 36 percent (6 percent per year)

CONSISTENCY   ★ ★ ★

Increased earnings per share: 9 of past 10 years
Increased sales: More than 20 consecutive years

SHAREHOLDER PERKS   ★ ★

Good dividend reinvestment and stock purchase plan: voluntary stock purchase plan allows contributions of $10 to $60,000 per year.

R. R. DONNELLEY & SONS AT A GLANCE

Fiscal year ended: Dec. 31
Revenue and net income in $ millions

	1989	1990	1991	1992	1993	1994	5-year Growth Avg. Annual (%)	Total (%)
Revenue ($)	3,122	3,498	3,915	4,193	4,388	4,889	10	57
Net income ($)	222	226	205	235	246	269	4	22
Earnings/share ($)	1.43	1.45	1.32	1.51	1.59	1.75	4	22
Div. per share ($)	.44	48	.50	.51	.54	.60	6	36
Dividend yield (%)	2.0	2.1	2.0	1.8	1.7	2.0	—	—
Avg. PE ratio	16.2	15.0	15.9	21.1	19.5	18.5	—	—

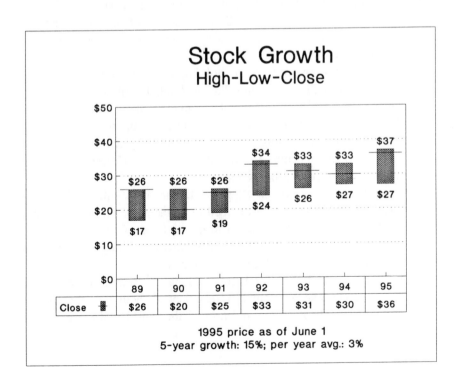

Stock Growth
High-Low-Close

	89	90	91	92	93	94	95
Close	$26	$20	$25	$33	$31	$30	$36

1995 price as of June 1
5-year growth: 15%; per year avg.: 3%

98
Manor Care, Inc.

10750 Columbia Pike
Silver Spring, MD 20901-4490
301-681-9400

Chairman, President and CEO:
Stewart Bainum, Jr.

Earnings Growth	★ ★ ★ ★	Dividend Growth	
Stock Growth	★	Consistency	★ ★
Dividend Yield	★	Shareholder Perks	
NYSE—MNR		**Total**	**8 points**

Whether you need a place for the night or for the rest of your life, Manor Care has a bed waiting for you. In addition to its chain of 164 nursing homes and rehabilitation facilities, the company owns or franchises more than 3,200 hotels and motels around the world.

The Silver Spring, Maryland, holding company operates Manor Healthcare, Vitalink Pharmacy and Choice Hotels International.

Manor Care's health care segment accounts for about 79 percent of its $1.16 billion in annual revenue. The company owns, operates or manages 164 nursing centers, including eight medical and physical rehabilitation centers. It also owns an acute care hospital, four assisted living centers and five nursing assistance training schools.

Manor Care also owns an 82 percent share of Vitalink Pharmacy Services, which operates 17 specialized pharmacies in Florida, Indiana, Illinois, Maryland, Ohio, Wisconsin, Iowa, New Jersey, Oregon, Colorado, California and Pennsylvania. Vitalink specializes in filling prescriptions and intravenous preparations for nursing homes.

The company's Choice Hotels International division accounts for 21 percent of revenue. The company is a franchisor of about 3,200 hotels and motels located in all 50 states and around the world under the names

Comfort Inn, Econo Lodge, Quality Inn, Clarion, Rodeway Inn, Friendship Inn and Sleep Inn. Nearly 600 of its hotels are located in 32 countries outside the United States. Manor Care's lodging division has been its fastest-growing area, with sales and earnings growing at more than 20 percent per year over the past 10 years.

Manor Care was founded in 1959 by Stewart Bainum, 74, who continues to serve as vice chairman of the company's board of directors. His son, Stewart Bainum, Jr., 47, succeeded him as company chairman, president and CEO. Manor Care has 26,000 employees and 3,200 shareholders.

EARNINGS-PER-SHARE GROWTH ★ ★ ★ ★

Past 5 years: 223 percent (26.5 percent per year)
Past 10 years: 231 percent (13 percent per year)

STOCK GROWTH ★

Past 10 years: 187 percent (11 percent per year)
Dollar growth: $10,000 over 10 years (including reinvested dividends) would have grown to $100,000
Average annual compounded rate of return (including reinvested dividends): 12 percent

DIVIDEND YIELD ★

Average dividend yield in the past 3 years: 0.5 percent

DIVIDEND GROWTH

Increased dividend: 0 consecutive years
Past 5-year increase: 0 percent

CONSISTENCY ★ ★

Increased earnings per share: 8 of past 10 years
Increased sales: 15 consecutive years

SHAREHOLDER PERKS

The company offers no dividend reinvestment and stock purchase plan, nor does it provide any other shareholder perks.

MANOR CARE AT A GLANCE

Fiscal year ended: May 31
Revenue and net income in $ millions

	1989	1990	1991	1992	1993	1994	5-year Growth Avg. Annual (%)	Total (%)
Revenue ($)	617.0	708.7	815.5	916.2	1,009.7	1,163.1	13	89
Net income ($)	23.0	26.7	32.1	62.5	59.4	78.4	28	241
Earnings/share ($)	.40	.46	.56	.83	1.04	1.29	26.5	223
Div. per share ($)	.09	.09	.09	.09	.09	.09	—	—
Dividend yield (%)	.009	.009	.006	.005	.004	.003	—	—
Avg. PE ratio	25.6	20.6	24.4	18.7	17.8	20.8	—	—

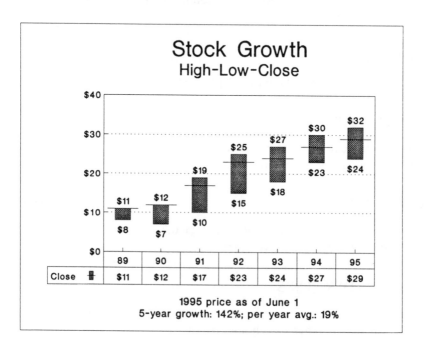

Stock Growth
High-Low-Close

	89	90	91	92	93	94	95
Close	$11	$12	$17	$23	$24	$27	$29

1995 price as of June 1
5-year growth: 142%; per year avg.: 19%

Dillard Department Stores, Inc.

1600 Cantrell Road
P. O. Box 486
Little Rock, AR 72201
501-376-5200

Chairman and CEO: William Dillard
President: William Dillard II

Earnings Growth	★	Dividend Growth	★
Stock Growth	★ ★	Consistency	★ ★ ★ ★
Dividend Yield		Shareholder Perks	
NYSE—DDS		**Total**	**8 points**

At age 80, William Dillard is still the heart and soul—and chairman and CEO—of the department store chain he founded in 1938. He is one of the few founders of a major U.S. corporation who has managed to keep the company a family affair. His son William II is the president and chief operating officer, sons Alex and Mike are executive vice presidents, and daughter Drue Corbusier is a vice president.

Keeping it in the family has worked wonders for Dillard Department Stores. While the company stock suffered as part of a retail sector downturn through 1993 and 1994, the firm continued to add to its long-standing record of increased profits. Dillard has posted 14 consecutive years of increased revenue, book value and earnings per share.

The Little Rock, Arkansas, retailer operates about 230 stores in 20 states, predominately in the South and Southwest. Its biggest concentration is in Texas, where it operates 62 stores, followed by Florida with 27 and Louisiana and Missouri with 16.

Dillard traditionally opens about five to 10 new stores a year and has made several key acquisitions in recent years.

Dillard specializes in middle to upper range priced merchandise, with emphasis on apparel and home furnishings. It recently switched to an "everyday low price" strategy, rather than the traditional approach of occasional special sales.

Revenue by category breaks down this way: women's clothing, 36 percent of sales; men's clothing and accessories, 18 percent; children's clothing, 12 percent; home furnishings and appliances, 12 percent; and shoes, cosmetics, lingerie, accessories and other products, 22 percent.

While Dillard's stores vary in size from 30,000 to 370,000 square feet, most of its newer stores are in the range of 140,000 to 225,000 square feet. The company has 36,000 employees and 7,400 shareholders.

EARNINGS-PER-SHARE GROWTH   ★

Past 5 years: 54 percent (9 percent per year)
Past 10 years: 266 percent (14 percent per year)

STOCK GROWTH   ★ ★

Past 10 years: 251 percent (13 percent per year)
Dollar growth: $10,000 over 10 years (including reinvested dividends) would have grown to $28,000
Average annual compounded rate of return (including reinvested dividends): 13.5 percent

DIVIDEND YIELD

Average dividend yield in the past 3 years: 0.2 percent

DIVIDEND GROWTH   ★

Increased dividend: 2 consecutive years
Past 5-year increase: 67 percent (11 percent per year)

CONSISTENCY   ★ ★ ★ ★

Increased earnings per share: 14 consecutive years
Increased sales: 14 consecutive years

SHAREHOLDER PERKS

The company does not offer a dividend reinvestment plan, nor does it offer any other type of shareholder perks.

DILLARD DEPARTMENT STORE AT A GLANCE

Fiscal year ended: Dec. 31
Revenue and net income in $ millions

	1989	1990	1991	1992	1993	1994	5-year Growth Avg. Annual (%)	Total (%)
Revenue ($)	3,049	3,606	4,036	4,714	5,131	5,546	13	82
Net income ($)	148.1	182.8	206.2	236.4	241.1	251.8	11	70
Earnings/share ($)	1.45	1.67	1.84	2.11	2.14	2.23	9	54
Div. per share ($)	.06	.07	.07	.08	.08	.10	11	67
Dividend yield (%)	.3	.2	.2	.2	.2	.3	—	—
Avg. PE ratio	14.1	16.0	21.8	19.4	17.5	13.4	—	—

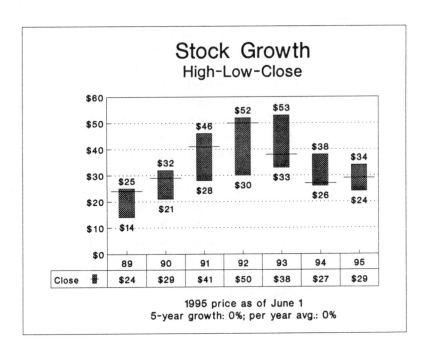

Stock Growth
High-Low-Close

	89	90	91	92	93	94	95
Close	$24	$29	$41	$50	$38	$27	$29

1995 price as of June 1
5-year growth: 0%; per year avg.: 0%

100

Computer Sciences Corp.

2100 E. Grand Ave.
El Segundo, CA 90245
310-615-0311

Chairman and CEO: William R. Hoover
President and COO: Van B. Honecutt

Earnings Growth	★	Dividend Growth	
Stock Growth	★ ★ ★	Consistency	★ ★ ★ ★
Dividend Yield		Shareholder Perks	
NYSE—CSC		**Total**	**8 points**

For many years, Computer Sciences earned most of its money designing, installing and servicing computer and communications systems for the U.S. government. But the El Segundo, California, operation has been steadily pushing into both the private sector and the international arena. In 1994, it cut its biggest deal outside the U.S. market when it signed a contract to provide computer outsourcing for British Aerospace Corp. for $1.5 billion.

Founded in 1959, Computer Sciences claims to be the nation's largest independent provider of information technology consulting, systems integration and outsourcing to industry and government.

The company's push beyond the federal government has been adding to its bottom line. As recently as 1992, some 57 percent of its revenue came from U.S. government contracts. By 1994, that figure had slipped to just 48 percent of its $2.58 billion in annual revenue. U.S. commercial customers account for 39 percent of revenue, state and local governments make up 1 percent and international customers account for 12 percent.

For the federal government, Computer Sciences designs computer-based systems and communications systems for the aerospace, defense and satellite communications industries.

In the commercial market, the company provides consulting and technical services in the development and integration of computer and communications systems, and comprehensive information technology services, including systems analysis, applications development, network operations and data center management. Computer Sciences has 29,000 employees and 8,000 shareholders.

EARNINGS-PER-SHARE GROWTH

Past 5 years: 62 percent (10 percent per year)
Past 10 years: 302 percent (15 percent per year)

STOCK GROWTH

Past 10 years: 541 percent (20.5 percent per year)
Dollar growth: $10,000 over 10 years (including reinvested dividends) would have grown to $64,000
Average annual compounded rate of return (including reinvested dividends): 20.5 percent

DIVIDEND YIELD

Pays no dividend

DIVIDEND GROWTH

Pays no dividend

CONSISTENCY ★ ★ ★ ★

Increased earnings per share: 10 consecutive years
Increased sales: 15 consecutive years

SHAREHOLDER PERKS

The company offers no dividend reinvestment or stock purchase plan, nor does it provide any other shareholder perks.

COMPUTER SCIENCES AT A GLANCE

Fiscal year ended: March 31
Revenue and net income in $ millions

	1989	1990	1991	1992	1993	1994	5-year Growth Avg. Annual (%)	5-year Growth Total (%)
Revenue ($)	1,500.4	1,737.8	2,113.3	2,479.8	2,582.7	3,372.5	18	125
Net income ($)	65.5	64.9	68.2	78.1	90.9	110.7	11	69
Earnings/share ($)	1.21	1.34	1.37	1.55	1.77	2.09	12	73
Div. per share ($)	–	–	–	–	–	–	—	—
Dividend yield (%)	–	–	–	–	–	–	—	—
Avg. PE ratio	14.4	12.1	16.6	15.2	17.3	19.5	—	—

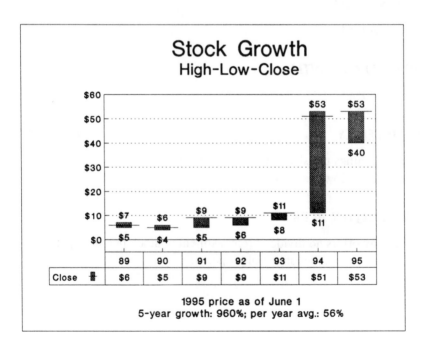

Stock Growth
High-Low-Close

	89	90	91	92	93	94	95
Close	$6	$5	$9	$9	$11	$51	$53

1995 price as of June 1
5-year growth: 960%; per year avg.: 56%

Appendix

The Honorable Mentions List
(40 Companies)

Alco Standard Corp.
825 Duportail Rd.
Wayne, PA 19087-5589
610-296-8000

Alco Office Products is the largest distributor of copiers in North America. Its Unisource subsidiary is North America's largest marketer and distributor of paper and imaging products and supply systems—disposable paper and plastic products, packaging systems and janitorial supplies. Annual revenue: $8 billion.

Andrews Corp.
10500 W. 153rd St.
Orland Park, IL 60462
708-349-3300

Andrews is a global supplier of communications products and systems for industrial, governmental and military customers. Products include coaxial cables, microwave antennas, electronic radar systems, communication reconnaissance systems and related items. Annual revenue: $558 million.

Bausch & Lomb, Inc.
One Chase Square
Rochester, NY 14604
716-338-6000

Bausch & Lomb manufactures personal health products such as health and beauty aids, contact lenses, ophthalmic pharmaceuticals, hearing aids, dental implants and biomedical supplies. It also manufactures sunglasses, binoculars and telescopes. Annual revenue: $1.8 billion.

...son & Co.
...rive
...es, NJ 07417
201-84, ...0

Becton Dickinson manufactures a broad range of medical supplies and devices. It is a world leader in the production of disposable syringes, hypodermic needles and other single-use medical devices designed to reduce the spread of infection. Other products include surgical gloves and blades, presurgery patient prep kits, thermometers, intravenous catheters, suction devices and elastic support products. The company is the leading producer of intravenous catheters. Annual revenue: $26 billion.

Circus Circus Enterprises, Inc.
2880 Las Vegas Blvd. South
Las Vegas, NV 89109-1120
702-734-0410

Owns and operates several hotel casinos in Nevada, including the Circus Circus, Luxor and Excalibur in Las Vegas and the Circus Circus Hotel and Casino in Reno. Annual review: $1.2 billion.

Cisco Systems, Inc.
170 W. Tasman Dr.
San Jose, CA 95134
408-526-4000

Cisco Systems is the world's leading supplier of multimedia, multiprotocol internetworking systems. Its technology is used to build enterprise-wide networks that link an unlimited number of geographically dispersed local area and wide area networks to form a single information infrastructure. Annual revenue: $1.2 billion.

The Clorox Co.
1221 Broadway
Oakland, CA 94612
510-271-7000

Clorox manufactures a broad range of consumer products, including Clorox laundry soaps, Liquid Plumr, Kigsford charcoal, S.O.S. soap pads, Stain Out stain remover, Hidden Valley Ranch salad dressings, Formula

409 all-purpose cleaner, and related products. Annual revenue: $18.4 billion.

Cordis Corp.
14201 N.W. 60th Ave.
Miami Lakes, FL 33014
305-824-2000

Cordis manufactures medical devices, including angiographic catheters, neuroscience devices and related products. Annual revenue: $337 million.

Danaher Corp.
1250 24th St., N.W.
Suite 800
Washington, D.C. 20037
202-828-0850

Danaher manufactures hand tools, process and environmental controls and automotive parts. It has manufactured Sears, Roebuck and Co.'s Craftsman line of mechanics' hand tools for more than 50 years. Annual revenue: $1.3 billion.

Deluxe Corp.
1080 W. County Road F.
St. Paul, MN 55126-8201
612-483-7111

The nation's leading check publisher, Deluxe also provides electronic funds transfer, automated terminal machine card services and credit services. Annual revenue: $1.7 billion.

Equifax, Inc.
P.O. Box 4081
1600 Peachtree St., N.W.
Atlanta, GA 30302
404-885-8000

Equifax provides credit information on consumers for merchants and other businesses. Related services include credit card marketing, risk management, fraud detection and prevention services, check guarantee services, credit card auithorization, insurance information, workers' compensation audits and related matters. Annual revenue: $1.4 billion.

Gannett Company, Inc.
1100 Wilson Blvd.
Arlington, VA 22234
703-284-6000

Gannett is the nation's largest newspaper group, with 83 daily newspapers (including *USA Today*) and 50 nondaily publications. The company also owns 10 television stations, six FM radio stations and five AM radio stations. Its Gannett Outdoor Group is North America's largest outdoor advertising company. Annual revenue: $3.8 billion.

GTE Corp.
1 Stamford Forum
Stamford, CT 06904
203-965-2000

GTE operates the nation's largest non-Bell telecommunications sytstem, with about 23 million customers in 29 states. (It also offers service in Canada, Venezuela and the Dominican Republic.) It's the second largest provider of cellular service. Annual revenue: $20 billion.

Helig Meyers Company
2235 Staples Mill Rd.
Richmond, VA 23230
804-359-9171

Helig-Meyers operates a chain of home furnishing stores located mostly in smaller cities in 24 states (primarily in the Southeast). Annual revenue: $1.2 billion.

Invacare Corp. ✓
899 Cleveland St.
P.O. Box 4028
Elyria, OH 44036-2125
216-329-6000

Manufactures a broad line of home medical equipment, such as walkers, wheelchairs and beds. Annual revenue: $411 million.

Jefferson-Pilot Corp.
100 North Green Street
Greensboro, NC 27401
910-691-3382

Jefferson-Pilot is a holding company of several insurance agencies, including Jefferson-Pilot Life and two property and casualty companies. The firm's communications division operates three television stations and 13 radio stations. Total assets: $6.1 billion.

Kaydon Corp.
Arbor Shoreline Office Park
19345 U.S. 19 N.
Clearwater, FL 34624
813-531-1101

Kaydon manufactures custom-engineered products such as antifriction bearings, filters, filter housings, sealing rings, balls, shaft seals and lip-rings. Its products are used in a wide variety of medical, instrumentation, material handling, aerospace, defense, construction and other industrial applications. Annual revenue: $205 million.

Kimberly Clark Corp.
P.O. Box 619100
Dallas, TX 75261-9100
214-830-1200

The company manufactures a number of paper products, such as Kleenex tissues, Huggies diapers, Kotex and New Freedom feminine care products, Depend and Poise incontinence care products, Hi-Dri household towels, Kimguard sterile wrap, Kimwipes industrial wipers and Classic premium paper. Annual revenue: $7.8 million.

Luby's Cafeterias, Inc.
2211 Northeast Loop 410
P.O. Box 33069
San Antonio, TX 78265-3069
210-654-9000

The company owns and operates 176 cafeterias in the southern United States. Annual revenue: $390 million.

Minnesota Minning & Manufacturing Co. ✓
3M Center
St. Paul, MN 55144-1000
612-733-1110

3M is a diversified manufacturer of tapes, adhesives, coatings, sealants, abrasives, fasteners, plastic films, floor coverings, fabric, paper products, graphic arts and photographic supplies, and medical and dental products. Annual revenue: $14 billion.

Nike, Inc.
One Boweman Drive
Beavertown, OR 97005
503-671-6453

Nike is a major worldwide designer and marketer of athletic shoes and related footwear. Its shoes are sold in 14,000 U.S. outlets and in 82 countries around the world. Annual revenue: $3.8 billion.

Old Kent Financial Corp.
One Vandenberg Center
Grand Rapids, MI 49503
616-771-5000

Old Kent Financial operates 207 branch banks in Michigan and Illinois. It is the 57th-largest banking organization in the U.S. and has posted 13 consecutive years of record earnings. Total assets: $11 billion.

Omnicom Group Inc.
437 Madison Avenue
New York, NY 10022
212-415-3600

Omincom Group is a holding company of a number of world-class advertising agencies, including BBDO Worldwide, DDB Needham Worldwide, and TBWA International Networks General.

Annual revenue: $1.8 billion.

Oracle Systems Corp.
500 Oracle Parkway
Redwood City, CA 94065
415-506-7000

Oracle makes computer software products for a wide variety of uses, including database management and network products, applications development productivity tools and end user applications. The company's principal product is the Oracle relational database management system. Annual revenue: $2 billion.

Owens & Minor, Inc.
4800 Cox Road
Glen Allen, VA 23060
804-747-9794

Owens & Minor is a wholesale supplier of medical and surgical supplies and drugs for hospitals and other health care facilities. Annual revenue: $3.1 billion.

The Pep Boys—Manny, Moe & Jack
3111 West Allegheny Avenue
Philadelphia, PA 19132
215-229-9000

The Pep Boys operates about 400 automotive parts stores throughout the U.S. It also provides maintenance and installation services. Annual revenue: $1.2 billion.

PPG Industries, Inc.
One PPG Place
Pittsburgh, PA 15272
412-434-3131

PPG manufactures a broad range of glass products, fiberglass, coatings, resins, paints, stains and specialty chemicals. Annual revenue: $6.3 billion.

Premier Industrial Corp.
4500 Euclid Avenue
Cleveland, OH 44103
216-391-8300

Premier supplies electronic components for industrial and consumer products as well as essential maintenance and repair products for industrial, commercial and institutional applications. It is also a manufacturer of firefighting equipment. Annual revenue: $740 million.

T. Rowe Price Associates, Inc.
100 East Pratt Street
Baltimore, MD 21202
410-547-2000

The company provides investment advisory services and management for the T. Rowe Price family of mutual funds and for private and institutional accounts. Annual revenue: $382 million.

Quaker Oats Company ⌄
Quaker Tower
P.O. Box 9001
Chicago, IL 60604-9003
312-222-7818

Produces a wide range of well-known foods, including Quaker cereals, Gatorade, Snapple and pet foods. Annual revenue: $6 billion.

Rollins, Inc.
2170 Piedmont Rd. NE
Atlanta, GA 30324
404-888-2000

Rollins is a leader in termite and pest control, plantscaping, lawn care and protective services. It is the parent company of Orkin Exterminating, Orkin Lawn Care and Orkin Plantscaping. Annual revenue: $605 million.

Russell Corp.
1 Lee St.
Alexander City, AL 35010
205-329-4000

Russell is a leading manufacturer of athletic uniforms for professional, collegiate, high school and other teams and individuals. Annual revenue: $1.1 billion.

SouthTrust Corp.
P.O. Box 2554
Birmingham, AL 35290
205-254-5509

SouthTrust is a bank holding company with 24 banks and 177 offices in Alabama, eight banks and 113 offices in Florida, and other banks in Georgia, South Carolina and North Carolina. It is the nation's 40th-largest bank holding company and has posted increased earnings 14 of the past 15 years. Total assets: $17.6 billion.

Stanhome, Inc.
333 Western Avenue
Westfield, MA 01085
413-562-3631

Stanhome makes a line of giftware and collectibles, such as Hamilton dolls, plates and figurines, and the Enesco Precious Moments collection. Annual revenue: $780 million.

Tambrands, Inc.
777 Westchester Avenue
White Plains, NY 10604
914-696-6000

Tambrands is the dominant player in the U.S. tampon market, with a 60 percent share. It is also well-established abroad, where it generates about 50 percent of its $645 million in annual revenue.

Toys "R" Us, Inc.
461 From Road
Paramus, NJ 07652
201-262-7800

Toys "R" Us has more than 600 toy stores in 46 states, and adds new ones at the rate of about 40 per year. But the real growth is outside the United States, where the company adds 65 to 70 new stores a year. In all, Toys "R" Us has about 300 foreign stores in 17 countries. The company also operates a chain of more than 220 Kids "R" Us clothing stores for children in 30 states. Despite the volatile nature of the toy industry, Toys "R" Us has posted 14 consecutive years of record earnings. Annual revenue: $8.8 billion.

Teleflex, Inc.
630 West Germantown Pike
Suite 450
Plymouth Meeting, PA 19462
610-834-6301

Teleflex is a manufacturer of precision controls, systems and related products for military and commercial aircraft. It has posted 19 consecutive years of record sales and earnings. Annual revenue: $910 million.

U.S. Bancorp
111 S.W. 5th Ave.
Portland, OR 97204
603-275-6111

U.S. Bancorp is a regional multibank holding company. Its principal subsidiaries are the U.S. National Bank of Oregon and the U.S. Bank of Washington. Total assets: $22 billion.

V.F. Corp.
1047 North Park Rd.
Wyomissing, PA 19610
215-378-1151

The world's largest publicly held apparel company, V.F. boasts the second, third and fourth largest selling brands in the jeans market—Lee, Rustler and Wrangler, respectively. The company's jeanswear accounts for slightly more than 50 percent of its $5 billion in annual revenue and about one third of the total U.S. jeans market. The company also makes casual wear and intimate apparel.

WMX Technologies, Inc.
3003 Butterfield Rd.
Oak Brook, IL 60521
708-572-8800

WMX is the worldwide leader in providing environmental and waste management services for industry, government and consumers. Annual revenue: $11 billion.

The 100 Best by Industry

Industry	Ranking
Alcoholic Beverages	
Anheuser-Busch Companies, Inc.	51
Apparel	
Reebok International Ltd.	87
Automotive	
Bandag, Inc.	90
Cooper Tire & Rubber Company	41
Genuine Parts Company	76
Harley-Davidson, Inc.	65
Chemicals, Coatings, Glass & Plastics	
Crompton & Knowles Corp.	19
Great Lakes Chemical Corp.	58
International Flavors & Fragrances, Inc.	70
Nordson Corp.	69
RPM, Inc.	36
Schulman A., Inc.	68
Sherwin-Williams Company	47
Valspar Corp.	44
Computers and Office Equipment	
Computer Associates International, Inc.	67
Computer Sciences Corp.	100
Intel Corp.	42
Microsoft Corp.	64
Novell, Inc.	79
Pitney Bowes, Inc.	74
Consumer Products	
Colgate-Palmolive Company	28
Gillette Company, The	1

	Ranking
Procter & Gamble Company, The	85

Corporate Services

Automatic Data Processing, Inc.	46
Cintas Corp.	26
Electronic Data Systems Corp.	31
FIserv, Inc.	88
H&R Block, Inc.	10
Interpublic Group of Companies, Inc., The	30
Olsten Corp., The	89

Electronics

Federal Signal Corp.	20
Hubbell, Inc.	86
Thermo Electron Corp.	84
Thermo Instrument Systems, Inc.	82
Sensormatic Electronics Corp.	71
Vishay Intertechnology Inc.	81

Entertainment

Disney, Walt Company	55

Financial

Banc One Corp.	62
Cincinnati Financial Corp.	72
Fifth Third Bancorp	22
First Financial Management Corp.	56
Franklin Resources	3
Norwest Corp.	13
State Street Boston Corp.	35
Sun Trust Banks, Inc.	50
Synovus Financial Corp.	38
Torchmark Corp.	93

Food and Beverage Production

Coca-Cola Company, The	4
ConAgra, Inc.	33
CPC International	43

Industry	**Ranking**
General Mills, Inc.	17
H. J. Heinz Company	73
Hershey Foods Corporation	39
Kellogg Company	45
PepsiCo, Inc.	12
Sara Lee Corporation	27
Sysco Corporation	29
Tyson Foods, Inc.	80
Wrigley, Wm. Jr., Company	2

Food and Drug Retail

Albertson's, Inc.	5
McDonald's Corporation	60
Walgreen Company	16

Health Care and Medical

Abbott Laboratories	15
American Home Products Corp.	61
Bristol-Myers Squibb Company	52
Cardinal Health, Inc.	57
Hillenbrand Industries, Inc.	59
Johnson & Johnson	21
Manor Care, Inc.	98
Medtronic, Inc.	7
Merck & Company	8
PacifiCare Health Systems, Inc.	77
Pfizer, Inc.	34
Schering-Plough Corp.	9
Sigma-Aldrich Corp.	92
Stryker Corp.	53
United HealthCare Corp.	66
U.S. Healthcare, Inc.	25
Warner-Lambert Company	48

Household and Commercial Furnishings

Emerson Electric Company	75
General Electric Company	49
Loctite Corp.	83

Industry	Ranking
Newell Company	40
Rubbermaid, Inc.	32
Shaw Industries, Inc.	54

Industrial Equipment

Donaldson Company, Inc.	24
Grainger, W. W., Inc.	96
Pall Corp.	37

Insurance

American International Group, Inc.	91

Paper Products and Packaging

Bemis Company, Inc.	23
Crown Cork & Seal Company, Inc.	94

Printers and Publishers

R. R. Donnelley & Sons Company	97

Retail Department Stores

Dillard Department Stores, Inc.	99
Home Depot, The	18
May Department Stores Company, The	63
Michaels Stores	95
Office Depot, Inc.	78
Wal-Mart Stores, Inc.	14

Tobacco

Philip Morris Companies, Inc.	11
UST, Inc.	6

The 100 Best By State

State	Ranking
Alabama	
Torchmark Corp. (Birmingham)	93
Arkansas	
Dillard Department Stores, Inc. (Little Rock)	99
Tyson Foods, Inc. (Springdale)	80
Wal-Mart Stores, Inc. (Bentonville)	14
California	
Computer Sciences Corp. (El Segundo)	100
Disney, Walt Company (Burbank)	55
Franklin Resources (San Mateo)	3
Intel Corp. (Santa Clara)	42
PacifiCare Health Systems, Inc. (Cypress)	77
Connecticut	
Crompton & Knowles Corp. (Stamford)	19
General Electric Company (Fairfield)	49
Hubbell, Inc. (Orange)	86
Loctite Corp. (Hartford)	83
Pitney Bowes, Inc. (Stamford)	74
UST, Inc. (Greenwich)	6
Florida	
Office Depot, Inc. (Delray Beach)	78
Sensormatic Electronics Corp. (Deerfield Beach)	71
Georgia	
Coca-Cola Company, The (Atlanta)	4
Genuine Parts Company (Atlanta)	76
Home Depot, The (Atlanta)	18
Shaw Industries, Inc. (Dalton)	54
SunTrust Banks, Inc. (Atlanta)	50

State	Ranking
Synovus Financial Corp. (Columbus)	38

Idaho

Albertsons, Inc. (Boise)	5

Illinois

Abbott Laboratories (Abbott Park)	15
Donnelley, R. R., & Sons Company (Chicago)	97
Federal Signal Corp. (Oak Brook)	20
Grainger, W. W., Inc. (Skokie)	97
McDonald's Corp. (Oak Brook)	60
Newell Company (Freeport)	40
Sara Lee Corp. (Chicago)	27
Walgreen Company (Deerfield)	16
Wrigley, Wm. Jr. Company (Chicago)	2

Indiana

Great Lakes Chemical Corp. (West Lafayette)	58
Hillenbrand Industries, Inc. (Batesville)	59

Iowa

Bandag, Inc. (Muscatine)	90

Maryland

Manor Care, Inc. (Silver Spring)	98

Massachusetts

Gillette Company (Boston)	1
Reebok International, Ltd. (Stoughton)	87
State Street Boston Corp. (Boston)	35
Thermo Electron Corp. (Waltham)	84

Michigan

Kellogg Company (Battle Creek)	45
Stryker Corp. (Kalamazoo)	53

Minnesota

Bemis Company, Inc. (Minneapolis)	23
Donaldson Company, Inc. (Minneapolis)	24

State	Ranking
General Mills, Inc. (Minneapolis)	17
Medtronic, Inc. (Minneapolis)	7
Norwest Corp. (Minneapolis)	13
United HealthCare Corp. (Minnetonka)	66
Valspar Corp. (Minneapolis)	44

Missouri

Anheuser-Busch Companies, Inc. (St. Louis)	51
Emerson Electric Company (St. Louis)	75
H&R Block, Inc. (Kansas City)	10
May Department Stores Company, The (St. Louis)	63
Sigma-Aldrich Corp. (St. Louis)	92

Nebraska

ConAgra, Inc. (Omaha)	33

New Jersey

American Home Products Corp. (Madison)	61
Automatic Data Processing, Inc. (Roseland)	46
CPC International (Englewood Cliffs)	43
Johnson & Johnson (New Brunswick)	21
Merck & Company (Rahway)	8
Schering-Plough Corporation (Madison)	9
Warner-Lambert Company (Morris Plains)	48

New Mexico

Thermo Instrument Systems, Inc. (Santa Fe)	82

New York

American International Group (New York)	91
Bristol-Myers Squibb Company (New York)	52
Colgate-Palmolive Company (New York)	28
Computer Associates International (Islandia)	67
International Flavors & Fragrances, Inc. (New York)	70
Interpublic Group of Companies, Inc., The (New York)	30
Olsten Corp., The (Melville)	89
Pall Corporation (East Hills)	37
PepsiCo, Inc. (Purchase)	12

	Ranking
Pfizer, Inc. (New York)	34
Philip Morris Companies, Inc.	11

Ohio

Banc One Corp. (Columbus)	62
Cardinal Health, Inc. (Dublin)	57
Cincinnati Financial Corp. (Fairfield)	72
Cintas Corp. (Cincinnati)	26
Cooper Tire & Rubber Company (Findlay)	41
Fifth Third Bancorp (Cincinnati)	22
Nordson Corp. (Westlake)	69
Procter & Gamble Company, The (Cincinnati)	85
RPM, Inc. (Medina)	36
Rubbermaid, Inc. (Wooster)	32
Schulman, A., Inc. (Akron)	68
Sherwin-Williams Company, The (Cleveland)	47

Pennsylvania

Crown Cork & Seal Company (Philadelphia)	94
Heinz, H. J. Company (Pittsburgh)	73
Hershey Foods Corp. (Hershey)	39
U.S. Healthcare, Inc. (Blue Bell)	25
Vishay Intertechnology, Inc. (Malvern)	81

Texas

Electronic Data Systems (Dallas)	31
Michaels Stores (Irving)	95
Sysco Corp. (Houston)	29

Utah

Novell, Inc. (Provo)	79

Washington

Microsoft Corp. (Redmond)	64

Wisconsin

FIserv, Inc. (Brookfield)	88
Harley-Davidson, Inc. (Milwaukee)	65

Index